The Prestons *of* East Street

The
Prestons
of East Street

THE STORY OF
A 19TH-CENTURY
AMERICAN FAMILY

Alan Maddaus

EPIGRAPH BOOKS
RHINEBECK, NEW YORK

To Barbara and our feline companions Josh, Lucy and Simba.

Hardcover ISBN 978-1-948796-98-9

Library of Congress Control Number: 2019917626

Book and cover design by Colin Rolfe

Epigraph Books
22 East Market Street, Suite 304
Rhinebeck, New York 1572
(845) 876-4861
epigraphps.com

— Contents —

— Author's Note —

I NEVER INTENDED to write a book. This enterprise was the result of the confluence of a number of factors: interest in the history of my childhood home stimulated by a book published by the local historical society; enjoyment in reading the works of noted American author Paul Horgan, whose focus was on historical fiction and non-fiction of the American southwest; lifelong employment in technology research and development for a global industrial equipment manufacturer; and, finally, retirement. After I retired for the second time in 2012, I worked sporadically as a consultant and discovered during that period a personal need to pursue some project that made use of the skills and interactions common to research. While during my employment I had written a number of technical articles, the influence of Paul Horgan's writings drove me in the direction of history.

The idea for the book came slowly. At first I was content with doing some high-level research and writing short articles for the Galway Preservation Society newsletter. The result of that activity was the realization that the first occupants of my childhood home, the Preston family, had lived interesting lives with, in most cases, stories worth telling. Examples:

Calvin, the youngest son of Dr. and Mrs. Preston, participated in two apocalyptic events, the Battle of Gettysburg and the 1900 Galveston hurricane. Both events were noteworthy not only as the causes of massive carnage and death, but also as catalysts for change—in the case of Gettysburg, the beginning of the end of the Civil War—and due to the latter, improvement in weather forecasting and protection of the City of Galveston by a seawall. During the Galveston hurricane Calvin acted heroically to rescue his family, moving them from their home to a place of apparent safety and accepting great risk in doing so. But with his heroism came the unexpected outcome that they would have survived by sheltering in place (definitely not recommended in preparation for hurricanes). Evacuate, evacuate, evacuate!

Charles, the oldest son, was groomed from early childhood to be a Presbyterian missionary to China. At the age of twenty-five he traveled there on a merchant vessel, enduring six months at sea while looking forward to the opportunity to preach the Christian doctrine to the Chinese in their native language. Much to his disappointment, his plan was sidetracked by an assignment to teach children English in a mission school, an alternate approach toward facilitating the conversion of the Chinese that he opposed on philosophical grounds. Rescued from this endeavor by the outbreak of the Second Opium War, he relocated to Macao for the duration and used this as an opportunity to learn the Chinese language to make it possible to pursue his interest. This put him at odds with a well-connected member of the Mission leadership and arguably hastened his death at an early age.

But perhaps the worthiest story is that of the third-oldest son, William, who heeded the call of Manifest Destiny to settle the West. After several false starts, he found his fortune in the beautiful Touchet River Valley of the southeastern Washington Territory and used his wealth to provide needed comfort and support for his siblings in future years.

Research—supported by the internet; local and regional works of history; contacts with libraries, museums, historical societies, and individuals located in widely separated regions of the country—progressed in fits and starts. Some of the historical details of the Prestons' lives were found in self-contained documentation; other details were scattered among the archives of a single site. And bits and pieces emerged here and there, contributed by acquaintances in the form of "this may be of interest to you" or surfacing by chance due to a variation in the input for a search function.

Some of the most interesting aspects of the research were the interactions with people in libraries, historical societies, and museums—as well as with those who made contributions without relevant organizational connections. Aside from an occasional remark in the realm of "you certainly are persistent" in response to follow-up by e-mail or voice contact after a reasonable waiting period, I received no negative feedback; the majority of contacts were friendly and exceedingly helpful, and several I contacted who did not have the information I was seeking went out of their way to help locate parties who did.

Roughly two years into the project, it became apparent that there existed sufficient material to support a book. Starting with a segment devoted to each of the seven Preston children's lives, I filled in the blanks available in summary accounts, then organized the entirety into a cohesive chronological narrative, beginning with the family of origin and continuing until the last of the occupants of my childhood home had passed away.

In writing this book I found it hard to disguise and/or restrain my background as an engineer. This is most apparent in the chapter related to the Galveston hurricane, although I admit to a similar indiscretion when discussing the steps required to load a model 1861 Springfield muzzleloader and the related firing rate, or the underlying economics supporting William's decision to acquire an interest in Wait's Mill.

With respect to the Galveston hurricane, there were a number of areas of technical interest. While it probably exists somewhere, I have not seen an attempt to express the major characteristics of a hurricane (wind speed and direction, atmospheric pressure, and storm surge or tide as experienced by a stationary observer in time from storm onset to departure) in a single diagram. The basis for the example contained in this book related to the 1900 Galveston hurricane is the National Weather Service memo written following the storm by Galveston Bureau chief meteorologist Isaac Cline. Although the information is cryptic (with exception of that for pressure), there is sufficient detail to provide a reasonable perspective of the storm characteristics' time signature.

Knowledge of the storm's characteristics makes it possible to understand the challenges (particularly due to wind speed and direction, and water depth) that Calvin faced during his rescue mission. It also raises questions about the underlying cause of the legendary collapse of Ritter's Café, the singular harbinger of doom that led to the realization in the business district that this storm was unlike any other and probably convinced many to seek shelter, thereby saving lives.

Finally, that Galveston suffered the worst natural disaster in US history to date is reasonably well-known. However, looking at data available on hurricane damage since then shows ominous trends in lives lost and property damage related to: some combination of seacoast communities' expansion into harm's way, rising ocean level, and increased intensity of storms. These factors, combined with failure or inability to accomplish full evacuation of threatened regions, has led to a recent increase in hurricane-related deaths—those associated with Katrina (August 2005) and Maria (September 2017) being cases in point.

In summary, writing this book was an interesting, if at times challenging and tiring, experience. Long periods of struggling to get all the facts straight and write meaningful sentences, paragraphs, and chapters were punctuated by instances in which a key piece of information or insight fell into my lap as if the book were writing itself. Without the availability of the internet and search engines such as Google, much of the scattered information would not have been found. I believe that this work would have been impossible to complete prior to the advent of the Web.

I will miss the activity connected with this work but feel a sense of relief that it is has been completed.

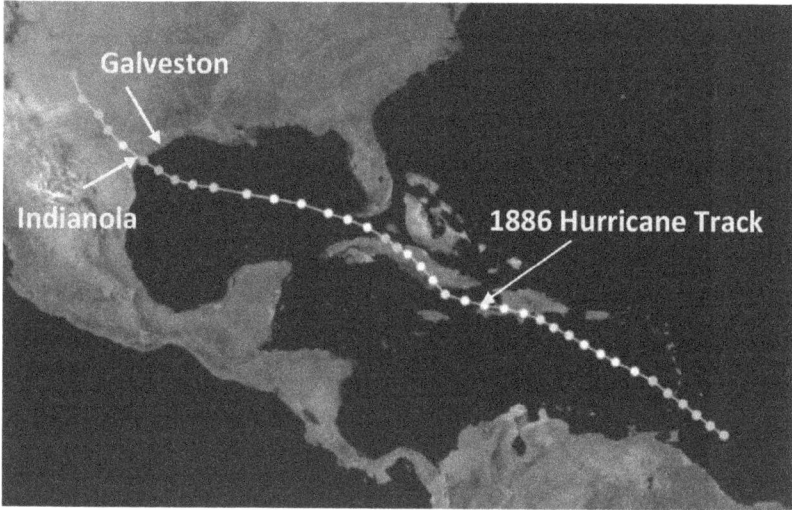

Track of 1886 Hurricane that led to abandonment of Indianola, Texas. Image courtesy of Wikimedia Commons. https://commons.wikipedia.org/wiki/User:Nilafanion

*H*istory, a record of what has happened in the past, contains repetitive patterns of similar events having similar outcomes. The well-known ominous warning: "Those who do not learn history are doomed to repeat it" is attributed to George Santayana, Spanish-born writer and philosopher and contained in his *Sense of Beauty*, published in 1896. Applying to cases in which the outcomes are negative, as clearly indicated by the use of the word "doomed", in some extreme instances the adjective "similar" can be replaced by "identical." The alternative, positive outcomes, may be viewed as guidance for the imagination and related action—e.g., if a vaccine can be developed to prevent smallpox and polio, why not cancer?

Two examples of repetitive events with distinctly negative outcomes—the first identical, the second very similar—occurred on the Texas coastline during the latter part of the nineteenth century and dawn of the twentieth. In September of 1875, the eye of a hurricane passed over the city of Indianola, population six thousand, on Matagorda Bay. Several hundred lives were lost and the city was completely destroyed. Viewed as a freak occurrence, the city was rebuilt only to be destroyed by another hurricane in 1886. This time—lesson learned—it was abandoned. The citizens of Galveston, Texas, a thriving city and center of commerce perched precariously on a large sandbar at the Gulf's edge one hundred miles to the northeast considered the consequences to their city of a similar event and debated construction of a seawall for protection. In due course the project was set aside on the basis that a hurricane could not possibly reach that area of the coastline, a perspective unfortunately given credibility by the National Weather Service—politics trumping science, not to mention common sense. In September of 1900 a hurricane came ashore in Galveston, destroying most of the city with a loss of life that remains the largest for any natural disaster in US history. *Lesson learned* at an extraordinary cost; a seventeen-foot-high seawall was built.

We are inclined to think of the major events of the present as unique. But if we look back in time, it is evident that events in centuries past have characteristics in common with those of our own. Consider the turmoil of present national politics on the issues of health care, abortion-rights, immigration, race relations, and gun violence—and the political map of the US with each state designated as either Red or Blue. The national discourse and divide approach the intensity of that associated with slavery and state's rights prior to the Civil War. While the outcome remains to be seen, one would hope that our leaders would reflect on the past and find a way to resolve the underlying issues peacefully—with wisdom, justice, and compassion, rather than acquiesce to continued defensiveness and divisiveness combined with the hostility that can only lead to violent and destructive acts.

In the nineteenth century there were positive events that in a general sense were repeated, some after a lengthy interval—nationwide transportation being an example. In 1869 the time required to travel from New York City to San Francisco was reduced, almost overnight, from months to a week by the completion of the First Transcontinental Railroad. A similar outcome, part of a continuing pattern of sudden travel time reductions, occurred when coast-to-coast travel graduated from railroad to jet aircraft during the 1950s—in this case reducing travel time from several days to a few hours. My grandfather, a businessman, referred to his trips by rail to the West Coast as the "Western Tour" taking several weeks; this ceased with the advent of high-speed air travel. In fact, well in advance of the century end it was possible to travel to Europe, attend a business meeting, and be back in the United States within twenty-four hours—or less if one booked a flight on the supersonic Concorde aircraft. Now, conceptual design of hypersonic aircraft is underway with the prospect of reducing flight time from New York City to Paris to one hour. Thus, when exploring the events of the nineteenth century it is always interesting to look for recent parallels and evidence of repetition.

A reasonable way to become immersed in the events of the nineteenth century is through the recorded experiences of individuals who lived during that era, and that is what this story is about.

The nineteenth century was a time of major change in America. "Manifest Destiny," the belief that the United States was destined by God to rule the North American continent, had taken hold, leading to westward migration; with westward migration came increasing conflicts between slaveholders and abolitionists. Civil war broke out as a result and threatened the existence of the nation. Medical knowledge advanced, driven in part by life-threatening diseases contracted by soldiers. Westward expansion accelerated by the discovery of gold led to the construction of the First Transcontinental Railroad. A Protestant movement based on the vision of a second coming of Christ brought excitement to religious practice and increased the size of congregations; related to this, a "spiritual manifest destiny" concurrently raised interest in converting "heathen" populations, notably that of China. The US Weather Service embarked on efforts to record data from instruments at hundreds of locations and transmit the information by telegraph to support predictions of major weather events. And opium use and elder abuse, then as now, reflected failings in human behavior. During the period 1829–1845, seven children were born to a young couple, raised in a small upstate New York village, and by 1875 (in the due course of their lives or through significant impact by national events) all but one had departed for distant destinations. Intelligent, talented, energetic, mature in personality and behavior, driven to succeed, and devoted to each other—they lived productive and interesting lives. This is their story, the underlying research and writing of which was purely accidental.

* * *

The Preston House, Galway, New York, 1950. Photo by Elsie Maddaus.

WHEN PHOTOGRAPHED IN the late afternoon of an autumn day in 1950, shadows had spread across the front lawn of my childhood home in rural Galway, New York. The house, its front still bathed in sunshine and sides in shadow, is of stark Federal style construction with a few subtle refinements that reflect the tastes of the original owner, a physician. In a village where homes formerly belonging to merchants are more splendid, it seems fitting; in my childhood, doctors invariably drove Buicks rather than Cadillacs, as if a display of wealth was unbecoming to an individual who made his living from the medical misfortunes of others—never mind the risks of failure, the sacrifices, and the related stresses of that career choice.

The shadows are a metaphor for my memories of that time and place. When moving there with my family at the age of five, the house was a dilapidated structure nearing the end of its useful life, with numerous problems ranging from leaking roofs, to a failing water supply and septic system and a backyard filled with farm buildings in worse repair—all squeezed onto a one-acre lot. My grandfather, on the occasion of his first visit from his home in New York City, likened the interior of the property to a small, rundown village.

The outbuildings deserve further mention, for when exploring the second floor of the barn with my father and brother, there was a loud crunching sound, and my father fell through the dry-rotted flooring up to his waist. He instinctively yelled for help as my brother and I looked on, momentarily paralyzed by fear; we were small children and he was six feet tall and weighed over 200 lbs. Fortunately, he was able to quickly extricate himself. Shortly afterward, my mother called the loan officer of the bank holding the mortgage and asked if the barn could be demolished. A representative from the bank took one look at it and said, "Tear that barn down before it falls on somebody."[1] And so began the process of renewal.

Beyond that, there was momentary excitement when a human skull missing most of its teeth was found in an adjacent outbuilding. How it got there is unknown but a solitary human skull lying abandoned in a dusty corner on the second floor of a decaying farm building is unusual, disturbing, and darkly symbolic of the neglect the property had suffered. My parents called the sheriff, who came to pick it up, but nothing was ever heard about related circumstances.

To his credit, my father successfully dealt with the frequently daunting challenges of restoration. As winter approached, the well and furnace failed at the same time. A mathematics professor at a local college, he took a second job as a hotel night clerk to pay for the cost of repairs and renovations, using slow periods in the early morning hours to prepare class notes and grade homework and test papers. How he found time to sleep is a mystery. Relationships he developed with individuals regularly frequenting the hotel in the night—waiters and waitresses, policemen moonlighting as security guards, and gamblers— were positive and rewarding. They visited our home from time to time, and I have clear and fond memories of them. And when we departed seventeen years later, the property was in vastly better condition. So it may not be surprising that later in life my wife and I purchased an aging farmhouse in a small upstate New York village that was in equally poor condition, built by a physician ca. 1850, and spent twenty years restoring it. History repeated itself. In any event unanswered questions related to my childhood home remained with me for half a century. Why the numerous upstairs bedrooms structured to accommodate multiple occupants, what use would a physician have with so many outbuildings, and were there any descendants living locally or did the family just disappear into the impenetrable darkness of unrecorded history?

The answers, on the surface, turned out to be simple: the bedrooms were intended to provide room for a large family, later to be used for overnight boarding of the next owner's stagecoach passengers; the doctor had acquired farm land nearby and had chosen to place the buildings for livestock adjacent to his residence; and most of the children, while having moved far away, became prominent in their adopted communities and thus the subject of newspaper articles, books, letters, and legal documents.

In 2014 the Galway historical society published a book on local history.[2] Included were scraps of information on my childhood home and some side glimpses of the house provided by photos sufficient to catch my interest. At my request for additional information, a Galway historian kindly forwarded an

excerpt from a document in the archives that became the starting point for extensive research into Dr. and Mrs. Preston's
remarkable family.

The document, entitled *Historical and Genealogical Notes of
Galway, New York*, by Elizabeth Robb Quinby, originally ca. 1920,
but with edits that were continued to the 1970s, contained brief
statements related to the Prestons based on personal recollections of acquaintances, by then elderly. Also included in the
notes, two letters from John Henry Hays (a local resident of
the same era) provided additional insights, some in the form of
interesting anecdotes. From the Notes the following is relevant:

- The house was built by George Hanford for Dr. Calvin
  Preston and his first wife, Margaret McAllaster Preston
  in 1838.
- Dr. Preston came to Galway from either North Gage in
  Jefferson County, New York or Connecticut.
- "His eldest son Charles went as a minister to China in
  the [1850s]."
- "His other children were: William, James, Sophia, Maria,
  Platt, and Calvin."
- "Two of his sons were at the site of Denver before it was
  built and had something to do with staking out the city."
- "Sophia married Stewart from the state of Washington" or
  "John Henry Hays [of Galway]"—or possibly both?
- Son Calvin Preston was a musician in the Northern Army,
  and his brother, James Preston who lived in Texas was in
  the Southern Army.

The above is informative, but generally vague, a bit confusing,
and ordinary. Here and there, after a small amount of research,
a few facts led to speculation. For example, Charles (the China
Missionary) graduated from nearby Union College. Perhaps the

two unidentified brothers reputed to have staked out the City of Denver had also attended Union, graduating as civil engineers and then traveling west to seek their fortunes? But by far the most interesting is the last item, which indicates that two brothers served on opposing sides of the Civil War; "brother against brother" seemed unusual for siblings born and brought up in upper New York State, far from the Mason-Dixon Line.

Mildly encouraged by the Civil War connection, I decided to start at the beginning and find more information about Dr. Preston's life prior to his moving to Galway. Given the choice between searching for his family of origin in either Connecticut or North Gage, New York, the latter seemed immediately more productive due to smaller size. An internet search revealed that a number of individuals with the Preston surname were buried in cemeteries in the North Gage area. I contacted the Town of Deerfield Historian who quickly sent me background on the family, as well as several short newspaper articles, including one dated July 1, 1905: the obituary of son Calvin, under the caption "Galway Boy Gained Honors in the South—News Received of Major Calvin W. Preston's Death—Prominent in Galveston Texas."[3] Amazing, I thought—a musician rising to the rank of Major in the Union Army and relocating to Galveston after the war; however, with further reading it became clear that the rank was associated with his membership in the Texas Militia. All right, so a Union soldier rose to a position of authority after the Civil War in a military organization of a former Confederate state. Interesting, but why Galveston? A reasonable speculation was that his brother James, the Confederate soldier, was somehow involved in that choice of location. An inquiry to the Rosenberg Library in Galveston revealed that James had settled there prior to the Civil War, serving in the Confederate Army and dying about four years after Calvin joined him there, and that the brothers were buried in adjoining plots in a section of a local cemetery reserved for Texas soldiers. Actually, the information was only partially correct, the truth turning out to be far more interesting. Nevertheless, it encouraged me to continue a research project that rapidly grew in scope, leading to contacts with historical societies in Galway, Saratoga, Ballston Spa, and Glens Falls, NY; Waitsfield, VT; and Waitsburg, WA—libraries at Union College/Schenectady, NY; and the University of Washington/Seattle—public libraries in Waitsburg, WA; Denver, CO; and Mechanicville, NY—the Presbyterian Historical Society in Philadelphia, PA—and the New York State Military History Museum and Veterans Research Center in Saratoga, NY—to mention a few sources. At times, progress in developing the story of their lives took an extensive amount of digging and luck. In other cases, it was simply a matter of providing input to a search engine in the form of a full name and location and pressing enter, (e.g., "William G. Preston Galway NY").

A reasonably complete historical account of the family was provided by information from these sources, supplemented by information contained in books on local history for Galveston, Waitsburg, Galway, and Denver; and on the Civil War and Western Settlement—as well as contained in legal documents archived in county clerks' offices and through contacts with historians. In the end, I found that the destinies of seven children— Charles, James, William, Platt, Calvin, Sophia, and Maria—were shaped by nineteenth century events including the Second Great Awakening, the Civil War, the opening of Nebraska and the Northwest Territories, the Gold Rushes, the completion of the First Transcontinental Railroad, the Galveston Hurricane of 1900, and the growth of legal rights for the mentally disabled.

And the Preston children's destinies were also influenced by individuals such as Horace Greeley, Colonel Elmer Ellsworth, General Horace Carpentier, and Reverend Charles Finney. Some of their lives ended too early, under tragic circumstances. Others, including the family patriarch, lived to prosper and survive to an age typical of average human mortality a century later. Their story, in the form of a cohesive narrative over time, was constructed from information pieced together from numerous sources. It includes topics regularly reported in the news of today and unfortunately part of human behavior, including sexual assault and elder abuse, as well as the destructive consequences of hurricanes and opium use. On the brighter side, it demonstrates the influence a man of energy, determination, and high moral standards can have on those close to him and his community in general.

Notes

[1] Elsie Maddaus, "That Old House," *Galway Preservation Society Journal* 2, no. 9 (May 1999): 1.

[2] "Galway 1900–1949: A Photographic History of Life in the Town of Galway, Saratoga County, New York," *Galway Preservation Society* (2014).

[3] "Galway Boy Gained Honors in the South," *Amsterdam Evening Recorder*, July 1, 1905, 2.

— Chapter One —

Family of Origin and Early Departures

Map of Galway Village 1866. Reprinted from *New Topographical Atlas of Saratoga Co., New York from Actual Surveys by S. N. & D. G. Beers*, (Philadelphia, 1866).

D R. CALVIN PRESTON Jr. was born in Deerfield, New York on February 2, 1799—the fifth of eleven children of Calvin and Rachel (Rice) Preston. His father, a Revolutionary War soldier and subsequently a farmer, had moved the family there from Ashford, Connecticut—lured, it is reasonable to believe, by the ready availability of inexpensive land. Deeply religious, he served as Deacon for Presbyterian churches in the area for about thirty years. Calvin Jr. and his brother, John, (ten years younger) received Medical Degrees— Calvin's from Fairfield Medical School in nearby Fairfield, New York, graduating with a two-year degree in 1825. He married Margaret McAllister (or McAllaster, or McAlister—the spelling varies with the source) of Antwerp, New York on September 17, 1827, and they resided there when their first child, Charles Finney Preston, was born in 1829. In 1830 they moved to Galway, a small hamlet with a growing population and a strong commitment to the Presbyterian religion. Noteworthy also was a family connection: Calvin's wife's sister was married to Reverend Adam W. Platt, who had grown up in Galway. So although the specific circumstances of their move are not available, Calvin and Margaret would have been comfortable relocating there, where he developed a substantial medical practice. In 1838 Dr. Preston had my childhood home built by George Hanford for a price of $1,000—an insignificant amount to pay for a house now, but a substantial sum then.

The Preston family grew rapidly. James Edwin was born in 1831, followed by William Goodell (1832), Sophia Jane (1835), Platt Adams (1837), Maria Chapin (1842) and Calvin Walbridge (1845). The 1850 Federal census lists all the Preston children at the home of their parents, ranging in age from five to twenty-one, hence the need for all those bedrooms. Sadly, Margaret Preston passed away of an unknown affliction in 1848, leaving the Doctor griefstricken and with young children to care for on his own. In 1850 he married Sarah Anderson.

At some point he became interested in farming, purchasing fifty acres of land a short distance along the roadway running east out of the village. This is the apparent reason for the barns that existed behind his home until demolished one hundred years later. His youngest son, Calvin, was listed as a farmer on his muster roll card when he enlisted during the Civil War at the age of sixteen—and evidently had a role in operating the farm.

Dr. Preston was active in the Presbyterian Church, liked flowers, and acquired one unfortunate habit—kissing his women patients, which would eventually make him the focus of prolonged legal action. He demonstrated a fondness for his children in several recorded instances and was cared for by a daughter in his old age. He died in 1885 and was buried in the Galway village cemetery in a plot shared with his two wives. His brother John's name is included on the monument, though John's grave is in a cemetery in nearby Schuylerville.

✳ ✳ ✳

IN 1792 THE Town of Galway was subdivided from Balls-Town, now the Town of Ballston. It is located approximately thirty miles NNW of Albany, the capital of New York State, which was settled by the Dutch in the mid-seventeenth century. The original settlers in the Galway area were all from Scotland. Shortly after their arrival in 1774 they named it New Galloway in honor of their former home, the shire of Galloway, Scotland. When the act creating the town was passed, the name was mistakenly or otherwise "Hibernicized" to Galway.[1] Galway Village was incorporated in 1838. A map of the Village dated 1866 shows a hotel, two churches, a female seminary and several businesses including a cabinet maker, cooperage shop and hub manufacturer. There were two physicians in the village at the time, Dr. Preston and Dr. Webb. To a great extent, the townspeople engaged in farming land cultivated for growing oats, corn, barley, peas, beans, and buckwheat—but very little wheat.

Parkis Mill, Galway, New York, 1974.
Photo by Arlene Rhodes.

With no large rivers, water power in the town was limited; thus, there was little manufacturing activity. Manufacturing facilities included two gristmills, six sawmills, and a combined foundry and plow shop. Levi Parkis' gristmill on Glowegee Creek, three miles to the northeast of the village, engaged in custom grinding and flour milling. The first gristmill in the town, it was built on this site in 1785 by Daniel Campbell and purchased in 1858 by Parkis.[2]

When Hiram Foster owned the mill, it was listed in the 1855 census as having "three run of stones, one employee, and works up about 6,000 bushels of rye and corn; but at what amount of profit it is difficult to determine". ... In 1870 the Parkis Mill was listed as a two horsepower, two stone gristmill with a capital investment of $1,500. The total output in that year was 500 bushels of corn, 150 bushels of oats, 300 bushels of buckwheat, 10,000 pounds of meal, 12,000 pounds of feed, and 7,500 pounds of flour with a total value of $1,670.[3]

Operated by members of the Parkis family until 1926, the mill was converted to a house in 1930. Eventually abandoned, partially fire-damaged and in badly deteriorated condition, it was deemed a safety hazard. In 1980 it was destroyed by the Galway Fire Department in a controlled burn.[4]

Twenty-two hundred miles west, in 1865 a similar gristmill in the heart of the Washington Territory wheat-farming region with abundant water power would have a profound impact on the lives of the Prestons.

⁎ ⁎ ⁎

Controlled burn of the Parkis mill.
Photo from the collection of Arlene Rhodes.

THE FIRST OF the Preston children to leave home was William. Born in Galway, New York on November 23, 1832, William Goodell Preston, his given name selected to honor William Goodell, abolitionist and reformer, was educated at Galway Academy, a private boarding school.[5] Working on his father's farm while growing up gave him experience in the use of mules and horses to pull machinery and wagons, skills he put to good use during the time he was a pack train operator in the western territories. His mother passed away on April 9, 1848. According to the program "at Public Exercises",[6] at Galway Academy two days later (on Friday evening, April 11), following Sacred Music and Prayer, William Preston was scheduled to speak on "Discipline of the Mind." The title is all that remains, but one might suppose the manuscript described how thoughts become spoken words that are subsequently transformed into

William G. Preston, ca. 1870, mill owner—Waitsburg, Washington. Photo courtesy of Rick Hamm and Waitsburg, One of a Kind by the Waitsburg Historical Society (1976).

actions, repeated actions become habits which in turn define character and shape one's destiny. Hence, the motivation for disciplining the mind to have positive thoughts. Or as the Buddha put it more succinctly: "We are shaped by our thoughts, we become what we think." One can only imagine William's state of mind as he prepared for the Exercises while his mother lay dying, but he ultimately either took his own advice to heart or inadvertently lived a life that reflects the power of positive thinking.

For the next two years he remained at his father's home in Galway; the 1850 Federal Census lists him among the occupants with the notation under occupation of: "laborer." William Preston may have become acquainted with gristmill operations there during that period—knowledge that would serve him well later in his life.

Then, perhaps with the intention of joining his brother Charles in a lifelong commitment to religion and thereby honoring his mother's memory, he went to live with his uncle, the Reverend Adam W. Platt, and wife Sarah McAllaster Platt (Margaret's sister) in Hector (Schuyler County, New York, near Ithaca) for two years. Reverend Platt grew up in Galway, joined the Presbyterian Church at the age of fourteen, graduated from Union College in 1817, studied Theology at Princeton, and became a missionary to the new states of Ohio and Indiana—a path similar to that taken thirty years later by Charles.[7] He moved with his wife to West Galway in 1829 as pastor of the Presbyterian Church, and their presence in the area may have been a factor in Dr. and Mrs. Preston's decision to relocate from Antwerp, NY to Galway in 1830. At the time of William's visit, Reverend Platt had ceased his pastoral activities due to poor health and only occasionally preached, very possibly limiting his effectiveness as a religious mentor. In any event, a career as a religious leader was not suited to William, because in 1852 he "went to sea—visiting New Brunswick, New Orleans and Liverpool, and other points in Great Britain and America."[8] Described in a passport issued in Boston, Massachusetts in [1853] "as five feet, eleven-and-one-half inches in height with a high forehead, blue eyes, Grecian nose, large mouth, short chin, sandy hair, light complexion and thin face,"[9] he evidently had a commanding presence, as his career as a business leader—not to mention as family and community patriarch—would attest.

* * *

CHARLES WAS NEXT to depart. Charles Finney Preston was born in Antwerp, New York on July 26, 1829,[10] the first child of Dr. and Mrs. Calvin Preston. His middle name was selected as a tribute to Charles Grandison Finney, a social activist and leader in the Presbyterian Church during the early- to mid-nineteenth century. Finney's background is similar in several respects to that of Dr. Preston.

* * *

CHARLES FINNEY, CHARLES Finney Preston's namesake, was born in Warren, Connecticut in 1792 into a large family typical of the period. His father was a farmer who relocated to Henderson on the frontier of west-central New York State after the American Revolutionary War. He was educated in a common school until the age of fifteen to sixteen years, and by his account he had learned enough to teach at that level.[11] At the age of twenty he returned to Connecticut, then relocated in New Jersey, teaching school. He went to New England twice, spent a season in high school, and engaged in self-education. In 1818 he returned to Henderson and settled there briefly at the request of his mother, who was in ill health,[12] then relocated in nearby Adams, New York (about forty miles southwest of Antwerp), joined a law office and studied law under Benjamin Wright. During this period, he was exposed to both the dry, Calvinistic preaching of the Presbyterian church and the emotional preaching of the Baptist Church—characterized by a raised voice, stomping of feet, and abuse of furniture, which was met by an equally emotional (groans, sighs, weeping, and confessions) congregational response.[13] It was this combination that shaped his approach when the time came.

In 1821 Finney had a sudden conversion experience, abruptly discontinued his practice of law, and joined the Presbyterian Church. He started studying for the Presbyterian ministry in 1822 and was licensed to preach in 1824. The Reverend Adams W. Platt, future brother-in-law of Dr. Calvin Preston and William's future mentor, performed the marriage of Finney and his first wife that same year.[14]

In the spring of 1824, Rev. Finney introduced "new measures" that he would practice in his revival services. Included were:

- Promoting the concept that the will of an individual is the determinant in securing salvation, rather than reliance on the Calvinistic position that God has preordained who would be saved and the individual has no recourse;
- Using religious music written in the style of the period to entertain and put the congregation in a receptive frame of mind;
- Allowing women to pray in the presence of men (!);
- Creatively advertising services and conducting them several times a day; and

- Preaching extemporaneously in language of the common man.

Controversial at first to say the least—one disgruntled soul commented that "female prayer is promiscuous" in assemblies with men and objected to use of "the language of unbecoming familiarity with God in prayer"[15]—these precepts have gained acceptance with evangelism today. The objective almost certainly was to make church attendance more rewarding and entertaining, thereby attracting more people to join the congregation. And it worked.

Finney began as a preacher in Adams, where his style and language when speaking to the congregation was noteworthy and controversial. He then took a position in the village of Evans Mills, where the conversion of two hundred people was attributed to his simple form of preaching—albeit with some question about the accuracy of the estimate. Tall, with angular facial features and piercing eyes which, when one was the focus of his attention, he or she could readily imagine a connection with God. The photo of him taken by an unknown source seems to hint at the differing perceptions of his character—dark and foreboding on the left, enlightened and kindly on the right. He preached in a powerful, exciting manner, with anecdotes

Charles Grandison Finney.
Wikimedia Commons/Public Domain.

taken from everyday life punctuated with gestures to make a point. His religious views led him to support social reforms, notably the abolition of slavery and equal rights for women and African Americans.

While his participation in revivals was limited to the period 1824–1832, when he contracted cholera and presumably required relief from the physical demands of life on the road, his revivals culminated in a series of extended events in western New York State that were well attended and wildly popular. As a result, he is recognized as a leader in the Second Great Awakening, a Protestant revival that gained strength during the period 1800–1840 and swelled attendance at congregations.[16]

In 1832 he took the position of pastor of the Chatham Street Chapel in New York City, followed by a teaching position at Oberlin College. During the period 1851–1866, he was president of Oberlin College and continued to teach theology. He died in Oberlin, Ohio in 1875. Coincidentally, much later, a daughter of Charles Preston and her husband moved to Oberlin after serving as missionaries in China.

※ ※ ※

A NOTEWORTHY EXAMPLE of an increased religious commitment during the Second Great Awakening is described in a history of Galway: [17]

In 1820 at a time when the church [Presbyterian Church of Galway] was without a pastor, a remarkable revival of religion occurred. It originated among school-children, who, from discussing some doctrine of the Bible, fell to studying the scriptures, and the interest grew until within the space of two months one hundred and fifty-two names were added to the church roll.

One might question that the increase in the size of the congregation was solely related to the curiosity of children, but the net result was typical of the excitement caused by the movement.

An influential personality in Galway's response to the revival was the Reverend Eliphalet Nott, president of Union College in nearby Schenectady. During 1820 he was the supply pastor at the Galway Presbyterian Church.[18] His philosophy was that of the evangelical millennials: by improving themselves and society within the framework of Christian beliefs, the day on which Christ would return and rule the earth for one thousand years prior to its destruction would be advanced.

> In a sermon preached to the General Assembly of the Presbyterian Church in 1806, Union College president Eliphalet Nott asserted that the millennium was near and that it was "to be introduced by Human Exertions." And Charles Finney, the most famous and successful of the Second Great Awakening preachers, argued that if "... people were united all over the world" the millennium might be brought about in three months.[19]

Possessing exceptional skills as an educator and preacher, it is not surprising that attendance at the Galway Presbyterian Church benefitted from his brief presence, and that school children were involved. Later, during the period 1823–1829, his brother Samuel Nott would serve the church as pastor.[20]

The Second Awakening resulted in an increased interest in Christian missionary activities in Asia, particularly China. The

Presbyterian Church looked upon itself as a missionary society with a responsibility for its members to assist in the conversion of the world to Christianity. In 1837 the General Assembly resolved to superintend and conduct the work of the foreign missions by a board appointed for that purpose and accountable to the Assembly.

According to G. Thompson Brown,[21] the decision to start work in China was based on a number of perceived factors, including: a) size of the population amounting to 25 percent of the world's total; b) ignorance of the only true religion, Christianity; c) one common written language; and d) accessibility and interest of reasonably sized segments of the population. Enthusiasm for missionary service at that time in general has been characterized as a "spiritual manifest destiny" operating in parallel with the secular manifest destiny associated with US westward expansion.

Given the Preston family connection with the Presbyterian religion, the inspiring nature of Finney's sermons and leadership, and the Preston's location in the Jefferson area during the same period—the selection of Charles' middle name is not surprising. And further, strong evidence exists that he was groomed for a position in the Presbyterian Foreign Ministry at a very early age.

The following excerpt is taken from a 1918 letter written by J. H. Hays, Galway farmer and husband of Charles' sister Sophia, to Elizabeth Robb Quinby, Galway Historian.[22] The "Mrs. Chapin" referred to was Abby Chapin, wife of the Reverend Augustus L. Chapin, a neighbor of the Prestons.

> Mrs. Preston and Mrs. Chapin were wonderfully interested in the Foreign Missions, especially China, and they used to meet every week at one or the other's home and pray for China, week after week, month after month, year after year,

and that their first born son (each had one) might be spared and called to the ministry and become a missionary to China. This was talked before the two boys and they thought that it was the proper thing to do for "Mama says so."

Well, one day their mothers missed them, could not find them (they were about seven years old) and Doct Preston took his horse and carriage to hunt for them. Someone told him they had seen the boys going up the West road. The doctor followed on and overtook them about three miles and asked them where they were going. They were going to China as missionaries.

Well, those mothers' prayers were answered. Lyman Dwight Chapin went as missionary to northern [China] and [labored] There for years and then came back on account of his health and climate and [labored] with the Chinese at San Francisco l think for as long as he lived.

Charles F. Preston also went to China, labored in Canton for many years, likewise eventually encountering health problems, but with a less fortunate and more troubling outcome.

The above anecdote is charming and close enough to the truth as reflected in consistent historical records found elsewhere to be of interest. The timing of the incident was in the early 1840s, approximately seventy years prior to Mr. Hays' letter and was probably a story told to him by his wife Sophia, who passed away a year prior. Ample reason, one can conclude, for some distortion of the facts.

Actually, the Chapin's first son Edward, born in Jewett, New York, died there in 1838 at the age of six, two years before their relocation to Galway. Their second-born son also succumbed in his infancy, prior to their move. Rev. Chapin was supply pastor in Galway from 1841 to 1844, and during that period the Chapins lived in a house across the street from the Prestons. Thus, Abby Chapin was undoubtedly praying that her *third-born* would survive and fulfill her wish, sadly reminding one of the rules of the sport of baseball—three strikes and you're out. The Chapin's third child, Lyman Dwight Chapin, was born in Jewett in 1836, so would have been between the ages of five and eight years during their time in Galway, while Charles Preston's age during the same period was twelve to fifteen. Thus, some discrepancies exist. For example, while one can conceive of the two boys imaginatively setting out on foot for China, they were definitely not both aged seven.

While two mothers regularly praying that their sons would become missionaries to China may seem unusual, that Margaret Preston would bond with Abby Chapin on the vision of their sons' missionary involvement is believable—because as a scholarly source[23] states, during the Second Great Awakening:

> Conversion and subsequent church membership provided a common experience for American women .... The churches, or more broadly, religious interest gave women a respectable sphere outside the home for peer support and meaningful activity.

In addition,

> Nor did women confine their religious activities to church membership, the immediate family or female prayer societies; they also joined together in a range of formal and informal associations[24] such as the Maternal Association, founded in 1815 by Ann Louisa Payton, wife of the

Congregational Minister .... Members agreed to shape
their concern through systematic religious duties including "praying for each child daily" ....[25]

Finally, by default, mothers were the conscientious guardians
of the family's religious inheritance. For example, at the time of
the Second Great Awakening, initial revival records of one New
York State community show that women accounted for 70 percent of the church population.[26]

Charles Preston studied at the Galway Academy under the
guidance of the Reverend Gilbert Morgan, becoming a member of the Galway Presbyterian Church at the age of fourteen.[27]
He next attended Union College, graduating in 1850, and then
Princeton Theological Seminary, where he completed a three-
year course. He was commissioned missionary to China by the
Presbyterian Board of Foreign Missions in 1853 and left by sailing merchant ship, the Horatio, departing from New York for
Canton in November, 1853.

※ ※ ※

NEXT TO LEAVE was James Edwin. The first recorded mention of James Edwin Preston, born May 21, 1831, the second son
of Dr. Calvin Preston and wife Margaret McAllaster is found
in the Quinby archives in the program for Public Exercises
of Galway Academy, April 11, 1848. After Sacred Music and
Prayer, James' brother William's talk on "Discipline of the
Mind" was followed by James' "Influence of Music on the
Mind." While there is no additional information available, it
is reasonable to believe he, like his brothers and sisters, was
musically inclined.

The 1850 Federal Census lists James' occupation as "merchant," the first clue of the reason for his relocation to Galveston, Texas not long after.

It would not have been unusual for a merchant in the Hudson-Mohawk region of New York to be involved with the marketing of textiles, as that was a major product of industry there in the mid-nineteenth century and beyond. The irony is that textile manufacturing owed its existence to cotton produced in the southern states, Texas included, and cotton production was profitable due to slave labor. Yet the underground railroad, which provided a protected route to Canada for slaves escaping from the south, ran along the Hudson and Mohawk rivers—and undoubtedly, safe havens were in close proximity to textile factories in cities like Utica, Amsterdam, Troy, and Cohoes. Preceding the Civil War, there were conflicts between abolitionists and textile manufacturing interests. Northern factions of Protestant religions (for example, Presbyterian, of which James and family were members) denounced slavery to the point of suggesting that, if necessary, God favored a war to end the practice. All of this James and his family were undoubtedly aware of, and the association of James with the cotton trade may have made his life uncomfortable amongst family members and other people in his home town. But why Galveston, a city with a significant slave population in a state that strongly supported slavery? Interestingly, in a Galveston newspaper editor argued in 1856 that "bringing slave labor from Africa to work in the cotton fields of Texas was ordained by holy scripture."[28]

The practice of slavery in Galveston began with the first settlers, Louis-Michel Aury, who established a center for the illicit slave trade on the island, which was later taken over by the Lafitte pirate family. When the pirates were displaced by action of the US government in 1821, settlers began to arrive in the region (then controlled by Spain as part of Mexico) some bringing their slaves with them. This was also the year when Mexico achieved independence from Spain, complicating the situation for slave owners, because Mexico had laws forbidding slavery. The Texas Revolution of 1836, resulting in Texas independence from Mexico, put the matter to rest temporarily because the Texas Republic constitution provided a lawful basis for slavery.

In 1840 a traveler described Galveston as a rough and dreary place, but with potential for growth, and also warned of its susceptibility to damage from storms moving in from the Gulf. Growth would soon come (as eventually would horrific storm damage) in the 1850s.

> In the decade before the Civil War Galveston became a genuine city, the first in Texas. Merchants began importing ornate iron fronts for their buildings, and the town council constructed sidewalks, installed gaslights, and paved primary streets with shell. For the first time the Strand [the main street of the business district] took on the appearance of a modern eastern city, an affectation that galled Houstonians. The *New York Sun* reported that that the streets of Galveston were wide and straight and their cleanliness was about on a par with New York—"which is no compliment," the reporter added.[29]

So from James' viewpoint, Galveston must have represented an opportunity to move forward in his career in a location where economic growth was assured. And if he was seeking relief from the conflict in New York State between abolition and textile business interests and was able to ignore the abject cruelty and suffering associated with slavery, Galveston was a good choice—because the citizens of Galveston, for the most part, appeared to be pro-slavery. "As the Galveston Weekly News declared in 1857, those who are not for us are against us. There can be no middle ground. Those who denounce slavery as evil, in any sense, are enemies of the South."[30] No ambiguity in that statement, although the truth for Galveston turned out to be considerably more complicated.

From the Galway area to Galveston there was an established route of transportation: by water to New York City via the Hudson River (or alternately by railway), where the Galveston firm of E. S. Jemison, Bankers and Cotton Commission Merchants maintained offices at no. 10 Old Slip, and thence by ocean-going ship to Galveston. James arrived in Galveston in 1852 and found employment at A. J. Ward & Co., a cotton factor a.k.a. broker, as a bookkeeper. He joined the Free-Mason Society, San Felipe De Austin Commandery No. 1, and became an officer. His place of residence was on Avenue H, between Tenth and Eleventh streets.

* * *

MEANWHILE, WILLIAM EMBARKED on an adventure of his own and, shortly after, Platt joined him. Calvin (the son) would join the Union Army at the beginning of the Civil War and the sisters, Maria and Sophia, would remain in Galway for some time.

Oceangoing ships powered by steam engines were in use for travel between the United States and Great Britain during the mid-nineteenth century, and William must have learned enough during his short period at sea to become proficient at operating and piloting such a vessel, as evidenced by a future, apparently successful (albeit short-lived) commercial venture.

* * *

IN THE MID-NINETEENTH century the western territories were opening up for settlement, and "Go West, Young Man" was frequently spoken advice. One popular version of its origin is an editorial by John Soule in an 1851 issue of *Terre Haute Express*. The phrase was also reportedly coined by Horace Greeley, New York newspaperman, liberal politician, and presidential candidate who ran against Ulysses Grant in 1872 and died shortly before the electoral votes were cast. Recent research has cast doubt on this, however, because there is no clear evidence that Greeley ever used the phrase in a publication, nor did Soule, for that matter. Timothy Hughes writes:

> There has been some dispute, however general consensus is that Horace Greeley was the first to use the oft-cited phrase *"Go West, young man."* .... There are many, many citations on the internet that Greeley used this phrase in his July 13, 1865 editorial .... I've scoured through the issue yet never found the quote. The closest I could come is in "The Homestead Law" piece, page 4 column 4, where he mentioned: *"We earnestly urge upon all such to turn their faces Westward and colonize the public lands."*[31]

So although Greeley enthusiastically promoted westward expansion to the extent that he traveled from New York City to San Francisco and wrote a series letters to the *New York Tribune* describing his adventure, which were subsequently published as a collection in a book—he may not have coined the popular phrase.

He described his purpose for the trip, a time-consuming, challenging journey in these terms: "If any excuse for printing these letters were wanted, it might be found in the fact that much of the ground passed over by the writer was absolutely new—that is, it had never before been traversed and described." He added:

> But another reason for printing these hasty sketches is found in the fact that very great and rapid changes in most of the region lying directly between Missouri and California are inevitable. The Leavenworth Express route, through the heart of what in June is the Buffalo region, which was hardly four weeks old when I traveled it, was soon after abandoned, and has reverted to the domain of the wolf and the savage; while the rude beginning of a settlement I found, scarcely three weeks old, at "Gregory's Diggings," has since been "Mountain City," with its municipality, its newspaper, and its thousands of inhabitants; and is now in its decline, having attained the ripe age of nearly half-a-year.[32]

Greeley traveled to Gregory's Diggings, an area in the foothills of the Rocky Mountains just west of Denver in a small party using mules as a means of transportation. The difficulties he encountered with one in particular was described in one letter. It all seemed to start out well, as he wrote:

> When we reached Clear Creek on our way up three mornings since, though the current rushing from the mountains looked somewhat formidable, I charged it [on his mule] like a Zouave, and was greeted with three ringing shouts

from the assembled Pike's Peakers, as I came up, gay and dripping, on the north shore.[33]

But the effort on the part of the mule to carry Horace up a steep grade in the foothills soured the relationship.

The hill on which we were to make our first essay in climbing, rose to a height of one thousand six hundred feet in a little more than a mile—the ascent for most of the distance being more than one foot in three. I never before saw teams forced up such a precipice; yet there were wagons with ten or twelve hundred weight of mining tools, bedding, provisions, etc., being dragged by four to eight yoke of oxen up that giddy precipice, with four or five men lifting at the wheels of each. The average time consumed in the ascent is some two hours. Our mules, unused to such work, were visibly appalled by it; at first they resisted every effort to force them up, even by zigzags. My companions all walked, but I was lame and had to ride, much to my mule's intense disgust. He was stubborn, but strong, and in time bore me safely to the summit.[34]

Greeley's experience with the mule would later be mentioned in a Denver area newspaper article on the Prestons' activities in nearby Golden Gate City, a settlement to encounter the same change in fortune as Gregory's Diggings.

✻ ✻ ✻

ALL CONFUSION ON the originator of the phrase aside, William followed its advice, returning to Galway by way of Boston in

1854, then travelling to the recently opened Nebraska Territory by rail to Chicago and Rock Island—and since there was no rail service across Iowa—down the Mississippi River to St. Louis and up the Missouri River to Bellevue, Nebraska,[35] which was then the location of the legislature.

William's exact intentions in traveling to Nebraska are not clear, as there is no record that he intended to settle there, and he was only in that area for a short period of time. But at Bellevue he put his experience as a sailor to good use, becoming captain of Colonel Sarpy's steam-powered ferryboat in 1855. Colonel Sarpy, of Creole descent and originally from Louisiana, was a longtime resident of the Nebraska Territory. He was a successful fur trader who operated a trading post that served immigrants traveling west during the gold rushes as well as a ferry for transporting people, livestock, and goods across the Missouri river. Prior to his acquiring a steam-powered ferry, the ferry was poled across—in some instances reaching the opposite side well downstream of the dock.

His brother Platt Preston joined William the same year, at age seventeen, to assist with ferryboat operations.[36] When the capital was relocated to Omaha, the boat was sold to the Council

Double-engine, side-wheeler riverboat. Wikipedia.

Bluffs and Nebraska Ferry Company and the brothers accompanied it to Omaha. In 1857 William went to Steubenville, Ohio and built the Omaha City, a double-engine side-wheeler designed to haul freight and passengers. Returning to Omaha with Platt, he ran a passenger and freight operation.[37] During the summer of 1857 his father, accompanied by the Reverend H.L. Grose from Galway, New York visited him, boarding the Omaha City at Pittsburgh and traveling the length of the Ohio River to St. Louis—a distance of approximately six hundred miles. In an article published in the September and October issues of the *Galway Home Register*,[38] the Reverend speaks in glowing terms about travel by steamboat, the journey, and the character of William Preston:

> We have tried various modes of conveyance—coaches, railroads, steamboats, hacks, lumber wagons, ox carts, and saddled horses—to say nothing of floating down the Mississippi in a skiff and out of a skiff—and we are prepared to express our preference for steamboats over all other inventions for the comfort and pleasure of travel. Perhaps our preference was determined by our good fortune in falling in with just the right captain, and just the right fellow voyagers, for the entire trip from Pittsburg to St. Louis. There may be better boats than the Omaha City; but if in all Nebraska there is a finer specimen of a whole-souled man than Captain W. G. Preston, we would like to know his name. Our only regret is that we did not have time to go with him from St. Louis to Omaha. With his father, C. Preston, M.D. of Galway, for a Bon Compagnon Du Voyage; having a commodious state room at our service; with several gentlemen of intelligence on board who knew almost everything of interest related to the settlement and growth of the west, nothing was wanting to make the passage delightful and profitable.

Platt Preston, ca 1860. Courtesy of the family of Laura Preston Chase.

Interestingly, there was no mention of Platt, perhaps because he was engaged in ferryboat operations at the time.

Apparently, William had found an occupation that was a perfect match for his skills and temperament, so it is somewhat surprising that in 1858 he turned the business over to his brother and journeyed to Colorado, evidently swept up in the excitement of the Pikes Peak Gold Rush. A factor in his decision may have been a decline in river commercial traffic due to the panic of 1857 and the recession that followed combined with a relatively safer period for crossing the plains associated with diminished hostilities involving Native Americans. Or it may have been something more substantial. Perhaps his decision to leave a situation of stable employment was influenced by the knowledge that four onetime residents of his small home town—Sam Davis, James Jones, John Allen, and Horace Carpentier—had joined the 1849 California gold rush, and several had achieved some measure of success.

Notes

[1] Nathaniel Bartlett Sylvester, *History of Saratoga County, New York*, (Philadelphia: Everts & Ensign, 1878), 359.

[2] Parkis Mill. Saratoga County Historical Society/Brookside Museum, by "ADMIN," filed under "Remember When...," (April 15, 2014). http://www.brooksidemuseum.org/the-grist-mill-2/

[3] "Gristmill was an area anchor: Galway business was just over the Milton line," *Ballston Spa Life*, (April 26, 2010), excerpted from Timothy Starr, *Lost Industries of Saratoga County*, (Charleston, SC: The History Press, 2010).

[4] Arlene Rhodes (Archivist/Galway Preservation Society), in discussion with the author, August 26, 2019.

[5] W. Bronson Taylor, *Stories and Pictures of Galway*, (Middle Grove, NY: published by author, 1966), 35-36.

[6] Elizabeth Robb Quinby and Ethel Robb, *Historical and Genealogical Notes of Galway, New York*, 2 vols., Galway Preservation Society Archives, section entitled: "F. Saxton 1918 West Street North Side," 1.

[7] Joseph M. Wilson. *The Presbyterian Historical Almanac and Annual Remembrances of the Church*, (Philadelphia, 1860) 2:121–122.

[8] Frederic Ambrose (1862), and Richard F. Shaver and Arthur P. Rose, (1875-1970). *An Illustrated History of Southeastern Washington, including Walla Walla, Columbia, Garfield, and Asotin Counties, Washington.* (Spokane, WA: Western Historical Publishing Co.), 244.

[9] Sandra Torres, *The Waitsburg Family: 1858-1900*, (Bloomington, IN [online publisher]: Authorhouse, 2014), 191.

[10] The Essex Institute, (October 1930), 66: 547-548.

[11] Charles G. Finney, 1868 Memoirs (restored text), (Orange , CA: Gospel Truth Ministries, copyright 1900 and 2000), 4.

[12] Marianne Perciaccante, *Calling Down Fire: James Grandison Finney and Revivalism in Jefferson County, New York, 1800–1840*, (Albany, NY: State University of New York Press, copyright 2005), 38.

[13] Ibid., 78.

[14] Ibid., 40.

[15] Rev. Wayne R. Brandow, *Finney's New Measures: The Controversy and Its Effect*, (Albany, NY: Albany Bible Institute, November 19, 1984), appendix.

[16] Perciaccante, *Calling Down Fire: James Grandison Finney and Revivalism in Jefferson County, New York, 1800-1840*, 75.

[17] Sylverster, *History of Saratoga County, New York,* 364.

[18] Ibid.

[19] Stephen D. O'Leary, *Arguing the Apocalypse: A Theory of Millennial Rhetoric*, (New York and Oxford: Oxford University Press, 1994), 85.

[20] Quinby and Robb, *Historical and Genealogical Notes of Galway, New York*, catalogue: "Pastors of the Church."

[21] G. Thompson Brown, *Earthen Vessels and Transcendent Power: American Presbyterians in China, 1837-1952*, American Society of Missiology Series (Maryknoll, NY: Orbis Books, 1997), 13.

[22] Quinby and Robb, *Historical and Genealogical Notes of Galway, New York*, letter from Mr. J. H. Hays, December 19, 1918.

[23] Susan Hill Lindley, *"You Have Stept Out of Your Place" A History of Women and Religion in America*, (Louisville, KY: Westminster John Knox Press, 1996), 61.

[24] Ibid., 62.

[25] Ibid., 63.

[26] "A Woman's Awakening: Evangelical Religion and the Families of Utica, New York, 1800 to 1840," *American Quarterly* 30, no. 5 (Winter 1978): 614.

[27] Necrological Reports and Annual Proceedings of the Alumni Association of the Princeton Theological Seminary, (1875–1889, 1891), I: 57–58.

[28] Gary Cartwright, *Galveston—A History of the Island*, (New York: Atheneum, 1991), 87.

[29] Ibid., 85.

[30] James M. Schmidt, *Galveston and the Civil War: An Island City in the Maelstrom*, (Charleston, SC: The History Press, 2012), 19.

[31] "Go West, young man ..." *Timothy Hughes Rare & Early Newspapers, (Williamsport, PA, 2019),* www.rarenewspapers.com.

[32] Horace Greeley, *An Overland Journey from New York to San Francisco in the summer of 1859*, (New York and San Francisco: C.M. Saxton, Barkley & Co., 1860), 4–5.

[33] Ibid., 45.

[34] Ibid., 42.

[35] Ambrose et al., *An Illustrated History of Southeastern Washington...*, 244.

[36] "Waitsburg, 'One of a Kind,'" compiled by Vance Orchard, Waitsburg Historical Society, (1976), 41.

[37] Ambrose et al., *An Illustrated History of Southeastern Washington...*, 244.

[38] *Galway Home Register*, September–October 1857, 50–51.

Chapter Two

Charles: The Chinese Presbyterian Mission and the Opium War

Merchant sailing ship Horatio watercolor by Benjamin Russell (1855). Courtesy of New Bedford Whaling Museum, New Bedford, Massachusetts.

ETWEEN THE TIME William and Platt headed west to pursue their destiny and their decision to abandon riverboat operations, much had happened in Charles' life. Charles arrived at the port of Hong Kong seventy miles from Canton on May 12, 1854 after a voyage of 160 days.[1] To put the matter into perspective, 160 days is the length of time to go twenty thousand miles at an average speed of 5 mph which is probably what the trip from New York City to China amounted to in speed and distance terms, bringing to mind the phrase "slow boat to China." Another report of sailing on the Horatio to China, mentions an unusually rapid trip of 102 days to Hong Kong, reflecting the extent to which passage time was dependent on the variability of wind and current. By contrast, clipper ships were capable *on the average* of 90–100 days.

The *Horatio* was of a design preceding that of the faster clipper ships, which were intended primarily for trade and not passengers. Built in New Bedford, Massachusetts in 1833, it was about 120 feet long with a maximum width of 29 feet, and had 3 masts and a square stern. In size it was small, compared with current oceangoing yachts.

> She was safe but not very comfortable, having no portholes or other ventilators between decks and the only opening for fresh air was though the companionway and hatches. When rough weather required these to be battened down, the sufferings of the passengers was intense.[2]

Depending on the cargo, the ship could be very stiff, which greatly increased pitching and passengers' seasickness.

> Those were the days of long sailing voyages around the Cape of Good Hope, fifteen years before the opening of the first railroad to San Francisco and the line of steamers across the Pacific Ocean, and the sufferings of passengers were endured as a matter of course.[3]

And sufferings may have been emotionally aggravated by the tortuous route that the sailing ships took from New York City to China. Forced to take advantage of existing ocean currents and prevailing wind directions, instead of sailing south-southeast for the Cape of Good Hope at the southern tip of Africa: they proceeded southeast toward the Mediterranean Sea—then (at perhaps at two-thirds of the distance to Africa) turned southwest toward South America, eventually turning south-southwest to parallel the coast until reaching the thirty-eighth to fortieth degree of south latitude—then (abruptly due east) pass Cape Horn—then (on a course east-northeast) crossed the Indian Ocean—and finally turned north to China. So the Atlantic was crossed three times in the process, adding considerable distance to the voyage and creating the impression of going nowhere fast.[4]

To his credit, Charles Preston took the time required to reach China in stride, writing to the Walter Lowrie, Esq., Corresponding Secretary of the Mission Board, upon arrival on May 18, 1954 that:

> Our good ship *Horatio* after a long passage of over 160 days landed us safely at Hong Kong last Friday evening. The Reverend Dr. Johnson came aboard very soon after dropping anchor....There were no events of especial interest. There was an extraordinary uniformity of good feeling in all the interactions of the passengers with each other and with the Captain. The time I trust was profitably spent in preparation for the great work upon which we are entering—the opportunities for solemn reflection and quiet study were of unspeakable value ....[5]

On the long voyage he was accompanied by Dr. and Mrs. (Abby) John G. Kerr. Dr. Kerr was also a missionary of the Presbyterian Mission Board, who on arrival took over management of the Canton Ophthalmic hospital, the services of which were broadened to include all branches of medicine.[6] Kerr would accomplish much in a forty-seven-year career there and become a close associate of Charles'.

While Charles did not specifically make mention of it, a reason for his "solemn reflection" probably included the failure of his plan to be accompanied by a wife. What became of the relationship is not known, but one could imagine that the reality of leaving home, traveling for six months to reach a foreign land where customs and language were unfamiliar and challenging, combined with the prospect of an eventual return uncertain and perhaps nonexistent, may have caused his "intended" to reconsider.

Charles Finney Preston, ca. 1855. Courtesy of the family of Laura Preston Chase.

Charles' most direct allusion to his failed relationship is contained in a letter to Mr. Lowrie:[7]

Macao—October 6th, 1854

My Dear Mr. Lowrie,

I am most happy to inform you that what I considered a most bitter providence has finally resulted in great good—I know it was a severe discipline for me—my coming to China alone—but God has not forgotten—He has sent one of the best wives—I am enjoyed to be married to Mrs. Brewster of the A. B. C. F. M. (American Board of Commissioners for Foreign Missions). This is an open sanctification of Devine Providence which I hardly dared to hope to see—all our mutual friends seem to be very much delighted—I know that I am—you manifested in a letter interest in my affairs and I believe you will join with me in praise for this dispensation. I do not expect to be married until spring—but I wish to have a box sent as soon as possible. One of the enclosed letters is for Mr. Gus E Byrne—91 Liberty St. New York—a brother of Mrs. Brewster. It contains an order for a variety of articles to the amount of about $75. I would be glad to have the bill paid by you and charged to my account—and the box sent by the very first opportunity.

I expect to return to Canton in a few days to prepare myself to take charge of the Boy's School during Dr. Happer's absence.

I am with the greatest respects yours very truly,
C.F Preston

Mrs. Brewster (a.k.a. Mary Byrne Brewster) was the wife of Rev. Frederick H. Brewster, who died on January 29, 1853 of smallpox—one month after they arrived in Canton, China, having been married for less than one year.[8] They, like Charles Preston, endured a long voyage to Canton, followed by a sad and sudden end for the Reverend.

Canton, seventy miles north of Hong Kong, was reached via the Pearl River by "steamer." Having been unsuccessful in establishing a mission within the city, the Canton mission at that point in time was located on a leased property on the river-front—consisting of a school, chapel, residence, and dispensary. Dr. Kerr immediately took over management of the dispensary to relieve Dr. Andrew Happer, a minister and medical doctor who was overworked, being responsible at that point in time for the school as well as the dispensary. After an absence of sixteen years from the US, Dr. Happer immediately requested a furlough—stating "thinks Mrs. Happer needs it"[9]—turning management of the school over to the Reverend Charles Preston and left for a "health vacation" in Macao en route to the US. Twenty-three years later Charles would request a health vacation to seek relief for a chronic disease – which was declined with a tragic outcome.

Initially Preston accepted the sudden and unexpected assignment of the boys' boarding school with positive resignation, reflecting on it in the following terms in a letter to the corresponding secretary of the board dated February 9, 1855:

> Since I last wrote to you my relation with the Board has very much affected by the change in at our mission—The Charge of the Boys' Boarding School has placed me in a position of responsibility which I little expected to occupy at so early a stage of my missionary life & which but for the plain Direction of Providence I should not thought of assuming. I fear it will very much impede my progress in the acquisition of the languages as I have not thought of dividing my attention to teaching hereafter it will not aid me directly in preparation for my particular sphere of labor—preaching the gospel. But the indications of Providence were too plain to admit of a doubt as to this path of destiny & I cheerfully engage in their service....[10]

Rev. Preston's view of the change in direction would become decidedly negative as time progressed, as written on May 6, 1856:

> During the first months the school was no little burden on me—the boys were exceedingly refractory—the Chinese teacher was very inefficient—One of the assistants gave much trouble, by his dissolute conduct. I had been there but a short time, & had but few words of the language at my command. My introduction was anything but agreeable—The very day I came into the school the boys broke their rice bowls in a fit of anger—the next day they came in a body and demanded a holiday—One of them told me before the school & his father, the science teacher, that he would not obey me—I mention these things to show you the nature of the difficulties, with which I have had to contend—You may be surprised at such a state of things, but it is to be explained by the fact that, for some time previous to Dr. Happer's leaving, *his attention had been called away from the school & the atheism unrestrained was bringing forth its legitimate fruits.* I am happy to say that for a long time there has been no evidence of insubordination & I have no difficulty in maintaining proper discipline—the boys also are making commendable progress in their studies—What I have to complain of now is the difficulty of keeping them in school—Three of the first class have left this year to go with business—It is really against their best interests but all attempts to keep them have been in vain they could not resist the temptation of four or five dollars per month. This is the great complaint of the schools in Hong Kong—the boys cannot be kept long enough to get even a tolerable acquaintance with English—I assure you that it is wrong

to place such a temptation, as a knowledge of English is, into the missionary schools—there is a kind of intoxication about it—at least to a Chinese of which but too surely, prevents attention to our blessed religion. I say again, I do not believe that teaching English is true missionary work. I feel sure that there is better work to do here ....[11]

This attitude would not endear him to Dr. Happer, who coincidentally extended his furlough to the US for another year. In a letter dated July 7, 1856, Rev. Preston voiced his frustration at this news:

I consented to take that school for a time because I thought under the circumstances there was no other way—I was not able to preach during the first year of my missionary life— I took the school hoping and praying for success—I am ready to continue for another year—I will do as well as I can. There may be individual instances of success in labors which are not the most wisely directed—I feel that I shall be called to give an account for my relations to these boys. I ask for your prayers that I may have wisdom & patience to perform my whole duty with a willing mind. But hope I may be sent to preach the gospel—I have said at various times more upon this subject than any perhaps seem proper for one so young in missionary work—It has been because the subject has weighed upon my mind. I have thought that if in the Providence of God Dr. Happer should not be permitted to return to this field of labor which is clearly possible it would be much better that my view & feelings should be known: I should be sorry to have it expected that I should continue to take charge of the school in such a case."[12]

In due course Dr. Happer responded with his position on the school, in the context of "on place of Missionary Education in the work. My deep sense of the importance of it."[13] This squabble was indicative of an unpleasant relationship between the two gentlemen, which may have contributed indirectly to Rev. Preston's death at middle age. However, immediate relief for Dr. Preston was on its way, driven by the commercial interests of Great Britain's opium trade with China, resulting in armed conflict referred to as the Second Opium War.

✳ ✳ ✳

THE OPIUM WARS were two conflicts in the mid-nineteenth century fought in China, involving the Qing Dynasty and Great Britain.[14] The following is an attempt to meaningfully describe the conflicts in greatly abbreviated format – it relies heavily on selected details provided in Julia Lovell's thoroughly researched and scholarly work.

The principal cause was the desire of Great Britain to freely exploit a large market for opium produced in India, in opposition to China's attempts to eliminate opium distribution by banning use and sale. Great Britain's interest in opium sales was related to its huge consumption of tea imported from China, which resulted in a large trade imbalance threatening the nation's silver reserves. Marketing of manufactured products from Great Britain to offset the trade imbalance was not successful, but the demand for opium by the Chinese was strong and the profits large enough to single-handedly reverse the trade deficit.

In the 1820s Britain's started pursuing the sale of Indian-grown opium from the East India Company, which managed hundreds of thousands of acres devoted to poppies production, processed the poppies into opium cakes packed for shipment, and auctioned this produce to private merchants in Calcutta. The merchants transported the opium in chests to Lintin Island near the Pearl River mouth of the Chinese mainland. Chinese wholesalers used silver to purchase certificates from trading offices located in "factories" outside the walled city of Canton and exchanged them for opium. The silver was used by British merchants to purchase tea. The wholesalers then smuggled the opium into China (where it had been illegal since 1729) with the knowledge and assistance of government authorities in exchange for bribes.

The Chinese government was understandably concerned about loss of silver as well as the effects of the drug culture— but it was internally conflicted regarding use of the drug to the extent that, during the Opium War, opium was actually being produced in China. Part of the problem with opium was that, aside from recreational use to provide euphoria, it had medicinal uses that were at the time exclusive; there simply was no recognized, readily available drug to treat pain, diarrhea, dysentery, coughs, diabetes, malaria, or arthritis. For its part, Great Britain wanted opium legalized to eliminate the black market and provide a lawful and respectable basis for trade—as well as freedom to move within the country of China for sales and marketing purposes. Interestingly, the missionaries favored the latter while ignoring the impact of the drug on Chinese society.

The conflict in China's and Great Britain's positions came to a head in 1838 when Chinese soldiers from Canton underperformed during a battle with rebels, and the emperor blamed their battlefield shortcomings on the influence of opium. He took action by appointing an official, Lin Zexu, to the position of Imperial Commissioner to Canton, and directed him to annihilate the evil influence of opium. Lin Zexu commenced by threatening the population with one-year-suspended death sentences for smoking the drug. In addition, shortly after his March 1839 arrival in Canton, he had: 1,600 citizens arrested for opium related offenses, 14 tons of opium and 43,000 pipes seized, and put pressure on the Hong merchants to abandon sales.

To keep the peace, 20,283 chests of opium were given up by the British. These were destroyed as ordered by Lin Zexu by dumping them in the Pearl River, a combined practical and symbolic act, as that was where raw sewage from Canton flowed.

In reaction to the unrest and interruption of trade Britain sent a fleet of twenty-two warships, twenty-seven transports and thirty-six hundred troops to China, which arrived at Canton in mid-June 1840. The key objective was to protect the honor of the British flag, preserve the dignity of the British crown, and secure an agreement for long-term trade with China.

In the initial battle at Zhoushan, the large disparity in military strength was apparent: the British troops had muzzle-loading rifles similar to those used in the US Civil War, while most of the Chinese soldiers fought with bows and arrows and spears. (The few guns available to the Chinese were ca. fifteenth-century match-loaders.) Perhaps the greatest difference in military equipment were the warships. Great Britain's had as many as 120 guns, Chinese junks typically had only ten. Great Britain sent its latest technology: the ironclad, steam-driven warship, Nemesis. One junk was blown to bits by the first rocket from the Nemesis.

The forts on the river designed to protect Canton were roofless with no provisions for protection from land assaults. They fell quickly when attacked, being no match for British firepower. And while the Chinese troops outnumbered the British one hundred to one, they lacked discipline and would scatter immediately upon attack. To make matters worse, the Chinese military leadership was corrupt, indecisive, and incompetent.

The war ended in 1842; the terms of disengagement included: ceding of Hong Kong to the British, payment of $21 million for damages and war reparations, and reopening of trade. However, opium was not legalized. And there was a big discrepancy in the treaty terms from the perspective of the opposing sides. The British interpretation was that they were granted access to the "treaty ports" on a permanent basis, although the Chinese view was that access was prohibited outside of the "trading season," September through January. Further complicating matters was a feeling of distrust and negative characterizations on both sides— the British looking upon the Chinese as stupid, greedy, stubborn, and conceited—and for their part, the Chinese considered the British to be uncivilized, brutal, and paranoid.

The main issue of contention was British entry to the busy port of Canton, specifically the desire for unlimited right of residence, which was met with strong Cantonese opposition. Canton was opened as a treaty port; however, prospects for acceptance of missionaries were not favorable due to the British occupation and bombardment during the war. Nevertheless, in 1847 Dr. Happer, accompanied by Rev. John French, attempted to move a boarding school of thirty students to quarters in the city, but were driven out and forced to settle in the Dutch compound, and eventually at a riverfront property near the foreign factories. Although a typhoon had initially succeeded in blowing their roof off, by 1850 the mission property contained a day school, chapel, and residence. Yet for all practical purposes mission occupants were confined to their grounds. After a period of two years, bad feelings subsided to the point that two chapels could be opened in the city. In one instance, the chapel building was rented with neighborhood consent and the understanding that a dispensary would be opened. Later in the same year, a boarding school for boys was opened by Mrs. Happer.

The uncomfortable relationship between foreigners and the Chinese continued. The former—which included France, Russia, the United States, and England—were intent on opening the Chinese market to unrestricted trade.

Matters came to a head on October 8, 1856 when the Governor of the province took control of a Chinese pirate ship, the *Arrow*, that was registered in Hong Kong and flying the British flag. The ship turned out to be a storage facility for stolen goods, but the British, ignoring the questionable nature of its activities and validity of registry and ownership, equated seizure with disrespect for the British flag.

Reacting quickly to this affront, the British took action to beat the Chinese out of their "superiority complex" and drew up a plan to destroy the forts protecting Canton. On October 23, the British took possession of the forts. Anticipating the worst would happen, the Presbyterian mission boarding schools were dismissed the following day. In rapid succession, the British captured a Chinese warship and shelled Canton, breaking through city walls and destroying government offices—then withdrew to Hong Kong. Consequently, the mission houses and property were destroyed. Apparently, there was no loss of life because mission staff had safely departed by boat to the Portuguese colony of Macao, at the mouth of the Pearl River, seventy miles away.[15] It was here that Rev. Preston found the time to study the Chinese language, as well as to preach the Gospel.

It is worth mentioning that the Americans played a small role in the Canton assault. Three warships (the San Jacinto, Portsmouth and Levant) were in Chinese waters when the war broke out. The

American consul in Canton requested military assistance to protect lives and property to which a force including a contingent of Marines responded. On November 15, an unarmed boat from the San Jacinto was fired upon from one of the four Chinese-manned barrier forts that protected the approach to the Canton harbor, killing the coxswain. The incident quickly escalated into a battle in which the American force took control of the forts. Seven US Marines were killed in the battle, while it is estimated that 500 Chinese defenders also died.[16]

Dr. Kerr was nearby when the forts were attacked; he filed a report that provided insight on the conflict, as well as his own basic decency in being willing to put his life at risk to assist the wounded, mostly Chinese:

Macao, 12th December 1856—

I wrote you [Mr. Lowrie] a hasty note from Whampoa on 22nd Nov. I was there for the purpose of getting at the Chinese who were wounded at the taking of the Barrier Forts by the Americans. On the 24th I visited these forts which had been a few days before the Scene of deadly conflict, but not a soldier was to be seen. I went in a field nearby one of the forts which was garrisoned by [American] marines & talked with some men who were busy gathering their crop of rice; they said my object was a very good one, but that all the soldiers had returned to Canton & had taken the wounded with them. Having made every effort I safely could in Canton I was compelled to give up all hopes of doing anything during the continuance of hostilities for those who might be injured by the weapons of their enemies.

The Americans have been engaged in destroying the walls of the four barrier forts, while a diplomatic correspondence has been going on between Gov. Gen Yeh & Com. Armstrong. On the 26th Nov. Dr. Parker issued a notice stating [that] Com A. would not desist from those measures that were forced upon him by the obstinacy of the Gov Gen until satisfaction was obtained. The opinion of all Americans & English was that the destruction of the forts was enough. It is more reported that the Gov Gen has sent a letter to Com. A. quite satisfactory, but I cannot say how true it is. The English are keeping up a blockade of the water approaches to Canton, while orders are waited for from London. What will be the end or when is still hidden in the dark & unknown future. The Suffering and Starvation of thousands who are driven from businesses & home must be inconceivable. The Rebels or pirates are collecting in force on the rivers & it is feared that the Scenes of two years ago will be renewed. Rev. French has gone to Shanghai. The rest of us are together in Macao enjoying health and peace. No missionary except myself has got his teacher to continue with him. We have been looking for a room in which to open a chapel & dispensary here. The Wesleyan Mission have kindly offered us a room in their house & we will use it until Mrs. K's return.

Respectfully Yours,
John G. Kerr[17]

Property and lives aside, the Americans, like the English, were there in part to protect business interests. During the period of the Opium Wars, American businessmen were likewise struggling to develop profitable trade with the Chinese. Warren Delano II, the grandfather of Franklin Delano Roosevelt was among them. He arrived in China in 1833 and eventually became involved in the Opium trade. Returning to the United States in 1846 after the first Opium War, he invested in real estate, railroads, and other respectable ventures—living comfortably until the Panic of 1857, when he found himself in a precarious financial condition. Returning to China, he restored his fortune by trading in Opium. His attitude toward the trade is summarized as follows: "I do not pretend to justify...the opium trade in a moral and philanthropic point of view... .As a merchant it has been fair, honorable and legitimate,"...[similar to] "the importation of wines and spirits into the United States"[18] (not to mention enormously lucrative). *Where you stand depends on where you sit*—Nelson Mandela.

The English at the time of the assault on Canton were in negotiations with Russia, France, and the United States in an attempt to secure allies in the military operation to open the Chinese market. France agreed to terms of cooperation and participated in the campaign that followed. The United States pursued a course of neutrality, which in isolated instances resulted in limited armed combat, while the Russians cooperated in diplomatic efforts only. The American stance presumably contributed to access to Canton prior to ratification of the treaty ending the war.

Following an English Parliament debate in March 1857, a decision was made to pursue a military solution. An Anglo-French fleet was sent to Canton, issued an ultimatum to surrender, and when that was not accepted, on December 29, 1857 heavily bombarded the city, setting roofs on fire throughout. In early January, French and British troops entered and occupied the city, capturing the Governor and taking him to India, where he died shortly afterward.

The following May the combined fleet sailed for Beijing, destroying forts along the way and forcing the emperor's negotiators to accept the Treaty of Tianjin. When the British team returned in June of 1859 to ratify the agreement in Beijing, the Chinese blocked the river from Tianjin. A fierce engagement ensued in which the Chinese showed improved capability to wage war, killing and wounding hundreds of British troops.

The British response was to send the fleet back for a vengeful reengagement at the forts of Tianjin in which many Qing soldiers were slaughtered, with relatively low British losses. Following the battle, talks were arranged which the Chinese used as a ploy to kidnap the British negotiating team and subject them to torture. Although they were later returned, some had died in captivity and were transported back in coffins. In retribution, the British and their French partners fought their way overland to Beijing and—upon reaching the location of the Emperor's summer palace—engaged in looting and desecration, and eventually burned it down. At that point the Qing saw the hopelessness of continuing the hostilities, particularly in view of ongoing revolts of their subjects in the south and central regions.

The Treaty of Beijing, ratified on October 16, 1860 ended the conflict with very favorable terms for the British: a fourfold increase in indemnities; the right to establish an embassy in Beijing; freedom to travel, trade, and work beyond the treaty ports; and legalization of Opium.

For the Chinese, the humiliating "resolution" of the conflict is, according to a scholarly source, the root and continuing motivation of Chinese nationalism prevalent today.

* * *

WHILE THE WAR gave Rev. Preston relief from responsibilities of managing the boys' school, allowing him to focus on learning the Chinese language and preaching the gospel, he and his wife suffered greatly from the death of an infant son. In his own words:

> Macao, 12th December 1857
>
> My Dear Mr. Lowrie,
>
> It is but a short time since I wrote to you asking for your sympathy in my joy at the birth of a little son—I have now to ask for your sympathy at his loss—The same hand which gave, has been stretched out to take away—His young spirit took flight on the morning of the 6th. He was with us only two months and six days and yet we loved him dearly, and we are deeply afflicted—We had devoted him to the cause of missions God grant that his death may make us better fitted for our work—He was not too young to teach a solemn lesson on the bed of death. We are not without consolation as we believe he is now learning the song of saints in the praise of Christ by whose merits he is saved—We feel that it is another warning of our mortality—a summons to be up and doing our Master's works.[19]

To this day, the grave of the son, Charles Hodge Preston (named out of respect for Charles Hodge, principal of Princeton Theological Seminary during Rev. Preston's studies there) in the Old Presbyterian Cemetery, Macau is marked by a small

Monument of Charles Hodge Preston.
Courtesy of Chris Nelson.

monument with the inscription: "In memory of Charles Hodge infant son of Rev C. F. Preston—died 6th Dec 1857—aged 2 months and 6 days—*suffer little children to come unto me—Jesus Christ.*" How painful it must have been to leave him there. And it was not to be their last loss of this kind.

The return of the Presbyterian missionaries to Canton proceeded in fits and starts, long before ratification of the treaty ending the war. The difficulties related to the political situation and living conditions of the general population and the missionaries are described in Rev. Preston's letter of March 12, 1858:

My Dear Mr. Lowrie,

Since the last dates, an answer has been received from the Emperor to the communications sent by the Chinese officers, after the capture of Canton. The document is exceedingly barren of information as to the future policy of the government. The notorious "Yeh" is of course degraded for not doing one of two things—driving away the barbarians or making peace with them. All the other officers retain their places (instead of being punished as they requested) upon the grounds that they were never taken into the counsel of "Yeh" and they are thus very charitably judged not to be participants in his guilt. A new governor general has been appointed Wong Trung How, a native of the province of Fukian. He is empowered to manage the affairs of the barbarians. But the commissioners of the several foreign powers now especially interested in the affairs of this country viz the United States—England, France & Russia have agreed to send communications to Peking requesting a commissioner empowered to settle existing difficulties and to revise the Treaties to be sent to meet them at Shanghai— the communications have been sent and are doubtless by this time receiving the consideration of the Emperor and his advisors. We have made the matter a subject of special prayer in our religious meetings of late. If a favorable answer should not be received and any delay be occasioned in opening negotiations the foreign commissioners will doubtless proceed forthwith to pay their respects to the Emperor "in propria persona" It is generally believed that there is a disposition to peace but it is thought that it will be necessary and best to visit the Northern Capital. This is a proper subject for prayer for the hearts of princes are in the hand of God and He disposes them to the accomplishments of His own glorious purposes.

In the meantime the Cantonese have a bitter pill to take. It is exceedingly humiliating but there is no help for it as the "City of Rams" is under martial law. It is rather an aggravation to many that the rulers so gentle and so much care is taken that it should not be offensive. The police force is well organized. The allies are making the most of their opportunities—reforming the prisons & even the names of the streets are translated and painted in blazing colors at the corners, proclaiming in English and French the introduction of a new order of things.

There has been a wide field for the exercise of charity and it has been cultivated to some extent. The city is thronged with beggars—multitudes reduced to want by the late hostilities. The chaplain of the English forces has been active in raising funds and applying them for the relief of the distress. Several of the missionaries who have returned have taken part in this good work. Two chapels have already been rented within the city. One by the Rev. H. Cox of the English Wesleyan Society in East College St. D. Wong the Chinese educated in England and sent out by the London Missionary Society distributes medicines daily in the building—The Rev H. Guillard has also obtained a commodious chapel for the Southern Baptist Religion. The few missionaries who are there have very poor accommodations—mostly on the ground. The houses in the city are represented as much inferior to those in the suburbs— the people are respectful within the limits reached by the foreign police – beyond it is evidently unsafe to go unarmed. Upon the whole however the prospects are exceedingly favorable—indeed beyond the most sanguine expectations. Bro. French or myself will take an early opportunity to make a visit—It has been raining for a week. I shall feel myself away from home until I get back with my family—In the meantime we have great accomplishments in Macao—the chapel is filled every day.

I am My Dear Mr. Lowrie, Yours Truly

C.F. Preston[20]

Rev. Preston and family returned to Canton on November 16, 1858, followed by Dr. Kerr and family in early December. Dr.

Kerr wrote of his attempts to find housing, which included his anguish over the legalization of Opium:

Canton Dec 11th 1858

Mr. Lowrie

My Dear Sir,

Soon after Mr. Rev & Mrs. French sailed, I came up to Canton with the Rev. Preston & family. Having spent about ten days looking for a house, I returned to Macao for Mrs. Kerr & brought her up Dec 2nd. We are occupying Mr. Preston's verandah for the present. It was not until yesterday that I succeeded in obtaining a house & it will require two or three weeks work before we can go into it. We pay $15 per month. It will be necessary to have more room for a chapel, hospital & school & we are negotiating for the next house & expect to get it for 12 or 13 dollars per month. These two will afford us all the rooms we need to present & can be made to accommodate two families without a very large outlay

You can readily understand we have many difficulties to contend with in resuming our work here & it is often hard to decide what to do but we look to God for his blessing & hope we will be guided in understanding taking what we trust is his own work. I was the last of the missionary circle in obtaining house and I have had to some extent the advantage of all their experience

I am inclined to think that Christians at home are too Sanguine as to the good that is to result from the recent war. The country was open to missionary effort far beyond what the force in the field was able to undertake. The prejudice that has long existed against the English is greatly increased & missionaries of that nation cannot escape the odor that rests upon them in the eyes of the people. The opium trade has been legalized and now all our foreign merchants can impose the poisonous drug under the sanction of law. I look upon this as a disgrace not only to the nation that has brought it about but to all Christendom. Nevertheless God can make the calamities of war and all the evil growing out of it work together for the accomplishment of his own gracious prospects of mercy to our fallen grace.

While we are without a Chapel Mr. Preston & our young assistant preach in temples & in the streets, sometimes to attentive audiences. We are all well.

With great Respect,
Yours,
J. G. Kerr[21]

In 1859, the missionaries reestablished a presence in Canton while the war involving the Chinese, English, and French continued in areas to the North. There were issues raised by the missionary board in decisions made regarding new housing. Rev. Preston responded bluntly: "Sorry the Board disapproves housing situation ... because you do not understand. ... We have made the best bargain of any of the Missions."[22]

Dr. Kerr supported Preston with a letter "justifying steps taken in securing the houses. ... The Mission has two good houses in the best locations along the river."[23] This was followed by another letter from Rev. Preston in which he "defends Mission action on securing the houses. It will be remembered, we had no definite rules. Left to our own judgement."[24]

The issue apparently was resolved or perhaps quietly died when mission claims against the Chinese Government for damages to mission property resulting for the war were allowed in the amount of $43,330.[25]

In the meantime, after an absence of five years, Dr. Happer returned with the intent of opening boys and girls boarding schools. Rev. Preston quickly weighed in with his opinion that English should not be taught, but his advice was apparently disregarded— with Dr. Kerr coming to Dr. Happer's defense[26]—though in all probability it did nothing to endear him to Dr. Happer. Preston's ongoing feud with the well-connected Dr. Happer would result in consequences unintended by both, leading to a tragic end.

Notes

[1] Necrological Report presented to the Alumni Association of the Princeton Theological Seminary, (April 27, 1875), 57.

[2] Rev. L. S. Foster, *Fifty Years in China—An Eventful Memoir of Tarleton Perry Crawford, DD*, (Nashville: Bayless-Fullen Company, 1909), 50.

[3] Ibid.

[4] Rev. R. S. Maclay and Rev. D. W. Clark, eds., "To China by Way of the Cape" in *The Ladies Repository*, (1862) 22:204–205.

[5] Rev. Charles F. Preston, letter to Walter Lowrie—May 18, 1854. Presbyterian Church in U.S.A. Foreign Mission Correspondence and Reports: 1833–1911, China, 1837–1911, letter book vols. 4,5,8, 9: calendar entry 340, (Philadelphia: Presbyterian Historical Society).

[6] G. Thompson Brown, *Earthen Vessels and Transcendent Power: American Presbyterians in China, 1837-1952*, (American Society of Missiology Series (Maryknoll, NY: Orbis Books, 1997), 36.

[7] Rev. Charles F. Preston, letter to Walter Lowrie—October 6, 1854. Presbyterian Church in U.S.A. Foreign Mission Correspondence and Reports..., letter book vols. 4,5,8, 9: calendar entry 351.

[8] Historical Catalogue of the Theological Institute of Connecticut, (Hartford, CT: Case, Lockwood & Brainard Company, 1881), 61.

[9] Dr. A. P. Happer—May 20, 1854. Presbyterian Church in U.S.A. Foreign Mission Correspondence and Reports..., letter book vols. 4,5,8, 9: calendar entry 341.

[10] Ibid., 363. (C. F. Preston—February 9, 1855).

[11] Ibid., 395. (C. F. Preston—May 6, 1856).

[12] Ibid., 401. (C. F. Preston—July 7, 1856).

[13] Ibid., 408. (A. P. Happer—November 7, 1856).

[14] Julia Lovell, *The Opium War: Drugs, Dreams, and the Making of China*, (New York: The Overlook Press, 2014).

[15] J. B. French—December 5, 1856. Presbyterian Church in U.S.A. Foreign Mission Correspondence and Reports..., letter book vols. 4,5,8, 9: calendar entry 411.

[16] "The Barrier Forts: A Battle, a Monument and a Mythical Marine," Marine Corps Historical Reference Series/Historical Branch G-3, (Washington D.C.: Division Headquarters–US Marine Corps), no. 6 (1962): 4-9.

[17] John G. Kerr, MD—December 13, 1856, Presbyterian Church in U.S.A. Foreign Mission Correspondence and Reports..., letter book vols. 4,5,8, 9: calendar entry 413.

[18] Joseph E. Persico, *Franklin & Lucy—Mrs. Rutherford and the Other Remarkable Women in Roosevelt's Life*, (New York, Random House, 2008), 12–13.

[19] Rev. Charles F. Preston—December 12, 1857. Presbyterian Church in U.S.A. Foreign Mission Correspondence and Reports..., letter book vols. 4,5,8, 9: calendar entry 443

[20] Ibid., 451. (C. F. Preston—March 12, 1858).

[21] Ibid., 471. (J. G. Kerr—December 11, 1858).

[22] Ibid., 485. (C. F. Preston—August 8, 1859).

[23] Ibid., 486. (J. G. Kerr—August 22, 1859).

[24] Ibid., 490. (C. F. Preston—October 10, 1859).

[25] Ibid., 495. (J. G. Kerr—December 26, 1859).

[26] Ibid., 504(a). (J. G. Kerr—March 10, 1860).

— Chapter Three —

William and Platt:
The Colorado Gold Rush

Golden Gate City, ca. 1860.
Photo courtesy of the Gardner family collection.

N 1858—AS Charles anticipated his return to Canton—William, eventually joined by Platt, was on his way to the future site of Denver as one of the early participants in the Pikes Peak Gold Rush. His decision was very possibly influenced by the knowledge that four onetime residents of his small hometown—Sam Davis, James Jones, John Allen, and Horace Carpentier—had joined the 1849 California gold rush, and several achieved some measure of success.

A "gold rush" is the rapid movement of people to a place where gold has been discovered, which may extend over a period of years, starting with the first rumors of gold discovery and ending when easily accessible gold has been exhausted. By this definition, the California Gold Rush began in January, 1848 with discovery of placer gold at Sutter's Mill near Sacramento and ended in 1852. The California Gold Rush was the largest in US history, with major impacts including: establishing California as a state in two-years' time without the intermediate step of becoming a US territory; quadrupling the population of the state in a ten-year period; hastening the development of transportation systems for movement of people from the East to the West coast, starting with a railroad across the Isthmus of Panama and culminating in the US with the First Transcontinental Railroad; and greatly increasing the nation's wealth while making a small number of ordinary individuals instantly rich. Unfortunately, all of the progress was accompanied by mistreatment of the indigenous population, ranging from indifference to their plight associated with displacement from ancestral lands, to abjectly cruel and brutal treatment.

One further, but intuitively obvious, aspect related to rushes: if one decides to go, sooner is better than later, as William had evidently concluded.

The little that is known about the experiences of Messrs. Davis, Jones, or Allen in California from a document in the Galway Preservation Society archives is summarized below. It is remarkable that four individuals from an isolated town in upstate New York, population at that time about 2,400, would go—and that three of the four would prosper from the experience. To put it in perspective, at that time in history the population of the US was approximately 23 million, of which an estimated 230,000 (or

1 percent) would participate in the migration, and most came back home empty-handed. Galway's participation based on the historical archive was four out of a town population of 2,400 (or less than 0.2 percent, but with a 75 percent success rate). The latter might have been a factor in William's decision to go to Colorado, the odds of success looking pretty favorable.

Returning to the experiences of the Galway Argonauts—Sam Davis "was a 49er, became very wealthy, lived the life of a hermit, did his own cooking, never married and left several millions."[1] He had three sisters who remained in Galway, the last of which, Jane, died in 1905 just after she inherited over a million dollars from Sam. Wealth is a definitely a poor substitute for good health.

James Jones "went [to] California during the gold rush and returned to Galway. He was a next-door neighbor of the Davis family on South St. His wife Olive, nee Davis, was the daughter of Benjamin Davis, probably related to Paul Davis, the father of Sam,"[2] It is not known if he had success as a prospector, and he was possibly one of many, many "go-backs" who, having arrived late, became discouraged by the amount of labor frequently required to obtain a very small amount of gold dust.

By contrast, John Allen went to California during the gold rush, was reportedly successful, came back to Galway, and carried on a wagon-making shop on West Street until his untimely death in 1857.[3]

*   *   *

REGARDING HORACE CARPENTIER, the story is distinct, and there exist clear and detailed accounts of his life and business activities. The son of James and Henrietta Carpenter, he was born in Providence in 1824, the youngest of eight children. Sources differ on the change of last name from Carpenter to Carpentier. Shortly after receiving a law degree at Columbia University, he left for California by sailing ship, arriving in San Francisco via Cape Horn in August 1849. The ship, *Panama*, was purchased as a joint venture by two hundred young men and was sold upon arrival in California.[4] He quickly became involved in local politics and set up a law office. A trip to California gold country followed two unsuccessful campaigns for political office and amounted to nothing. However, he did achieve success in real estate transactions, though not without controversy. Through development of political connections, during the incorporation of the city he was able to gain control of the entire waterfront. He was the first Mayor of Oakland and served on the boards of a railroad, bank, and the company that completed the first transcontinental telegraph line. Along the way, he acquired the title of "General." While his "ownership" of the Oakland waterfront was contentious and, after many years, dissolved by legal action—through skillful maneuvering he was able to amass a fortune of $20 million before he left California in 1880. He travelled to China, engaged in business ventures there and employed a Chinese valet, Dean Lung, who returned with him to the United States. In 1893 he established permanent residence in a brownstone on East Thirty-Seventh Street, New York City, and subsequently remodeled and maintained a summer home in Galway. In 1901 Dean Lung sent a letter with a check for $12,000 to Columbia University as a contribution to the Fund for Chinese Learning. Out of respect for his companion and servant, General Carpentier, a trustee, subsequently donated $200,000 to set up an endowment for Chinese Studies, in memory of Dean Lung.[5]

In 1905, he began to stay year-round at his home in Galway. His philanthropic actions there were numerous, among them:

donating the family property in the Town of Providence to Saratoga County for a tuberculosis hospital; providing funds for improvements to roads including one still bearing the name Dean Lung Road; and installing a water trough for use by Galway village animals, which still exists. He died at the age of ninety-four, leaving a considerable amount of his fortune to Columbia University, Sloane Hospital for Women, New York Presbyterian Hospital, University of California at Berkeley, and American Society for Prevention of Cruelty to Animals.[6]

* * *

HOW MUCH WILLIAM Preston knew of the success of Sam Davis, John Allen, and Horace Carpentier is a matter of conjecture, but certainly some information would have been provided to him by his father, who remained in touch with him. Thus, William's involvement in the Pikes Peak Gold Rush may have simply reflected his knowledge in what could be achieved, either by mining for gold, or related business development. In the end, during the time he was there he more closely pursued Carpentier's approach toward accumulation of wealth, rather than Davis' approach, and later in life became a noteworthy philanthropist. It is tempting to think he had a plan; he would go first to get an understanding of the opportunities while his brother disposed of the river freight and ferry business. Then his brother would join him and share the effort required for searching for gold while William would also get involved in territorial politics and business development.

* * *

To BRIEFLY SUMMARIZE, beginning in the 1820s, rumors of extensive gold deposits in the front range of the Rocky Mountains persisted for decades. Finally, some individuals with the determination and knowledge to make an evaluation traveled there. The Colorado Gold Rush was triggered by the discovery of placer gold (fine particles of gold, "gold dust," interspersed in soil) by a group of prospectors led by William Russell of Auraria, Georgia in the summer of 1858. Not coincidentally, Auraria, Georgia is one of only two places east of the Mississippi River that had significant gold deposits, so Auraria was the name given to one of the first towns established at the present site of Denver.

After the initial discovery of gold, there was an explosion of immigration to the region, that is, "the Gold Rush." Perhaps one hundred thousand individuals came—mostly men discouraged by their current employment (or lack thereof), excited by exaggerated newspaper reports of the riches to be found in the gold fields, and enticed by the prospect of adventure travelled to the area. Some made the twenty-to-thirty-day trek from the Missouri River to the future location of Denver—with minimal provisions and means of transportation. There they found that, in general, prospecting for gold was hard work; the gold was in isolated areas, and one day of effort could yield less than that necessary for a good meal. Faced with these harsh realities many, perhaps 40–50 percent, lost their enthusiasm and returned east. Labeled "go-backs" they were a common sight on the trails encountered by westward-bound travelers who caused confusion by citing news reports of ever-increasing discoveries, with the result that some go-backs reversed their direction and returned to the Denver area.[7]

In fact, more deposits of lode gold (seams of gold in rock) were found in January of 1859 in the same general location near the present city of Denver, resulting in thousands of new prospectors traveling overland through the territory of Nebraska by different routes from cities on the Missouri River. There were several trails across Nebraska north, central and south—the northern trail starting from Omaha, following the Platte River to the branch with the South Platte River, and thence along the South Platte River to the future site of Denver.

❋ ❋ ❋

ACCORDING TO INFORMATION contained in a regional biographical sketch, William Preston was among the earliest arrivals on the site of Denver and built one of the first houses there, in the gold mining town of Auraria,[8] This is vaguely consistent with information in the Galway archives that he and his brother Platt had something to do with laying out the city of

Denver. However, the brief but detailed records in the archives of the Colorado Historical Society indicate that he first resided in the town of Douglas City, and subsequently in Golden Gate City.

William Preston arrived at the current site of Denver shortly after gold was discovered in July 1858. He had a contract to build a house there dated December 6. Whatever his interest in mining for gold, it seems to have been secondary to politics and land and business development. Perhaps his brother Platt, who arrived there later, was the prospector. In 1859 there was strong interest in forming a government for the territory to be named Jefferson, after Thomas Jefferson. William became a delegate to the constitutional convention from Douglas City, one of the settlements that quickly sprang up near the gold mining area. The convention met as scheduled on June 6, 1859, then adjourned until August when a constitution was drafted for the proposed Jefferson State. Meanwhile, he became involved in the development of Golden Gate City, located on a 640-acre parcel of land in the vicinity of Golden City and Denver.

Founders of 'cities' at the foot hills within sight of Auraria-Denver persisted in their activities through the last half of the year 1859. About the middle of July, the Golden Gate Town Company was formed by Thomas J. Golden, J. S. Rogers, Charles Fletcher, H. S. Hawley and W. G. Preston who had selected for their purpose 640 acres of land lying about two miles north of Golden City and hidden from the plains by the northward extension of the mesa-like elevation known as "Table Mountain." There they plotted a town upon which they bestowed the name 'Golden Gate' because it was situated near the point where the easier route from Auraria-Denver to the diggings on the North fork of Clear Creek entered the mountains.[9]

As one of five permanent appointed officers of the convention, it is reasonable to assume that he chose to represent Golden Gate City.

Evidence of progress in developing Golden Gate City is found in this brief statement by a reporter in the *Rocky Mountain News*, dated September 10, 1859:

> Fording the river at the point made famous by the passage of Horace Greeley on a refractory [stubborn] mule, we diverged from the old road, and in a short distance entered the mountains at Golden Gate, a city with ambitious name and some 8-10 houses, occupying a commanding site, overlooking its rival—Golden City and the plains for many miles.

It was followed by an announcement in the same newspaper, dated September 26, 1859, under the heading:

> Miners and the Public generally TAKE NOTICE: The Golden Gate Town Company are now donating lots and will continue to donate during the winter to all who will improve them. Golden Gate is one of the most pleasant places in the whole country for winter quarters with wood, water, good grass, building timber, saw mills and the best hunting grounds the country affords, convenient.
>
> Golden Gate being situated at the foot of the mountains, immediately at the mouth of the canon, on the road to the largest, rich and most extensive gold region in the west,

range of mountains is positively the best business point in the whole country.

All who wish building lots will do well [to] call on the secretary and make their selections as early as possible.

By order of the Board of Directors, W. G. Preston, Sec'y.

At about the same time the state constitution was rejected by a popular referendum in September because a territory would be funded by the US congress while a state would be self-funded. And unlike the circumstances of California ten years prior, a direct path to statehood was not available. The constitutional convention met for a third time in October 1859 to draft a constitution for the "*territory* of Jefferson." A provisional government for the territory was established the same month and officials elected. Included in the proposed territory of Jefferson was all of the current state of Colorado but with a major difference that the northern boundary was approximately 140 miles further north than the current one. Governor Steele opened the first session of provisional territorial legislature in November 1859, with a second session scheduled for January 1860 in Denver City.

While the steps were being taken to form a government, William Preston was actively pursuing a business venture. By early February 1860, he had conveyed to other parties his interest in seven lots in the cities of Denver, Auraria, and Golden City, and was engaged in building a hotel in Golden Gate City with his brother Platt. The *Western Mountaineer* and *Rocky Mountain News* issue of March 30, 1860 contained the following ad for Gate City Hotel:

The undersigned have opened a Hotel at Golden Gate, where we are prepared to receive guests. Every effort will be made by the proprietors to establish the reputation of the Gate City Hotel as one of the best Hotels in the mining region. The patronage of our friends and the public generally is respectfully solicited. Preston & Bro.

In the April 6, 1860 *Western Mountaineer*, it was reported:

A grand inauguration ball was given on Friday evening last by Capt. W. G. Preston & Bro., on the occasion of the opening of the Gate City Hotel, at Golden Gate. A large number of ladies were present, whose gay dresses, ringing laughter and winning smiles forcibly reminded us of our younger days, when, in far off America, we essayed to "Trip the light fantastic toe" and thought we were "some". The supper was to be quite a surprise—such an array of delicacies we did not expect to see in this region; the tables, (to use an original expression) literally groaned beneath the weight of good things. Dancing was kept up till the "wee sma' hours" when all went home apparently surfeited with pleasure. Success to the Gate City Hotel.

And then the situation slowly but surely deteriorated:

Originally the Golden Gate Canyon Road went straight up and across the mountain to the North, following native trails of old. In 1860 Daniel L. McCleery took it upon himself to blaze a new Golden Gate Canyon Road through Golden Gate Canyon itself. It was built as a toll road leading to the gold fields of today's Gilpin County and the

Central City/Black Hawk area and was one of the main roads to the Gold regions of Colorado.

The new Golden Gate Road was quite successful and Daniel McCleery was elected the Second Mayor of Golden Gate City in June of 1860. However, all was not well, as Golden Gate resident Alfred Tucker lodged a legal challenge to the Golden Gate Town Company. He alleged that the town company had illegally entered upon his ranching claim and he sought control of the Golden Gate City townsite and the canyon road that McCleery had just built. This spurred a bitter lawsuit between Tucker and his allies and McCleery and his allies, which included the Golden Gate community which backed their Mayor. Prevailing in the Arapahoe County Court of Kansas Territory, Tucker ultimately gained control of the road.[10]

Well, at least for a short time.

In July of 1860, a Denver saloon owner, James Gordon, murdered John Ganz in Denver and escaped to Leavenworth, Kansas where he was apprehended and brought before the Supreme Court of Kansas Territory, which included the provisional Jefferson Territory. The October 1860 decision by the Court held that the crime took place where no official court had jurisdiction and ordered him released.[11] Though Gordon was subsequently removed to Denver by quick action of local authorities, tried and convicted by an extralegal "people's court," and hanged for the crime—the legal precedent established by the Supreme Court ruling put the Golden Gate City property dispute resolution in limbo because rule of law was in serious doubt.

Further complicating the matter, Rick Gardner, Golden, Colorado historian, writes:

Golden Gate's people claimed the townsite under jurisdiction of Jefferson County, Jefferson Territory (the extralegal provisional government) while Tucker claimed the
road and townsite as his ranch under Arapahoe County,
Kansas Territory (the legal but operationally ineffective
government). It is quite recently I discovered that, as
a legal matter, in the end both were wrong, because the
Kansas Territorial government had reorganized the area
as Montana County before either claim was made and
the court decision setting murderer James A. Gordon free
effectively legally vaporized both of their claims. This
might be why Tucker himself ultimately peacefully settled in Golden Gate City. Ironically Montana County was
stillborn because the legislature failed to fund it (therefore
no one to hand Gordon over to). Both Tucker and Golden
Gate City were, in legal effect, squatters! The developed
part of the Golden Gate townsite is now owned by the
Brunel family and there could be archaeological remains
there.[12]

And if that weren't enough to sink the Preston brothers' business venture, an attempt to legitimize the provisional Jefferson
Territory stalled when, in August 1860, the Kansas Territory
rebuffed a proposal for a merger. It was not until February
1861 that the Colorado Territory was created by act of the US
Congress and signed into law by President James Buchanan,
just days before President Abraham Lincoln was inaugurated.
Lincoln was a Republican—Governor Steele, a Democrat who
reportedly had been vocally opposed to Lincoln's positions and
therefore not likely to have much political leverage in organizing the new government. At this point the provisional Jefferson

Territory government was disbanded, undoubtedly leaving its officeholders and supporters, William Preston included, in a state of confusion and political uncertainty.

To make matters worse for the Prestons, the number of individuals seeking gold decreased in 1860 because most easily extractable gold had been mined in 1859, and the rush was ending. Then the Civil War began: troops in the territory were called back east, the routes connecting Colorado to the Missouri River became subject to attack by native-Americans and outlaws, leading citizens left to join the war effort, and a severe economic depression resulted.[13]

Golden Gate City showed promise for a brief period and was envisioned by some as a rival to Golden City. But its time of prosperity was limited, and it eventually disappeared. The Prestons probably saw evidence of their business prospects declining and started evaluating alternatives. Gold had been discovered in central Idaho in the Florence and Elk City region....

Back home, 1859 was a bad year for Dr. Preston.

Notes

[1] Elizabeth Robb Quinby and Ethel Robb, *Historical and Genealogical Notes of Galway, New York*, 2 vols., Galway Preservation Society Archives, Section D.

[2] Ibid., Section J.

[3] Ibid., Section A.

[4] "Galway 1900–1949: A Photographic History of Life in the Town of Galway, Saratoga County, New York," *Galway Preservation Society* (2014), 62.

[5] "Department History," Columbia University Department of East Asian Languages & Cultures, ealac.columbia.edu/department/short-history, September 1, 2019.

[6] "Galway 1900–1949," 62.

[7] Elliott West, The Contested Plains, (University Press of Kansas, 1998), 175.

[8] Vance Orchard, compiled by, *Waitsburg: "One of a Kind"*, Waitsburg Historical Society, (1976), 41.

[9] Jerome C. Smiley, Semi-Centennial History of the State of Colorado, vol. 1, (Lewis Publishing Co., 1913), 269

[10] Richard Gardner, "Golden Gate City Sesquicentennial—Road to the Gold," Gardner History & Preservation. www.gardnerhistory.com/sesquicentennialstories/goldengatecity

[11] Manfred Berg, *Popular Justice: A History of Lynching in America*, (2011), 64.

[12] Richard Gardner, in discussion with the author, February 21, 2018.

[13] Ibid.

— Chapter Four —

Dr. Preston versus
the Caverts

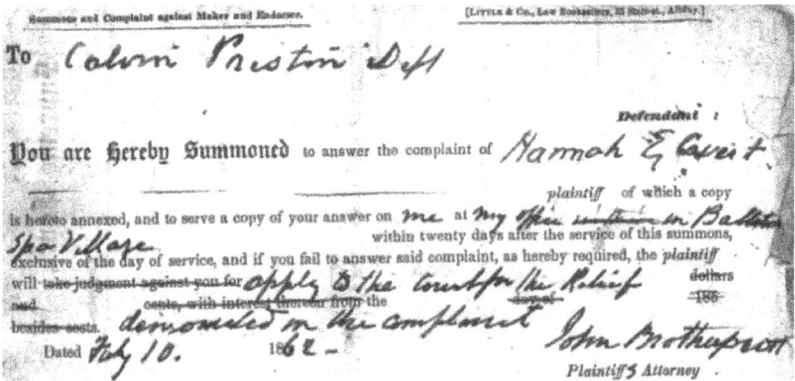

Summons—Hannah Cavert, plaintiff v. Calvin Preston, defendant. File A-135,
Saratoga Historian's Archive, Saratoga County Municipal Offices, Ballston Spa, NY.

*T*he oral history notes compiled by Elizabeth Robb
Quinby contain the following negative assessment of Dr.
Calvin Preston, Galway, NY physician from 1830 to 1877,
attributed to Harvey Crouch, local farmer: "He was the village
doctor with a large practice. He wasn't very brilliant or much
of a man, short, rather effeminate. He kissed Billie Cavert's wife
one time and Billie sued him. He was remembered for kissing his
women patients."[1]

Harvey didn't stop there, noting that "he was very fond of flowers"—not considered a very manly thing, one supposes—and "Rev. Charles Preston, son of Calvin Preston was educated and went to China about 1850. Never heard that he had very much success in converting the heathen Chinese." Apparently, Mr. Crouch was not impressed by the Preston family.

While oral history is a valuable source of information on the past, accuracy suffers when it is based on a mixture of incomplete facts, potentially flawed recollection, and prejudice—either positive or negative. The clarity of recollections fades with time, and some of the facts disappear or are altered in translation, but prejudices tend to remain strong, which may have been what happened in this case. Therefore, verification is important. Fortunately, the reference to a lawsuit identified a path to documentation in the form of legal records carefully archived by the Saratoga County Clerk and Historian's office, going back to the date of the Cavert incident, and from that emerges a more complicated but sympathetic view of the situation relative to the Doctor.

According to a civil complaint by Hannah Cavert against Dr. Preston dated February 1862, for several days in early April 1859, Dr. Preston (age 60) made visits to the Cavert home to provide treatment of an undefined illness of Mrs. Hannah Cavert (age 28), a recent bride. During one visit, upon entering Mrs. Cavert's bedroom he allegedly assaulted her with violence while she was too sick to defend herself, kissed her many times against her will, and endangered her health.[2] Her husband, William W. (Billie) Cavert must have learned of the encounter later on from his wife—for he undoubtedly would have prevented the alleged attack by the doctor—and an individual later identified as a material witness was not approached to share information until years later. Billie Cavert made his version of the encounter public in terms likely to damage Dr. Preston's reputation and business. And as later criminal and civil complaints would make clear, Mr. Cavert was prone to judgements that were accompanied by aggressive and occasionally violent behavior.

The initial legal action was an attempt to settle the dispute out of court. It is not clear why a case involving sexual assault would not immediately become a criminal matter, but in February 1862 the matter detailed in the complaint was submitted to arbitration. Two of the arbitrators selected, William Beers and Rev. Lane, were both associated with the Presbyterian Church of which Dr. Preston was an Elder and the Caverts were members. The third arbitrator was an attorney from Ballston Spa, John Brotherson, who was apparently known to be representing the Caverts. For whatever reason, Dr. Preston, perhaps overly confident in his position, consented to Brotherson's involvement in the arbitration.[3] The assignment of the arbitration team was to take statements from Hannah Cavert and Dr. Preston, and try to reach a settlement. The meeting was held in the Galway Hotel, a public gathering place and therefore a questionable choice for holding confidential discussions. Mrs. Cavert charged that the defendant had kissed her and imposed upon her in an unlawful manner. Doctor Preston said, "he was a man of very sympathetic manners that kissed her as he had other women under like circumstances or something to that effect."[4]

The truth generally lies somewhere between the two extremes represented by these opposing positions.

Two factors entering into this dispute that would not have the same legal consideration today are: the pain and suffering inflicted by mid-nineteenth-century medical procedures, and the legal weight given to the act of kissing.

Medical procedures, (for example, blood-letting) were frequently counterproductive in treating patients with ailments ranging from sore throats to seizures. While surgical tools to perform blood-letting improved with time, by current standards for blood draws, they were frankly gruesome and caused considerable pain while generally doing more harm than good. In addition, most of the drugs used to treat ailments were unpleasant to take and caused symptoms and damage that were worse than the disease. For example, calomel, or mercurous chloride, was prescribed as a laxative but with continued use caused extensive degeneration of the tissues of the mouth and jaw and major facial disfigurement. An anecdote recorded in the Quinby notes involving Dr. Preston dispensing medicine of the day illustrates the issue in humorous terms, but of course the effects could be much more serious.

> Dr. Preston once persuaded one his patients, a young boy, to take some medicine that was very distasteful. Seeing the boy the next day, the doctor said, "Well, you feel better, my little man?" "Yes, Damn you!" The boy replied.[5]

The point is that medical treatments of that era caused pain and suffering with potentially minimal or no benefits, compassion was undoubtedly a natural part of the care of patients, and expressions of sympathy were reasonable. Thus, a kiss delivered, perhaps with a hug, in non-sexual manner may have been common—as Dr. Preston admitted it was with him.

The other side of the issue is that kissing, as late as the early twentieth century, was taken very seriously in legal actions. An article in the November 12, 1903 *Amsterdam Evening Recorder*, entitled "Galway Kisses," describes a breach of promise suit won by a Miss Francis Petit against her suitor, a blacksmith by the name of Tittemore. He courted her for a period of fourteen years during which time, according to her diary, he kissed her 1,236 times. When he eventually lost interest in her she sued him for breach of promise in the amount of $59,000. The court ruled in her favor, providing a smaller judgement of $3,000, (or $2.37 per kiss) but enough to bankrupt him. It was noted that, although Miss Petit was not likely to collect anything, "this does not weaken the importance of the principle which the appellate division has established. *It is the first time that the Supreme Court has passed on the value of a kiss.* The decision affirming the trial court was reached on a vote of three to two." The defendant planned to appeal.[6]

Attorney Brotherson proposed a settlement of $500 to be paid by Dr. Preston to Mrs. Cavert.[7] The Doctor declined. After some negotiation a lesser amount was agreed upon, $250.[8] On March, 10, 1862, Dr. Preston paid $50 and then stopped payments possibly because the promised secrecy of the agreement had been breached by the Caverts, later taking the position that he thought the initial payment was a fee owed to attorney Brotherson.[9]

The award was to be kept secret. Evidently the breach in confidentiality was so pronounced and the details provided so explicit as to meet the accepted standard for a criminal complaint of Slander and Defamation against William W. Cavert. In June 1862 Dr. Preston engaged the authority of Brightman Briggs, Deputy Sheriff of the Town of Galway, to have Mr. Cavert arrested. Bail of $1,000 was paid jointly by Cavert and an associate, Reuben Jackson.[10] During that period, $1,000 was sufficient to purchase a house.

Much later, Reuben Jackson's wife would inexplicably provide a "get-out-of-jail card" to Mr. Cavert.

Dr. Preston also initiated legal action against one of the associate arbitrators, possibly to get information on the discussion during the arbitration session. Though the exact point at which he acquired legal representation is not clear, he evidently made an excellent choice: Jesse L'Amoreaux of Chapman and L'Amoreaux.

* * *

THE LAWYERS RETAINED by Dr. Preston and William "Billie" Cavert, Jesse L'Amoreaux and John Brotherson respectively, were as different personally as the individuals they represented; metaphorically they remind one of a Great Dane and a Pitbull.

Jesse L'Amoreaux, born December 11, 1837 in the town of Wilton, a descendent of French Huguenots, was educated in Wilton Public Schools and the Fort Edward Collegiate Institute.[11] He first was engaged in teaching at Wilton, then Schuylerville. While in Schuylerville he likely became an acquaintance of Dr. John R. Preston, Calvin's younger brother, who later may have influenced Calvin to retain him in the Cavert matter.

In 1856, at the age of nineteen, L'Amoreaux started studying law at the Schuylerville office of Lewis and Wells. Two years later he moved to Ballston Spa where shortly after he became a partner in the legal firm of Hill and L'Amoreaux. For most of the period of the Cavert v. Preston

Photo courtesy of the Saratoga County Historical Society at Brookside Museum

73

legal action he was in partnership with George Chapman, a prominent citizen of Ballston Spa. In his mid-twenties at that time, he displayed maturity and legal expertise in his handling of the case.

He continued practicing law, lastly as a partner in the highly regarded firm of L'Amoreaux, Dake and Whalen, until 1882 when he was elected to the office of county judge, which he held until 1889. L'Amoreaux then returned to legal practice as a corporation lawyer for businesses located in Pittsburgh, Cincinnati, Cleveland, and other cities in the Mississippi River Valley.

In legal practice he was known for his "knowledge of the law," "sound judgement," and "skillful management of litigation." Adjectives used to describe him on a personal and professional level include "cordial," "dignified," "methodical," "prompt," and "direct." In 1890 he built a large home at 199 Milton Avenue in Ballston Spa and also had a New York City residence at Central Park West and Ninety-Second Street. Married to Ellen Holbrook in 1865, he was a loving husband. A trustee of the First Presbyterian Church of Ballston Spa, upon his death in 1918 he left his Ballston Spa residence and furnishings to the mission societies of Church for use as a home for retired missionaries and their families. This act may have been influenced by the situation involving Dr. Preston's son Charles, a missionary to China who died in Hong Kong on the way home after twenty-three years of service, leaving his wife and six children traveling with him in a precarious position, had it not been for brother William.

By contrast, John Brotherson, born in Charlton in 1806, was a seasoned lawyer when, at age 55, he represented the Caverts. While biographical information[12] is limited, he is described as having "remarkable force of character" and "great physical energy"—and being "indefatigable in the interests of his clients" and "a formidable opponent." His actions in the Cavert v. Preston matter also suggest a tendency to abandon integrity when in pursuit of clients' interests and/or his own. Evidently his practice was not nearly as successful as L'Amoreaux's, a fact which is reflected in his choice of residence, as listed in several Federal censuses.

The 1850 Federal Census lists him among four lawyers living in a building with fourteen law students. The building was probably the San Souci Hotel, which housed the New York State and National Law School during the period 1849–1853. Among its attendees was Chester Arthur, a graduate of Union College in Schenectady, NY who became president of the United States upon the death of James Garfield. Interestingly, Arthur, who was apparently in a very limited financial position at that time, was unable to complete the three-year program, which cost three dollars per week for tuition, room, and board. Brotherson may have been one of the instructors, but there is no evidence to confirm this.

A bachelor, John Brotherson died in 1887 at the age of eighty-one.

✳ ✳ ✳

A COMPLAINT WAS submitted by Hannah Cavert in June, 1862 related to payment of the balance awarded by arbitration. In Dr. Preston's response, issues were raised about the arbitration process and actions by the arbitrators. Specifically, Dr. Preston complained that:[13]

1. The arbitrators "took into consideration matters and facts and circumstances not submitted to them by

submission (of the plaintiff and defendant) in which said award was found." Further, "arbitrators would not have found any damages had not matters not submitted to them by the parties [been considered]."

2. "[John Brotherson], one of the said arbitrators used threats and made false and malicious and improper allegations and statements against [Dr. Preston] to his associate arbitrators...and represented to them that he [Brotherson] was about to prosecute [Dr. Preston] for numerous wrongs alleged to have been committed by [Dr. Preston] upon other persons and that [if associate arbitrators] were to find for a [$250] award he would not [prosecute]."

3. "[Hannah Cavert] was at the time of making said award, and still is, a married woman living and cohabitating with her husband in Galway in the county. She was a married woman aforesaid and that said submission was improper. She had not the right or power to make said submission... ."'

4. "The fifty dollars mentioned in this complaint...was paid under a mistake of both law and fact."

In July, the pace of the legal confrontation accelerated.

On July 1, Seymour Chase, Justice of the Peace–County of Saratoga, found in favor of Dr. Preston in the civil case brought by the Caverts.[14]

On July 10, attorney John Brotherson had Dr. Preston served with a summons demanding an award of $2,000 and costs.[15]

On July 16 Brotherson appealed the ruling of the Justice and demanded a trial by jury in Saratoga County Court. The case came to trial on October 21, 1862.[16] The pleadings were interesting in again reflecting the legal position of women of that era, specifically: The defendant objected to reading the arbitration award into evidence on the ground that the plaintiff is a married woman and that she is incompetent to bind herself to a submission to arbitration. In addition, the only witness prepared to testify on Hannah Cavert's behalf was her husband, and his testimony was not accepted, presumably based on the prospect that it would differ little from her's.

It is not clear, what, if any the above influenced the Jury in finding in favor of Dr. Preston, but in addition, the court awarded costs of $49.49 to him. Perhaps, in the absence of witness testimony the conflict became a matter of *he said-she said* as far as the jury was concerned. However, the Caverts were not done yet.

An appeal of the verdict was filed by Attorney Brotherson on behalf of Hannah Cavert—and after at least one complaint on the part of Dr. Preston by attorney L'Amoreaux that the case had been abandoned—in June of 1864, five years after the incident, the appeal was denied.[17] That ended the civil action, but still to be resolved was the criminal case against William Cavert.

During the period that the civil case was active there was little activity on the criminal matter. Ironically, just before the judgement for final appeal in the civil case was recorded, a material witness was identified to support William Cavert in the criminal charges. She was Elizabeth L. Jackson, wife of Reuben Jackson, a Galway Hub Manufacturer who had helped William Cavert raise the funds required for bail and subsequently moved with his family to Niagara, New York. When Brotherson and Beach Attorneys filed a request for examination of Mrs. Jackson under oath on the 10th of June, 1864, it was found that she had moved to City of Hamilton, Province of Upper Canada. [18]

The Supreme Court of Saratoga County granted the request for an interrogation of Mrs. Jackson, stipulating that the attorney for Dr. Preston be permitted to join.[19]

The untimely revelation that Mrs. Jackson had information of substance to offer was never explained. Possibly as a result of this action the criminal case ended and it certainly disappeared from legal records. It seems likely that Dr. Preston had no way to counter the assertions of a witness, nor did he have any knowledge beforehand of what she might say, and he wisely abandoned the complaint.

And so, it ended with a whimper, with Dr. Preston victorious in a court of law but perhaps with consequences to his standing in the community. There is evidence that his involvement in church and civic affairs diminished following the first trial, and at the time of his death the obituaries were brief and muted, not what one would expect for a physician who served a community for almost fifty years. However, he did continue to practice medicine until 1877, and remained at his home in the village. Five years prior to his death in 1885, he transferred interest in that property to his daughter, Sophia Preston Hays, who retained it until the death of her stepmother and then moved with her family to Saratoga Springs.

Hannah Cavert remained at Galway until her death in 1914. She is buried in the Galway Village Cemetery not far from Dr. Preston.

As for Mr. Cavert, his darker side emerged in a very public way about fifteen years later in

Hannah Cavert Monument, Galway Village Cemetery. Photo by Author.

the form of two legal matters of record. According to a June 28, 1877 newspaper account:[20]

> Tuesday night of last week five men in the village of Galway made an assault on a half-demented woman by the name of Ann Gleason. She escaped from them and ran into the yard of Mrs. Gibson, a lady of the highest respectability, and sought shelter. Mrs. Gibson, hearing the commotion, opened her door, when the frightened creature begged admission and shelter. While talking with her the miscreants began to stone the house. This aroused Charles E. Gibson, son of Mrs. Gibson who arose, ran to the door and discharged a revolver into the midst of the crowd, which had the effect of scattering the villains in headlong flight. Four of them were identified as John Hudson, William Martin, Morris Shayne and George Moon [the fifth would be identified as William W. Cavert]. The matter was examined by the grand jury at Ballston Spa Friday and Saturday. A lawless gang of desperadoes has been disfiguring horses and performing similar acts for some time and it is hoped that an example will be made of the present case to prevent future outrages.

In advance of the grand jury deliberations, matters momentarily took a turn for the worse for the victim as reported in a separate article:[21]

> In the matter of Ann Gleason, under confinement for want of bail on a peace warrant, District Attorney Ormsby stated that is was a conspiracy on the part of certain fellows to prevent her appearing before the grand jury against

them for a riot, and to punish her for so doing. Judge Crane ordered her discharge.

And finally,[22]

John P. Hudson, George Moon, William W. Cavert and William T. Martin [were] indicted for assault and battery on Ann Gleason at Galway, pled not guilty and gave bail to the Sessions.

The disposition of the case was apparently not recorded, or the records were either lost or not readily available.

Then, several years later another altercation, as reported in the June 23, 1881 *Saratoga Sentinel*,[23] in curiously quaint and polite language:

This little village has not been so excited since Joseph Glasser shot Patrick Breen jr. twenty-seven years ago, as it was Saturday, June 11 over the acts of two hot blooded citizens. While John Cunning [age 51] was talking in the front of his residence with Deputy Sheriff Robert Shaw, his neighbor William Cavert [age 49] came up and commenced talking about Cunning's horses (note reference to horses as in the last incident—perhaps Mr. Cavert had a grudge against horses) running in the streets. To the latter's reply he re-joined in emphatic terms his belief in its falsity. Cunning having hastily laid a parcel of eggs that he held in his hands into the sheriff's wagon, felt for his opponent and hit upon one of his eyes. A rough and tumble [ensued] in which Cunning's beard was partially extracted and Cavert's eyes were blackened. The deputy sheriff, having a span of young horses, rheumatism and advancing years, was unable to do more than command peace, which was finally brought about by the intervention of bystanders. Cunning asserts that Cavert at the time of giving the lie had a knife in his hand and invited him to "come on" saying in terms impolite that he would let the daylight penetrate. Cavert, not satisfied with this demonstration, next got a warrant from Justice James H. Sexton for Cunning's arrest for assault and battery, but at the time, on Wednesday, that the issue was to be tried he absented himself and the charge was dismissed. At the same time he had gone to Ballston Spa to consult counsel about the propriety of beginning a civil action in the same premises. On his return that evening he was arrested and held to bail on a peace warrant sworn out by Cunning. It is understood that a Supreme Court action will eventuate from this matter with Cavert as plaintiff and Cunning defendant.

The legal conflict moved forward as a civil suit, William W. Cavert against John Cunning.[24] As in the Preston matter, Mr. Cavert chose John Brotherson to represent him, and Attorney Brotherson held little in reserve in the amended complaint[25] presented to the Saratoga County Supreme Court on or about June 13, 1882:

> [John Cunning] on or about the 11th day of June 1881, *being instigated by the devil,* wickedly, maliciously and then and there committed a violent assault and battery upon the person of [William Cavert] with great force and violence, in the public highway; and then and there knocked [him] down upon the ground with his fists; and when knocked

down [John Cunning] struck [William Cavert] with blows, in his face, and trampled upon his person, while [he] was down, upon the ground, and by reason thereof [Cavert's] face from his eyes downward to his chin became black and blue; and [his body] from head to foot became same , and sore and by reason thereof [he] became sick, sore, and lame; so that for a time he could not attend to his ordinary business, and on account of his injuries inflicted as afore-said by [John Cunning] upon [Willam Cavert]"

A demand was made for a judgement of $1,000 in addition to costs and disbursements.

In John Cunning's amended answers to the complaint sub-mitted by his attorney, Emmet Blair, is included some insight into the character of William Cavert, as well as details clarifying the sequence of events the day of the incident:

[John Cunning].....alleges and states the facts to be that at the time mentioned in the complaint and for a period of about two years previous and frequently repeated and continued down to the time of the alleged assault and battery [William Cavert] would meet [John Cunning] in the public street and the places of business in the town where they resided to wit the village of Galway, county of Saratoga N.Y. and in a threatening manner with clenched fists would use vile and abusive language and threaten to whip, beat and bruise [John Cunning] without and provo-cation whatsoever for the purpose of provoking [him] to commit an assault and that immediately before the alleged assault [John Cunning's] team [of horses] was standing [on his premises] and [William Cavert entered the premises] and maliciously struck said team and caused the same to run away for the purpose and with the intent of aggravating and provoking [John Cunning] to commit an assault. And [William Cavert] maliciously and without true claim or cause of action against [John Cunning] caused to be issued from a justice of the peace of the Town of Galway, one Charles Saxton, a summons in civil action wherein [William Cavert]was plaintiff and [John Cunning] was defendant and just before the alleged assault when the officer came upon the premises of [John Cunning] and had the same duly served for the purpose of aggravating and provoking [John Cunning while] he had no claim within the law or equity against [John Cunning]. All of the above facts are plead in mitigation of damages—

And [John Cunning] for a further amended answer alleges that [William Cavert] just before the alleged assault and battery and at the time mentioned in the amended complaint came to the shop or barn of [John Cunning]in the village of Galway and in an abusive and violent manner called [John Cunning] "a lying son of a bitch" and said he could lick him and with a deadly and open knife threatened to [cut?] up his guts, and struck [John Cunning] with his fists and made an assault upon [him] and could have beaten and bruised him if [John Cunning] had not immediately defended himself and that at same time [William Cavert] grabbed [John Cunning] by the beard and [William Cavert] fell pulling [John Cunning] by the beard and pulled out a large quantity of the same.

So here upon to make William Cavert let go of his beard and to avoid being beat, bruised and violated himself he did beat [William Cavert] as he lawfully might and so doing did necessarily and unavoidably a little beat and bruised [William Cavert] and if [William Cavert] sustained damage it is as occasioned by his first assaulting [John Cunning].

The facts above mentioned are the cause of which [William Cavert] complains—

Wheretofore [John Cunning] demands [William Cavert's] complaint herein be dismissed with the costs of this action.[26]

The case went to trial in June of 1882. The final disposition of the case was recorded in a Saratoga County Supreme Court judgement dated December 12, 1882, by Clerk James W. Horton.

The issues in this action having been brought on for trial before the Justice Chas G. Tappan and a jury at a circuit court held on the second Monday of June 1882 and the issues having been tried and a verdict for the defendant [John Cunning} having been duly rendered on the 14th day of June 1882 and his costs having been adjusted at Ninety Six dollars and nine cents—

Now on motion of Emmet Blair attorney defendant, it is adjudged that the defendant have judgment against the Plaintiff [William Cavert] upon the issues in this action with ninety-six dollars and nine cents costs and disbursements of this action.[27]

Based on the information available on two cases (one criminal, one civil) involving Mr. William W. Cavert, it is clear that he was prone to reckless and violent behavior. As a member of a small mob that terrorized a defenseless single woman, he displayed in a very general way the same kind of behavior described in the lawsuit he and his wife pursued against the doctor. The nature of the grudge he held against John Cunning, the village undertaker, is unknown. But, based on the evidence provided the jury, likely to be the same as that contained in the answer to his complaint, it is clear he was looking for revenge. Unfortunately for him, he underestimated his opponent. Never pick a fight with someone who has trained as a boxer.

How this behavior pattern influenced events leading to the earlier legal entanglement with Dr. Preston or for that matter his relationships with other individuals, including his wife, is a matter of conjecture—as is the reason that Mr. Harvey Crouch, the oral history source of a negative assessment of the doctor, took sides with him. Let the reader ponder...

A final footnote to the extended drama that linked Dr. Preston, Ann Gleason, and John Cunning to Billie Cavert is found in *Stories and Pictures of Galway* by W. Bronson Taylor, 1966:[28]

> The park in Galway once had an iron fence around it. Inside the fence was a row of shrubs. One night some prankster borrowed a bulletin board from in front of a store and placed it inside the iron fence. Behind the board they placed some overalls with a pair of boots projecting from the legs. The whole thing was partly hidden so that it looked like a man's body lying there. On the board was a verse carefully printed in chalk.
>
>> "We cannot have all things to please us.
>> Poor Billy Cavert has gone to Jesus.
>> But one cannot always tell.
>> Perhaps poor Billy has gone to hell."

Billy was a man easily aroused. He went to a justice, Mr. Kemp and tried to have certain persons arrested. The justice would not issue a warrant for lack of proof.

William Cavert passed away in 1906, predeceasing his wife. She was buried in an adjoining grave.

Notes

[1] Elizabeth Robb Quinby and Ethel Robb, *Historical, Genealogical and Supplemental Notes, Galway Historical Society*, Galway Preservation Society Archives, Section P.

[2] Cavert v. Preston, (1863), Civil Actions and Special Proceedings Box A-135, Saratoga County Clerk's Office, Ballston Spa, New York, item M-788.

[3] Ibid., item M-785.

[4] Ibid., item M-783.

[5] Elizabeth Robb Quinby and Ethel Robb, *Historical and Genealogical Notes of Galway, New York,* 2 vols., Galway Preservation Society Archives, Section P (F. Saxton).

[6] "Galway Kisses. Appellate Court Stands by Miss Pettit. Two Judges Dissent," *Amsterdam Evening Recorder,* (November 12, 1863).

[7] Cavert v. Preston, (1863), item M-783

[8] Ibid., item M-790.

[9] Ibid., item M-800.]

[10] Preston v. Cavert (1862), Civil Actions and Special Proceedings Box A-132, Saratoga County Clerk's Office, Ballston Spa, New York, item M-726.

[11] Biographical Sketch K of Nathaniel Bartlett Sylvester, Jesse L'Amoreaux, from "History of Saratoga County, New York with Historical Notes on its various Towns, together with Biographical Sketches of its prominent men and leading citizens" (Richmond, Indiana: Gresham publishing Co.,1893), 422–4.

[12] Edward F. Grose and John C. Booth, , Biographical Sketch of John Brotherson from "Centennial History of the Village of Ballston Spa: including the Towns of Ballston and Milton" A Souvenir of the Centennial Celebration held June 22-25, 1907, *Ballston Journal*, Ballston Spa, New York, 1907, 253.

[13] Cavert v. Preston, (1863), item M-800.

[14] Ibid., item M-779.

[15] Ibid., item M-787.

[16] Ibid., item M-826.

[17] Book of Orders, March 26, 1861 to August 24, 1867, Judgment of the Saratoga County Court, Hannah E. Cavert agst Calvin Preston, June 20, 1864, pages 265–6

[18] Preston v. Cavert (1862), item M-713.

[19] Ibid., item M-715.

[20] Galway, *The Saratoga Sentinel*, June 28, 1877.

[21] Adjourned Session, *The Saratoga Sentinel*, June 28, 1877.

[22] Circuit Court and Court of Oyer and Terminer, *Daily Saratogian*, June 30, 1877.

[23] Galway, *The Saratoga Sentinel*, June 23, 1881.

[24] Circuit Court and Court of Oyer and Terminer, *Daily Saratogian*, June 14, 1882

[25] Supreme Court—William W. Cavert agst John Cunning 1882, Saratoga County Clerk's Office, Ballston Spa, NY. Civil Actions and Proceedings Box A-313, Saratoga County Clerk's Office, Ballston Spa, NY, items M774-776, on or about June 13, 1882.

[26] Ibid., items M-778–M-782, on or about June 13, 1882.

[27] Ibid., item M-786, December 12, 1882.

[28] W. Bronson Taylor, *Stories and Pictures of Galway, Saratoga County, New York*, (Middle Grove, NY: published by author, 1966).

— Chapter Five —

Calvin, James, and the Civil War: "Brother Against Brother"

Muster roll abstract—Calvin W. Preston, New York State Archives.

s the case worked its way through the courts, there
was another departure from the Preston household:
Calvin Walbridge, born in 1845, the youngest of the
Preston boys. Not much is known of Calvin prior to his enlistment in the Union Army in September 1861, other than he
attended school in Galway, New York. The muster roll abstract
for the Union army describes him as five feet four-and-a-quarter
inches in height, in contrast to the five feet eight requirement
(the army evidently measured very carefully, then ignored their
own height criterion); light hair and complexion; eyes, blue;
age, seventeen; occupation, farmer; grade, drummer. His father
owned land suitable for farming adjacent to the family home in
Galway, hence the farmer designation seems appropriate; three
brothers and one sister were musically inclined, so presumably
that talent was in the family genes. His age at date of enlistment,
September 2, 1861 was sixteen years seven months, rounded off
to seventeen years, and in any event below the age requirement
of eighteen years—but that did not seem to make much difference to the Union Army recruiters, particularly when consider-
ing candidates for drummer.

Referred to as "the Boy's War" because many of the soldiers
were teenagers, it was common for the youngest to serve as
drummers. Army recruiters, probably under pressure to meet
quotas, tended to accept without proof the answer to the question about age, and many recruits simply lied about it. The
youngest, John Joseph Klem, a.k.a. Johnny Clem, was nine years
old (and four-feet tall) when he attempted to join the 3rd Ohio
Regiment in 1861 and was eventually added to the muster roll

of the 22nd Michigan in 1863. So Calvin Preston's case does not seem to be particularly noteworthy.

News of the Civil War resulted in a strong reaction from the missionaries in China. The Civil War in the US—which was precipitated by the election of Abraham Lincoln on December 11, 1860, and quickly followed by the secession of South Carolina on December 20—began with the bombardment by the US Army and surrender to the Confederates of Fort Sumter in Charleston Harbor on April 13, 1861. News travelled to the missionaries in China by the same sailing ships that carried passengers and merchandise, so it is not surprising that Charles Preston's first letter describing in passionate terms his anxiety related to the war would be dated July 9, 1861. The July letter described his concern related to the impact of the conflict on monetary collections to support the missionary effort and the separation of the Presbyterian Church into North and South regional factions in support of the Union and Confederate causes. In the South, the Presbyterian leaders Drs. Thornewell and Palmer defended slavery as "morally right and justified under the Christian religion" and "defended slavery and secession."

Charles Preston's letter to Walter Lowrie makes interesting reading, due to his passionate view and surprising comment about prior sympathy with the South's cause.

We thank you again very much for your kind & sympathizing letters, and so punctually every month. It is with the deepest grief that we hear of the troubles in our native land. The effect on our Board must be sad indeed— Receipts will fall off—our operations will be crippled, we cannot be reinforced & Religion at home will be very apt to suffer from this war. Spirits for some hearts it may develop—this war–a higher level of Christian life, but I fear too few will thus be affected. It cannot be disguised we sympathize in the enthusiasm which distinguishes the efforts to sustain the government against the traitorous designs of wicked men – if there be anything like civil government ordained by God, and any foundation for patriotism in the divine revelation then secession as supported by the south is only another name for rebellion—Alas for our country when such treason springs up, buds, flowers, and so arises in Washington and alas for our church when its ministers stand up to plead for such an unholy cause and express such sentiments as were ascribed to Drs. Thornewell and Palmer. I have always supposed I was doing right when taking up the cause of the South against the abolitionists but I never intended to uphold such principles."......[1]

An educated guess is that the reference to taking up the cause of the South against the abolitionists is related to the actions of the abolitionist leader John Brown that led to the deaths of pro-slavery settlers in Kansas.

A reasonable question is his father's role in Calvin's decision to volunteer; as a doctor he would have a heightened sense of the terrible toll bullets take on the human body in terms of death, diminished capacity, pain and suffering. Possibly strong religious beliefs influenced the decision, because the Prestons were devout Presbyterians, and in the North the Presbyterian Church was "supportive of moral reform movements such as abolitionism." Support of religion for abolition was expressed in the context of the Christian civilization doing battle for God and humanity to free the slaves. Or Calvin simply disobeyed his father's wishes, but most probably regional fervor over the death of a Union officer was the deciding factor. In any event, Calvin Preston's name was recorded in the muster roll of the 44th New York Infantry Regiment, also known as Ellsworth's Avengers, named in memory of Elmer Ellsworth. He was mustered in on September 2, 1861.

※ ※ ※

THE STORY OF Elmer Ellsworth may be summarized as follows: A young man from rural upstate New York, just over twenty years of age, gained widespread acclaim for training and exhibitions of volunteer militia drill teams in the tactics of an Algerian mountain tribe; became a lawyer in Abraham Lincoln's Springfield, Illinois law firm as well as a close friend of the family; travelled to Washington with Lincoln as he assumed the presidency of a divided nation; and was the first Union casualty of the Civil War. This brief biographical sketch of his life seems improbable, but thorough research[2] pursued one hundred years after his death, based on plentiful documentation in the form of letters and newspaper articles, confirms it.

Elmer Ephraim Ellsworth was born in Malta, New York on April 11, 1837 and raised in Mechanicville, both towns within twenty-five miles of Galway. The story of his short life reminds one of a Greek tragedy, a play in which the protagonist, an individual of outstanding character and importance, encounters evil and is overcome with disastrous consequences due to a fatal flaw. In the words of a friend after his death by an assassin, Ellsworth actually had two flaws: "too generous and too brave." Born to poor but loving parents, his lifelong dream was to care for them in much better circumstances during their old age. He was also devoted to his younger brother Charles (serving as his

mentor and protector from birth until the time of his death due
to smallpox) and to his fiancé Carrie, the beautiful, refined, and
well-educated daughter of a prominent Chicago-area family. As a
teenager he developed an intense interest in military tactics and
drills, organizing a military drill team he named the Black Plumed
Riflemen of Stillwater, New York. The two driving forces of his
personality—devotion to the persons he loved and to military service to his country—would be in conflict throughout his short life.

While attending public school in Malta he worked as a store
clerk, and at the age of fifteen, in Troy. Following the advice of
Horace Greeley, in 1852 he traveled west—residing in Kenosha,
Wisconsin. Subsequently, he returned briefly to Mechanicville,
relocated to New York City, and in 1854 finally settled in the
Chicago area. Having an interest in mechanical devices, he
applied for a patent of a railway car window latch and subsequently found employment as a patent agent in Rockford,
Illinois; based on his productivity and business acumen, he
became a partner in the business. Just short of the point where
his accumulated wealth could provide a more comfortable life for
his parents, he was bankrupted by an unscrupulous individual.

At the time of his association with the patent brokerage Elmer
had continued to pursue his military interest. He studied military training and tactics, gaining expertise in leading and training drill teams associated with volunteer militias that became
prevalent in the vacuum created by state government's diminished role in maintaining a military capability. Prior to the Civil
War, state governments had allowed official military organizations to dissolve and disperse. The only viable military capability
was in the form of volunteer militias of generally inferior training and equipment. Into this void stepped Elmer Ellsworth with
his vision of a well-trained, extensively drilled infantry.

Col. Elmer E. Ellsworth. Photo courtesy of the Mechanicville Public Library, Mechanicville, New York.

His first successful venture was the Rockville Grays drill team. As a consequence, he would meet the love of his short life, Miss Caroline (Carrie) Spafford, daughter and only child of a wealthy Rockville couple. While the Spaffords were fond of Elmer, they accepted the engagement on the condition that Elmer prove he was capable of supporting her in the manner to which she was accustomed. Encouraged by Mr. Spafford to become a lawyer, he found employment in a law firm as a copier of legal documents—a copier in those days being a person rather than a machine—while studying legal manuals as time permitted. He lived very economically, sleeping on the floor of the law firm and subsisting on a diet of crackers and water. His interest and activity in military matters intensified at the same time, and he became increasingly involved in training volunteer militias in tactics and maneuvers. While the legal work provided a small income, there was no direct income associated with training drill teams, but it resulted in public recognition and eventually an association with government officials at the state and federal level.

In the period October 1853 to March 1856 the Crimean War was fought, a power struggle resulting from the decline of the Ottoman Empire and Russia's interest in dominance in the region. It pitted the forces of Russia against those of the Ottoman Empire, Britain, France, and Sardinia. Ultimately the Russians were defeated and the war ended with signing of the 1856 Treaty of Paris. The war was noteworthy for the use of modern military weaponry such as rifled gun barrels and reporting by telegraph. As a result of the latter, the *New York Times* carried "live" reports of battles, and magazines of the period such as *Harper's Weekly* published related articles. Engaged in the conflict was a French regular army regiment that adopted the flamboyant uniforms and heroic battlefield tactics of the Zouave mountain tribe of Algeria. Adjectives describing the Zouaves in various sources included: elite, tough, exotic, daring, colorful, and reckless; their flamboyant uniforms were multi-colored, consisting of signature baggy trousers, leggings, shirts, and jackets.

"Pitching Quoits," oil painting by Winslow Homer, ca. 1863.

Colorful uniforms may have been the reason that Winslow Homer, an illustrator for *Harper's Weekly* prior to the Civil War, selected Zouave soldiers as the subject of one of his earliest commercial paintings. Homer was known throughout his prolific career for use of bright color (red his apparent favorite) as a focal point, as is evident in the Civil War painting "Pitching Quoits," in which a number of Union Army Zouave soldiers in full uniform with baggy red trousers are depicted in a camp-life scene.

Inspired by the *New York Times* reports and the Zouave approach, Ellsworth developed drills, which he described in a training manual. Ellsworth's drills reflected the Zouave's athleticism, incorporating rapid formation changes and expert handling of rifle and bayonet. He went on to convert the Rockford Grays militia into a competition drill team wearing Zouave-style uniforms that he personally designed. A performance of the drill team in September of 1858 at the Rockford fairgrounds was well received and led to Ellsworth's election to Captain of Cadets of the 60th Illinois Regiment, which was quickly renamed: the US Zouave Cadets. As a result, Ellsworth gained celebrity status resulting in an offer by the State Adjutant General of the position of Paymaster General of Illinois. Oddly, the position, which by its title seems lofty, had no salary connected with it but was Ellsworth's ticket to the State Capital, where he would meet Governor Bissell and Abraham Lincoln. Lincoln immediately took a liking to Ellsworth, treated him like a son and encouraged him to finish his study of law, be admitted to the bar, and join the firm. Concurrently, exhibitions by the Zouave Cadets caught the attention of the public and major newspapers in the area, as well as in the major East Coast cities where they performed. As the handsome and colorful leader of the Cadets, who performed fast-paced and intricate maneuvers in response to his commands, Ellsworth gained celebrity status akin to that of twentieth century icons like Charles Lindbergh, Muhammad Ali, and Martin Luther King.

Subsequently, Ellsworth became a close friend of Lincoln's and used his status as a celebrity to support Lincoln's 1860 campaign for president. When Lincoln was elected, Ellsworth accompanied him to Washington as a member of his staff, first on his protection detail, and subsequently as a military attaché with the rank of lieutenant—and at long last, a salary of $1,850 per year.

At the outbreak of the Civil War with the Confederate conquest of Fort Sumter, Ellsworth left Washington for New York City, where he formed the 11th New York Volunteer Regiment—enlisting many of its troops from the city's fire departments (hence, the "Fire Zouaves")—and returned with the regiment to Washington.

On May 24, 1861, the day after Virginia voters ratified the state convention's decision to secede from the Union, Colonel Ellsworth and his Fire Zouave troops entered Alexandria, Virginia to assist in the occupation of the city. A large Confederate flag had flown for weeks from the rooftop of a hotel, the Marshall House, and could be seen from the White House, seemingly mocking the president and calling attention to a lack of action in putting down the rebellion.

Ignoring premonitions of his own death and with the intent of providing his friend, President Lincoln, relief from the irritation caused by this readily visible symbol of the Confederacy, Ellsworth, accompanied by several soldiers, entered the hotel to remove it. Not taking the time to secure the hotel prior to scaling a ladder found in the

"Death of Col. Ellsworth," Currier and Ives lithograph print, ca 1861. Library of Congress/public domain.

attic to climb to the roof was a tragic oversight. Passing a supposed boarder on the way to the rooftop, they took down the
large, eight-by-fourteen-foot flag, which Ellsworth carried down
the stairs. While descending, they encountered the "boarder,"
who was actually James W. Jackson, the hotel owner—a genu-
inely unpleasant individual with strong proslavery views, presumably suicidal. Stepping out of the shadows adjacent to a stair
landing, at close range Jackson fired a shotgun at Ellsworth's
chest, killing him instantly. One of the soldiers accompanying
Ellsworth then killed Jackson with his rifle and bayonet.

Col. Ellworth's Tunic, entry wound encircled. Photo courtesy of the New York State Military Museum, Saratoga Springs, New York.

Ellsworth's tunic is stored at the
New York State Military Museum,
Saratoga Springs, New York. A half-
dollar-size circular hole shows the
entry wound at his heart. The remains
of the flag, severely damaged by souvenir collectors, resides there as well.

Lincoln was grief-stricken by the
death of his friend, referring to his
actions on the fatal morning as brash
and heroic. Whether he realized that
Ellsworth's death resulted from an act
of generosity directed toward reliev-
ing him of public denigration by a con-
federate sympathizer is unknown. Ellsworth's body lay in state
in the White House at Lincoln's direction, then was returned
by rail to Mechanicville, New York for burial with stops for citizens to pay their respects in New York City and Albany, remi-
niscent of the journey of Lincoln to Illinois after his assassination four years later. Thus, the lives of two worthy individuals
and close friends who had taken the journey from poverty to

high accomplishment and acclaim ended similarly. *Remember Ellsworth!* became a rallying cry for the Union, and formation of the memorial regiment, the Ellsworth Avengers, also known as the New York 44th Volunteer Infantry Regiment began immediately. Interestingly, although James Jackson was recognized as a martyr of the Confederate cause, apparently no similar effort was undertaken in the South. A plaque on the site of Marshall Hotel commemorating the incident and referring to Jackson as a martyr to the Southern cause and defender of his property and personal rights was quietly removed some time ago.

Ellsworth is buried in Hudson View Cemetery, Mechanicville, New York. An impressive obelisk monument marks the grave. His fiancé, grief-stricken, did not attend the funeral and was destined to encounter further sadness in her life with the death of a son and husband. Ellsworth's parents found some comfort in the benevolence of Abraham Lincoln, who ensured his father's employment by the government for the remainder of his life.

✳ ✳ ✳

THE EFFORT TO organize the Ellsworth Avengers regiment began the day after his death. An article appearing in an Albany, New York newspaper under the title "Retribution" proposed a plan in which every town and ward in the State would provide one man and provide a subscription of one dollar for equipment—the men selected to travel to Albany as soon as possible to join the regiment.[3] An association of prominent Albany citizens was quickly formed to guide formation of the regiment, with the stated criteria for candidates being "unmarried, not over 30 years of age or under 5 feet, 8 inches in height, and of military experience." Ironically, Ellsworth (at five feet six, described by the six-feet-four-inch tall Lincoln as "the biggest little man I ever met") would not have qualified. The plan was adhered to as far as possible, and on August 8, 1861 all members selected prior to that date assembled at Albany City Hall. From there they marched to a barracks, a three-story brick building in the western part of Albany on the northwesterly side of New Scotland Road. The regiment continued to draw members through September and into October, while those in attendance drilled for six hours a day under the guidance of officers, some of whom had originally belonged to the Ellsworth US Zouave Cadets of Chicago. Drills included execution of movements in close formation, as well those related to musket and bayonet use.

On October 21, 1861 the regiment, numbering 1,061 men dressed in Zouave uniforms, marched to the Hudson River boat landing, accompanied by a band, through a crowd of twenty thousand, "charmed by this intoxicating prelude to war." The horrors and carnage of battles to come (such as Malvern Hill, Antietam, and Gettysburg) were probably not imaginable on that sunny day. After speeches by dignitaries, and with the roar of cannons signaling their departure, they left Albany for New York City on two barges towed by the *Columbia*, a steam-driven towboat.

The journey to New York City, a distance of about 140 miles, took some eighteen hours. For most aboard the barges (Calvin Preston, Galway farmer boy included), it must have been a first-in-a-lifetime experience, and they certainly had beautiful scenery to

Towboat pulling passenger barges. Photo courtesy of the Hudson River Maritime Museum.

enjoy along the way. Upon reaching the city at 10:00 a.m. on the twenty-second, they were greeted by a large crowd at the pier near Fourteenth Street. From there they marched up Fourteenth to Broadway, and then down Broadway to City Hall Park, where barracks were located for use by volunteer regiments on the way to Washington. The next day, the old arms received in Albany were exchanged for new Springfield muskets.

The new muskets were originally scheduled to be delivered in Albany, but delivery may have been delayed due to the recent start of production by the Springfield Armory Company, coupled with high demand. The 1861 Springfield musket had a rifled barrel for a 0.58 caliber Minié "ball," which actually had a cone shape similar to current bullets. Rifling, a spiral set of grooves and lands machined into the length of the bore causes the bullet to spin at very high rotational speeds, improving its stability due to the gyroscopic effect, and thereby increasing the accurate range. Smooth-bore muskets like the Springfield 1842 have a useful range of about sixty yards; the range of the 1861 rifled musket was three hundred to six hundred yards. The 1861 Springfield had leaf sights for ranges of zero to one hundred, three hundred, and five hundred yards, while the smoothbores were sighted along the barrel, regardless of distance to the target. Percussion caps were used to ignite the propellant, black powder. A nine-step process was required to load the weapon, the following representing a greatly condensed form of the procedure described in the *Manual of Instruction for the Volunteers and Militia of the Confederate States* (1861):[4]

1. Position rifle vertically for loading, stock supported on ground, muzzle up, and open cartridge box.
2. Remove a cartridge and place it between teeth.

3. Tear open the cartridge paper down to the level of the powder.

4. Empty powder into the muzzle bore, followed by the bullet.

5. Remove ramrod from holder and position to insert in bore.

6. Insert the ramrod in bore, ram cartridge home, remove ramrod.

7. Return ramrod to holder.

8. Position rifle, move hammer to half cock position and insert primer.

9. Fully cock hammer white moving into position to fire.

Surprisingly, with all the required actions, an experienced soldier could reload and fire two to four times a minute, although in the heat of battle it must have taken a remarkable amount of concentration.

While soldiers preferred the newer-technology 1861 musket—older, smoothbore rifles may have been more effective in the close- range encounters typical of the Civil War. This is because they could be loaded faster, possibly five times a minute, and with multiple projectiles known as "buck and ball" (a combination of buckshot and a ball projectile), could do more damage than possible with a single projectile. In any event, "the 1861" was very popular with Union and Confederate soldiers (the latter acquiring them by capture), and became the small arms of choice during the Civil War.

At the same time, it is evident that there was better technology available than the muzzle loaders, in the form of breechloaders—rifles that were loaded through an opening adjacent to the hammer which increased the rate of firing and were also a matter of great convenience for the cavalry. In addition, repeating rifles such as the Spencer rifle, which had been developed (though resisted) by military leadership, found their way into the hands of a few select units, where they were used to devastating effect against the Confederate army. The Spencer repeating rifle reportedly had a capability of fourteen rounds per minute, and could therefore be used to hold off a much larger force equipped with "single shot" technology.

One can only wonder at Calvin's reaction to the new weapons. Drummers did not carry small arms, rifles, or pistols, and aside from their role as a primitive signal corps, were essentially noncombatants. However, Calvin came from a rural area where guns were commonplace and had an important use as a means of acquiring food for human sustenance. So he would have been impressed with the 1861 musket, which represented the latest technology, and envious of the soldiers who received them. Perhaps not enough to be interested in becoming an infantry member when the opportunity presented itself—although another circumstance before he reached the age of eighteen surely had an overwhelming influence.

From New York City, the route to Washington, D.C. took them by ferry to Jersey City, then by train to Philadelphia and Baltimore. The crowds were friendly in the City of Brotherly Love, but not so much in Baltimore, where verbal abuse was directed toward the soldiers, so consideration was given by the officers for issuing rounds. Continuing their travel by rail, they reached Harve de Grace, where twelve cars at a time were taken by ferry across the broad Susquehanna River and then on to Washington—the right of way there forward guarded by pickets. When the 44th arrived and was not met by greeters, official or otherwise, the night was spent sleeping on the railway station platform and adjoining sidewalks. The next day, they woke to see the magnificent capital building in the distance surrounded by nondescript buildings and adjacent streets in need of repair. That day they were reviewed by President Lincoln; the historical record does not indicate that he addressed them, though that might have seemed natural, given their status as a memorial regiment for his fallen companion. But later, Lincoln displayed a strong aversion to retribution and vengeance in accepting the surrender of the Confederacy, and this admirable character trait may have precluded such recognition

The 44th was quickly assigned to Brigadier General Daniel Butterfield's Third Brigade of Brigadier General Fitz John Porter's First Division of the Third Corps, (later to become the Fifth Corps) about fifteen thousand in number—part of Major General McCellan's Army of the Potomac—and then marched to a field in Hall's Hill, Virginia (disputed territory just beyond the Washington defenses) and set up camp. There they would remain through the winter, engaging in drills and preparations for the Peninsula Campaign.

* * *

Major General George B. McCellan became General in Chief of all Union armies, replacing Winfield Scott in November 1861. He was successful in transforming the inexperienced volunteer army into an effective fighting force, following the rout by the Confederate army at the first battle of Bull Run. He was also the driving force behind the Peninsula Campaign, which may have been doomed from the start. With Union planning and strategy caught up in a swirl of political forces, including clamor by the press for action, the apparent reticence of General McCellan to engage the enemy and Lincoln's search for decisive path forward, it is a small wonder that Lincoln later remarked of

Ulysses Grant "I can't spare this man, he fights." The Campaign was conceived by McCellan as an attractive alternative to facing off with the Confederate army, which was led by General Joseph Johnston and stationed at Manassas, approximately forty miles east of Washington. The plan was to move the Army of the Potomac by ship to Hampton, Virginia at the southern extremity of the peninsula formed by the confluence of the York and James rivers, then rapidly march approximately ninety miles northwest to Richmond, at the head of the peninsula, blocking the Confederate army's access to the capital of the Confederacy and occupying it. Ironically, later inspection of the Confederate army's Manassas works determined that the defenses had been far weaker than McCellan had believed, making the choice dubious at best. In any event, in early March 1862 President Lincoln reluctantly approved the plan (one can imagine him thinking: *okay, okay—do anything you want, just get on with it!*) but ultimately allocated one hundred thousand troops rather than the 150,000 that McCellan had requested. McCellan, demoted to General of the Army of the Potomac, was not happy, and seemingly retaliated by becoming more cautious and then blaming the failure on Lincoln. In a delayed emotional reaction, he ran against Lincoln for the office of President in 1864. Again, he lost. Lincoln, known for his wisdom, kindness, intelligence, and communication skills was also a tough and resourceful politician.

❊ ❊ ❊

THE MAP BELOW shows the route taken by McCellan's army during the Peninsula Campaign, which was conducted entirely within the eastern part of the state of Virginia, extending southward to Hampton, eastward to Richmond, northward to Manassas.

On March 10, 1862, at the start of the campaign, the New York 44th Regiment led the advance to the Confederate defensive works at Centerville, very close to Washington and roughly twenty miles southeast of the Hall's Hill camp, via Falls Church and Fairfax. There it found that the works had been abandoned so recently that campfires were still burning. There were obviously no complaints about these circumstances on the Union side. Among the defenses were wooden cannons, mutely testifying to the Confederate strategy of exaggerated strength.

From Centerville the 44th returned to Fairfax for several days, then on March 21 marched to the boat landing at Alexandria, where fifteen steamships were docked to transport troops to Fortress Monroe at the extreme end of the peninsula. The Union ships must have been very active for several weeks in order to transport one hundred thousand troops, associated equipment, and supplies over the two-hundred-mile distance. Upon landing on the 24th they marched to Hampton, and on the following day north to Big Bethel on the road to Richmond, where an assault was expected to capture the Confederate works. Similar to Centerville, no assault was necessary as a few cavalry men fired their carbines and rode away. While camped there, "considerable sickness" of an unspecified nature occurred, attributed to the "low, swampy condition of country". This was an omen of things to come.

The same situation of minimal resistance occurred at Howard's Mills, six miles from Yorktown. There, after a brief period of shelling, the enemy abandoned their position. Then came Yorktown, which ended any hope of a rapid conquest.

Originally, an assault had been planned, which was deferred as General McCellan maintained that he did not have sufficient troops. Instead, a siege commenced which continued for one month, during which there was much firing of guns and cannons but few casualties, though a member of the 44th was killed, the first to die in action. On May 4, with a delayed assault imminent, it was discovered that the defenders abandoned their positions and the town had been evacuated. Unfortunately for the Union side, in the meantime the Confederates had strengthened defenses at Richmond, so in retrospect it was a hollow victory.

The 44th was assigned to garrison Yorktown, finding numerous land mines placed at locations such as wells and springs, and magazines. Four or five soldiers were killed and several times that number were wounded. Land mines were looked upon as murderous, barbarous, and unethical weapons, and on occasion their use was banned. Under General McCellan's orders, twenty-five rebel prisoners were taken from the Yorktown prison and forcibly assigned to dig up the torpedoes, as they were called, including any that were concealed in the powder magazines. About fifty were found outside the magazines, and while the prisoners' cooperation was reluctant, no incidents occurred.

On May 8, 1862, General Porter's First Division, of

Peninsula Campaign—route of the Union Army.

which the 44th was a part, left Yorktown by steamship traveling up the York River to West Point, the eastern terminus of the
Richmond and York River Railroad, about forty miles due east of
Richmond. Then they moved by rail to White House, Virginia,
which was the Curtis estate where George Washington first met
Martha Curtis, and they later married. The organizers of the
44th were not comfortable with the regiment's assignment to
garrison duty in Yorktown, apparently feeling strongly that they
had sponsored a regiment that would have a direct impact on
the war, and petitioned for it to join the brigade in the advance
on Richmond, which was quickly ordered. The regiment's commander, Colonel Stephen W. Stryker (an appropriate name for
an infantry regiment commander, at least by present Hollywood
standards)—who had gone to Washington accompanying the
regiment's quartermaster to ship the Zouave uniforms in storage to Yorktown—protested, evidently favoring the comfort of
garrison life to life and death on the front (and who could blame
him)—but was overruled. It was a fateful decision promoted
by officials far from the battlefield and reminds one of the line
from Lord Jim, "there was not the thickness of a sheet of paper
between the right and wrong of the affair." And so, along with
glory, casualties (dead, wounded and missing)—from which
good fortune had so far largely spared them—were guaranteed.
On May 25 the 44th joined the brigade at White House, six miles
east of Richmond, with the Confederate army close by.

Colonel Stryker was twenty-six years old, previously a member of Ellsworth's Zouave Cadets of Chicago and then Ellsworth's
11th New York Volunteer Infantry, a.k.a. New York Fire Zouaves. A
close associate of Elmer Ellsworth, he was in charge of Ellsworth's
remains until burial. Evidently, he was fond of peacetime military life—uniforms, competition marching drills, privileges of

rank, and parades, but not the wartime role. Colonel Stryker's strong stated preference for a role removed from the front was the first strike (pun not intended) against him. Not long after he left his command during an engagement to get reinforcements, he was discovered sitting under a tree next to his horse by a wounded soldier seeking medical aid. In a following battle he led his command in a direction inconsistent with orders—away from the line of fire, one suspects. Eventually, he was forced to resign, and was replaced by Lieutenant James C. Rice, a brave and resourceful leader with a strong belief in God and His objective of freeing the slaves, using the Union army as a tool for that purpose. During an advance in a particularly hard-fought battle, Col. Rice shouted "Men, we are Christians and we can die" one soldier reportedly replying, perhaps under his breath "I don't see what the Hell is the use of his saying that for we are dying fast enough."[5] Col. Rice was promoted to Brigadier General for his heroic leadership at the Battle of Gettysburg. Mortally wounded at the Battle of Spotsylvania, his last words were, "Turn me over....Toward the enemy, let me die with my face to the foe."[6]

An advance toward the Confederate line from the Chickahominy River began in the rain at 4:00 a.m. on May 27 with a cavalry detachment in the lead, heading northwest on the New Bridge Road toward Hanover Court House, located approximately twenty miles due north of Richmond. The 44th was in light marching order with three days of rations and sixty rounds of ammunition. Sixty rounds of ammunition may not sound like much—at two rounds per minute firing rate it would be gone in thirty minutes, but that amount was apparently standard for major encounters: Malvern Hill, where all the ammunition was expended and the regiment forced into retreat; and Gettysburg, where a supply effort in the midst of the battle was fortunately successful. There was a fundamental perception in the military at that time that, without controls on ammunition supply and firing rate, aiming would be compromised and ammunition would be wasted. This is the reason for resistance to repeating rifles, the technology for which was available at the beginning of the war.

After six hours of rain, the road used by cavalry, artillery, and infantry became almost impassable. Progress was miserably slow, and then the sun broke through and it became unbearably hot. About fourteen miles from camp an intense, short-range firefight ensued and lasted for two hours. During this period another Division of the Union Army continued to advance toward Hanover Court House, having passed the Confederate troops hidden in the woods. When heavy firing began, the union troops in the lead reversed direction and engaged the rear and left flank of the Confederates, who soon retreated. It was the first battle in which the 44th participated; their Division com-mander, General Burnside, called it "Baptismal Fire." Union Casualties were 53 killed and 344 wounded, more than half of those killed belonged to the 44th. The 44th Regiment's casualties were 33 killed and 58 wounded. The Confederate Army had 200 killed, and 730 were taken prisoner. Termed a "rout" of the Confederate army by General McCellan in his report made at that time, contemporary analysis indicates that superior Union strength in terms of number of soldiers was a deciding factor—an irony, given McCellan's position that his army was outnumbered. In any event, it was a highpoint for the Union advance on Richmond; their situation worsened quickly and led to retreat and abandonment of the campaign.

Following burial of the dead, the troops returned to camp, finding the march back as difficult as during the advance due to muddy conditions. Firing was heard near the Chickahominy, but the 44th was not engaged. Heavy rain continued to fall, causing streams to overflow and water to rise in low lands and marshes. Adding to the misery, lightning struck a tent, killing one of the occupants and setting off a box of cartridges.

Several days later, on May 31 the Battle of Seven Pines or Fair Oaks began. The 44th's brigade was not engaged but attempted to cross the Chickahominy and attack the Confederate line there. However, pontoon bridges could not be erected across the swollen river. The major impact of the battle was the wounding of the Confederate General, Joseph E. Johnston. In accordance with the Law of Unintended Consequences (i.e., actions frequently have unfortunate effects that are unintended), he was replaced by Robert E. Lee, who took a more aggressive approach, building up defensive lines around Richmond and reorganizing for much of the month of June. This spelled the beginning of the end for the Union's Peninsula Campaign. During the same period that McCellan's army was inactive—waiting for the roads to dry out before resuming the advance on Richmond—the 44th Regiment was engaged in camp and picket duties along the Chickahominy. Again, there was much illness, attributed to hot weather and miasma, a poisonous atmosphere thought to rise from swamps and putrid matter.

The Seven Days Battle began on June 26. This included six separate battles in which the Union Third Brigade was engaged: Mechanicsville, Gaines Mills, Savage Station, White Oak Swamp, Turkey Bend, and Malvern Hill—the last occurring on July 1. The 44th saw action at Gaines Mills, where it sustained 61 casualties; Savage Station, 3; and Malvern Hill, 103. The path connecting the battlefields starts about three miles northwest of Richmond and continues in an arc to Malvern Hill, twenty miles to the southeast. Clearly, the Confederate army was successful in driving the Union army further from its objective. Early in the morning of July 2, the Union troops were awakened with orders to march away from Richmond. In the words of Captain Eugene Nash:[7]

> It was learned that for the first time that the army of the Potomac was moving from Richmond instead of towards it. No army ever experienced greater humiliation. Darkness concealed the evidences of its grief. The patience, endurance and bravery of the army had been superb. The blame did not rest with the rank and file.

They reached Harrison's Landing on the James River on July 7 and remained there until August 14 when it became clear that General Lee, sensing that the Army of the Potomac was abandoning the peninsula, planned an assault before reinforcements could arrive. Over the next five days the army marched seventy miles to Hampton, then to Newport News where the 44th boarded the steamship *New Brunswick* for Fortress Monroe, and subsequently northward toward Washington.

Acquia Creek, a tidal tributary of the Potomac River, forty-five miles south-southeast of Washington, was reached early on the morning of August 20 and from there, the regiment was transported by rail to Falmouth, near Fredericksburg, where it bivouacked. On the twenty-second, it began a march along the banks of the Rappahannock River in a northwest direction and continued that until the twenty-sixth at Kelly's Ford. At that point it was learned that the Confederate army had positioned itself between the Union army and Washington, captured supplies, and destroyed the railroad track. The Union army was forced to backtrack to Falmouth, return by rail to Acquia Creek, and travel by steamship to Alexandria. From there it marched to Groveton (south of Alexandria) and then to Manassas, where the first battle of Bull Run had been fought. A second battle occurred there on August 30 with the result that the Union army was forced to retreat. The 44th had seventy-one casualties. The 44th then returned to Halls Hill, Virginia, the location from which they had originated at the beginning of the campaign—unquestionably wondering if it had been worthwhile, or in the words of one of the survivors of the campaign: "Since striking camp on the 10th day of March had anything been accomplished? If so, what or where? If so where was the fault?"[8]

At this time, preparations for the September 17 Battle of Antietam, in which the Union army was able to force the Confederates into retreat, began. But it was a bloody brawl with combined casualties that exceeded all other encounters for a single day of battle in the war.

* * *

ACCORDING TO CALVIN Preston's muster roll abstract, he became absent due to sickness just before Antietam. The first part of the notation is "Absent sick since Sept 14.62 [September 14, 1862]," followed by, "Mo. Ret. [month of return] Sept 62 at Frederick, Md. Oct 62 Absent on d.l. [disabled list] at Frederick, Md. Since Sept 15.62 Nov, Dec, Jan, Feb, Mch [March], April, May, Absent sick at City Point Va [Virginia] Co [commonwealth?] Mo. Ret. [month of return] August." Embedded in the written record, perhaps as an indication of the authority behind the record keeping is: "Clerk of the Court Martial." One can infer that absences due to sickness or any other cause were taken very seriously. (Note: words in square brackets are the author's interpretations.)

While the notations are cryptic and subject to interpretation, it appears that Calvin was absent due to sickness starting on September 14, 1862, with expectations that he would return before the end of the month to Frederick, Maryland. Subsequently, when his condition did not improve, he was placed on the disabled list at the same location until May 1863 for a period of seven to eight months and then again in August at City Point. However, the Union army was not in control of City Point until May of 1864, when General Butler captured the town in preparation for the siege of Petersburg. So it is reasonable to conclude that Calvin returned to the regiment from his first illness in May 1863, and was available continuously until he became sick for the month of August 1864 at City Point. A check of the 44th Regiment's location in August of 1864 confirms that it was in the vicinity of Petersburg, a short distance from City Point. The locations and timing of his absence are of interest because they were places where the Union army maintained large general hospitals, and because this indicates he was with the regiment at Gettysburg in July 1863, and therefore exposed to the carnage of that battle.

❊ ❊ ❊

TYPICALLY, EACH REGIMENT had a hospital facility within camp staffed by a surgeon and assistants, with supplies and an ambulance. As the war developed, it became apparent that large general hospitals were needed (general meant open to the wounded from all regiments, including confederate soldiers) to handle the large volume of sick and wounded. The first general hospital, opened by the Federal government in August 1861, was at Frederick, Maryland. This site was chosen due to location relative to railway lines, proximity to Washington and Baltimore, paved roads, good drainage, water and gas service, and suitable existing buildings.[9] Eventually, there were seven general hospitals located there, which utilized twenty-seven separate buildings and two camps.[10]

After the Frederick General Hospital opened, the Confederate army took control of the town, paroling union soldiers who could not be moved and making use of the hospital for the Confederate sick and wounded. Just before the Battle of Antietam twenty miles distant, the Union army regained control. Ambulances transported the wounded from the battlefield to the hospital, where they were either treated or readied for transport to other hospitals in Washington or Baltimore. Soldiers who were wounded in the upper extremities walked to the hospital. (Imagine walking twenty miles with a large caliber bullet hole in your arm, or shoulder!) Confederate wounded were also treated there with reportedly the same quality of care as the Union. The Frederick General Hospital also cared for soldiers who were sick or otherwise disabled during that same period with complaints including: typhoid fever, dysentery, rheumatism, bronchitis, scurvy, hernias, pneumonia, undefined fever, and chronic diarrhea. One source[11] lists diseases as major contributors to soldier deaths with

the most widespread throughout the war being dysentery/ diarrhea, while initially, measles and typhoid fever were the most dangerous threat to recruits.... Pneumonia and "consumption" (tuberculosis) decreased in frequency in the later years while scurvy and measles occurred episodically. Malaria was prevalent in the summer and early fall particularly in coastal areas and along southern rivers.

It is generally accepted that approximately 620,000 soldiers, Union and Confederate, lost their lives in the Civil War, although a recent study indicates the total was higher. The figure of 620,000 is based on 204,000 battlefield deaths, 389,000 attributed to sickness, and 25,000 attributable to other causes—for a total of 618,000. This means that approximately 63 percent of the deaths were caused by illness. Breaking this down further on the Union side, there were 110,000 and 225,000 battlefield and sickness deaths, respectively; and similarly, for the Confederate side: 94,000 and 164,000.[12]

The causes of chronic dysentery and diarrhea were poor hygiene and unsanitary conditions at the army camps. Soldiers went indefinitely without the opportunity to bathe or even wash hands, and latrines were routinely placed in close proximity to drinking water supplies. In addition, food was of poor quality and preparation was haphazard. The same factors were responsible for typhoid. The majority of the diseases were attributed by doctors to miasmic conditions (foul air near the camps) and efforts were made to reduce the impact by locating camps upwind of swampy areas and lighting fires to control mosquitos. This may have been helpful because it reduced the insect populations in the camps, which were responsible for initiating and spreading diseases—for example, malaria. But lack of recognition that the water supplies were contaminated by the human and animal waste that caused diseases was very unfortunate, to say the least.

Treatments of the diseases were often worse than the diseases themselves. There was no understanding of causes; the germ theory of disease developed by European scientists such as Joseph Lister was not part of American physicians' skillset, and there were no antibiotics or intravenous/oral rehydration fluid therapy, so dysentery and typhoid fever were essentially untreatable.

Civil War physicians had a long list of drugs to choose from. The Union Army's formulary (supply table) listed more than 131 different preparations. However, most of these drugs were useless at best, and harmful too often; very few were effective in treating even the most common diseases. The most valuable drugs were the anesthetics (ether and chloroform) opiates (particularly morphine) and quinine (for malaria). Alcoholic drugs were also considered to be medicinal and not surprisingly, were the soldier's most popular remedy.[13]

The lack of effective medicinal remedies could lead to long periods of sickness in which the patient had one or the other disease, or perhaps recovered from one, and then got the other. The most common problems, dysentery and typhoid, were gastro-intestinal in nature and treated with calomel (mercurous chloride), a compound containing mercury taken orally, which had the effect of damaging oral tissues and causing permanent facial disfiguring—with probably no effect on the disease. In addition, quinine, which was successful for treating malaria, was used for treating typhoid fever—with no likely benefit. Opium was used to treat pneumonia, for pain relief and cough suppression.

Chronic dysentery responded to a diet of fresh vegetables and an extended period of rest, away from the contaminated situation in the camps. In the case of the Union soldiers this success and the fact that in many cases the soldiers were sent north to rest at home (the "Northern cure") led to a theory that climate was somehow involved.

In Calvin's case it is likely that he was sent back to Galway, New York to recover under the supervision of his physician father, for all the good that would have done, but in a much

healthier environment—the location of the privy (still in existence in 1950) being at least fifty feet from the well—the livestock barns, a similar distance.

Statistics of soldier status for the New York State 44th
Volunteer Infantry Regiment, from the first engagement in
November 1861 through January 1863 is as follows:[14]

	Number	Percentage
Killed	113	10.5
Wounded	201	18.6
Died of Disease	67	6.2
Discharged for disability	207	19.2
Detached from regiment	207	19.2
Promoted	32	3.0
Discharged by order	50	4.6
Present for duty	229	21.2
Present in camp	9	8.3
Absent, sick	125	11.6

So about 60 percent as many died of disease as by bullets, a
reversal of the statistics for the armies as a whole. Perhaps the
44th bore proportionally more of the burden on the battlefield
Noteworthy, also is the differentiation between "present, sick in
camp" and "absent, sick," leading to the conclusion that "absent,
sick" meant the individual was either at an army general hospital
or perhaps sent home.

The patient list for the Frederick, Maryland hospital consisting of records for 9,264 individuals does not include Calvin
Preston's name. The 44th Regiment surgeon could have recommended he stay at camp even if unfit for light duty, but it seems
unlikely given the length of his illness, and is not reflected in

his muster roll abstract, which clearly states "absent, sick" rather than "present sick in camp". The other possibility was a hospital located in Washington or Baltimore where many of the sick and wounded from Frederick were eventually transferred.

✳ ✳ ✳

What impact Calvin's illness had on his life after the war is a matter of conjecture, but the fact that he became a successful druggist in Galveston, Texas may have been related to his experience with prolonged illness and medications available to mitigate the effects.

Calvin returned to his regiment in June 1863. During the month of June, 1863, the New York State 44th Regiment, attached to the Fifth Corps, was on the march from Chancellorsville, where the outnumbered Confederate army forced the Union army into retreat. The Confederate army, commanded by General Robert E. Lee, headed northward to the border of Pennsylvania, a straight-line distance of approximately one hundred miles, in an effort to outmaneuver the Union army and force a fight on favorable terms. Also heading northward, the Union army maintained a position to the east of the Confederate army to protect Baltimore and Washington. On June 29 the Union army marched through the city of Frederick in columns by platoon with flags flying and drums beating (presumably including Calvin's). The citizens of Frederick were responsive and sympathetic, a reception totally unlike what the Union soldiers were accustomed to in Virginia—with buildings decorated with flags and bunting. Understandably so, because the day before, the Confederate cavalry had passed through and confiscated property, including horses and provisions. Upon reaching Hanover in the late afternoon it was learned that the First Corps and Eleventh Corps had engaged the Confederate army at Gettysburg and in a lengthy battle, suffered severe losses, and were driven back. Marching all night, the Fifth Corps reached the Battlefield at 7:00 a.m., July 2.

In the early morning of July 2, the alignment of the Union army assumed that the Confederates would attack at the right, leaving the left thinly defended. Fortunately, the strategic importance of that area, which included the rocky knolls of Little and Big Round Top, was recognized before it was too late. The Third Brigade, including the Michigan 16th, New York 44th, Pennsylvania 83rd, and Maine 20th was positioned, right to left, down from the summit of Little Round Top in a semicircular configuration facing an area of flat land between the two. Shortly after, the Confederate army began an assault, moving over the peak of Big Round Top and advancing toward the Union line.

The battle for control of that area raged for most of the day, with repeated thrusts by the Confederates repelled, but at the expense of large numbers of the defenders. With a final assault of the day in preparation and the sixty rounds of ammunition issued each soldier totally expended, Col. Chamberlain of the Maine 20th, positioned at the extreme left of the line, ordered a bayonet charge that swept in circular motion to the right and was successful in clearing the Confederate brigade from the area in front of the Union line.

The Battle for Little Round Top resulted in approximately 200 Confederate soldiers killed, 500 taken prisoner, and over 1,000 small arms confiscated. More importantly, it protected the remainder of the Union line from an assault that would have been difficult to repulse, and thus ranks as a key Union triumph. In the course of the battle the NY 44th sustained 116 casualties, including 37 killed.

On July 3, after a two-hour barrage with artillery, Confederate General Pickett led at least 15,000 troops on an assault of the left center of the Union line, on Cemetery Ridge. It was repulsed with huge losses to Pickett's Division. After a quiet day on July 4, reconnaissance on the fifth found that the Confederate army had departed during the night. Lee's Army of Northern Virginia survived to fight another day, but Gettysburg was the high-water mark for the Confederacy.

The accounting of battlefield casualties has shifted with time—one recent source,[15] apparently based on figures ca. 1883, is the basis for the following, rounded to the nearest thousand.

	Union	Confederacy	Total
Soldiers	102,000	78,000	180,000
Killed	3,000	2,600	5,600
Wounded	14,000	13,000	27,000
Missing/Captured	5,400	5,100	10,500

More recent tabulations provide lower estimates for number of soldiers involved, ~160,000, and higher estimates for Killed, Wounded and Missing (7000, 33000, and 11, 000 respectively). Whatever the actual figures, the resulting death and suffering was staggering. Carnage was indescribable: dead soldiers and artillery horses, wrecked guns and gun carriages, shattered buildings and trees, and unexploded shells.

From the diary of Sergeant E.R. Goodrich of Company A 44th New York State Volunteer Infantry Regiment:[16]

At night of July 2nd our company was on picket in our front at the foot of the hill. The ground was literally covered with dead and wounded. It was the worse picket duty

I had ever performed. Will never forget it. The Rebs were principally Texan troops. They said it was the first time their brigade had ever been repulsed. I spent all my time, while on picket, attending to the wounded, giving them water fixing them in easy positions, cutting off shoes and helping them in any way I could. It was terrible, some crying, some praying, some swearing, and all wanting help.

A report[17] by Colonel James Rice, Commander of the 44th, dated July 31,1863, contains the following statement regarding care for the wounded and burial of the dead:

It was now 8 o'clock in the evening, and before 9 o'clock we had entire possession of the enemy's ground, had gathered up and brought in all of our own wounded and those of the enemy, and had taken and sent to the rear over 500 prisoners, including 2 colonels and 15 commissioned officers, together with over 1,000 stand of arms belonging to the enemy.

The following morning the prisoners of the brigade buried all of our own dead and a large number of those of the enemy.

The fearful loss of the enemy during this struggle may be estimated from the fact that over 50 of his dead were counted in front of the Twentieth Maine Regiment, and his loss was nearly in that proportion along our entire line.

Although this brigade has been engaged in nearly all of the great battles of the Army of the Potomac, and has always greatly distinguished itself for gallant behavior, yet in none has it fought so desperately or achieved for itself such imperishable honors as in this severe conflict..........

Calvin Preston's role in the battle and its aftermath is not documented. But because he was attached to the regiment and an able-bodied noncombatant at that time, it is reasonable to assume he was involved in the gathering of the wounded and burial of the dead. His exposure to the sudden carnage and loss of life of this magnitude would be repeated thirty-seven years later as a result of the massive hurricane that struck his adopted home of Galveston, Texas in 1900. At that point in his life, it was too much to bear.

Burial of the 7,058 dead (the number appears to come from a tabulation made during burial) took a reported twelve days and was a gruesome task.[18] The bodies quickly began to decompose in the July heat, obliterating any normal human tendency to conduct the handling of the deceased with dignity. Graves dug by the work teams were shallow trenches long enough to accommodate up to one hundred bodies. The remains were handled with tools and unceremoniously hauled or pushed into position in the mass graves. In addition, there were thousands of horses and mules that died during the battle. Their remains were collected and burned.

Today, signs of the carnage gone long ago, the Gettysburg battlefield is a placid scene, an area of monuments and cannons located at significant places of interest in recognition of the fiercely fought conflict and the bravery of young men from the North and South. The words of the poet Stephen Vincent Benet from "John Brown's Body" poignantly connect then and now:

> Pickett came
> And the South came
> And the end comes,
> And the grass comes

And the wind blows
On the bronze book
On the bronze men
On the grown grass
And the wind says
"Long ago
Long
Ago"

The wounded were transported to field hospitals for treatment. Most of the homes in Gettysburg and the surrounding area served that purpose. The number of doctors available was limited by the need to have them available to support the Union army in anticipated battles as they pursued the confederates. One can imagine that care and treatment of the wounded was compromised.

Following Gettysburg, the 44th Regiment was involved in battles at Rappahannock Station, Mile Run, The Wilderness, Laurel Hill, Spotsylvania, North Anna, Bethesda Church, Cold Harbor, and Petersburg, Virginia. Calvin Preston's muster roll abstract records that he was "absent sick" for the Month of August 1864, during the siege of Petersburg. On September 24, 1864, an order was received to turn over ordinance and ordinance stores, and proceed with the regiment to Albany, New York to be mustered out. Transportation was by steamship from City Point to Washington, and then by rail via Baltimore, Philadelphia, and New York City.

* * *

WHILE CALVIN PARTICIPATED in the war on the Union side, his brother James was a member of the Texas army, first the Galveston Artillery Company, and then Debray's Cavalry Regiment.

Again, in August 1861, Rev. Preston expressed his concern about the war, this time in terms of the defection of a prominent Northern church leader, Mr. Wilson, to the Southern faction. Rev. Preston also expressed his anguish over his brother James joining the Confederate army. Lastly, he included a reference to the three villages on the Sea of Galilee which were cursed for not accepting Jesus Christ as the Messiah, and suggesting that the same fate might befall the rebels.[19]

> We were all very sorry to hear that Dr. Wilson declined a re-election to the office which he held on the Board. And we still more regret the combination of circumstances which led to this result—Alas for our beloved country so torn with internal division. *I feel it particularly as one of my brothers has become a volunteer in the Southern Army—Can I regard him as anything other than a rebel against one of the best—nay the very best governments in the world*—when I think of these troubles in the United States I cannot help bringing to mind the woes pronounced by our Lord against Chorazin, Bethsaida & Capernaum—Exalted to heaven and may it not come to pass that by not appreciating the teaching of the Devine Grace they meet the same doom. To me it seems foolish as well as wicked it can do no good—but must inevitably result in the very opposite of what they wish—It will not redress one of their supposed or real grievances....The Chinese heard of the news from America with astonishment for they have really believed something near perfection of the US. We shall stand in the much less favorable position now—

Curiously, he later failed to mention in correspondence the October 1862 enlistment of his brother Calvin in the Northern army.

In the period of unrest immediately preceding the Civil War, Texans were torn between remaining in the Union because they had worked hard for statehood but were deeply concerned about the abolition of slavery, which was seen as essential to their business interests. Galveston was no different, although during the war the attitude apparently evolved to one of ambivalence.

The issue of slavery came to a head in 1860 with the election of President Abraham Lincoln. Lincoln was not on the ballot in Texas. "Galvestonians overwhelmingly voted for Southern Democrat John C. Breckenridge"[20] who carried the state of Texas, but Lincoln carried the free states and won the election. By contrast, while Lincoln won James' home state of New York with a plurality of 50,000 votes of approximately 675,000 votes cast, over Fusion Candidates John C. Breckenridge and Stephen Douglas,[21] it was a surprisingly narrow victory in a Northern state, which one might assume was strongly abolitionist.

A week later, the *Galveston Weekly News* declared that the "people of Texas will receive the announcement of the election of a Black Republican President...with feelings of indignation and gloom that...pervaded the South when news of this national disaster was heralded abroad." The paper added that the "policy of waiting and submitting and compromising has gone far enough" and that unless the federal government could give "guarantees—constitutional guarantees—that the abolition fanaticism shall be crushed among yourselves" that Texas and the South would no longer be part of the Union.[22]

In February 1861, by referendum, Texas followed South Carolina, Mississippi, Alabama, Georgia, and Louisiana in seceding from the Union. "The statewide voting results were 46,153 for, 14,747 against. In Galveston the vote was 765 for secession with only 33 opposed."[23] After Texas seceded, the concerns were initially territorial—keeping the Union from occupying the state and gaining control of the economy, which was essential to the Confederate cause. Caught up in the excitement of the approaching conflict and evidently supporting the pro-slavery stance of his adopted hometown, in February 1861 James enlisted in the Confederate army Galveston Artillery Corps First Brigade under William T. Austin, which had been, before the civil war, more of a social club than a military organization. The primary military purpose was to protect the harbor from intrusions by Union warships, as described:

> The Company voted to join the Confederacy as six-months men, and having had "rebored the two small iron 4-pounders...were now ready for action with two brass and four iron guns, all six pounders (the smallest having been enlarged in the foundry of Morgan Perry, on 18th and B, so that the entire battery could use uniform balls and ammunition). Land forces under General E.B. Nichols of Galveston and some companies in West Texas under Colonel J. O. Ford were ordered to invest and attack Fort Brown. The Morgan liner, "Gen. Rusk" was seized by local troops and the greater portion of the Artillery Company, under Captain Van Buren, made the trip to Santiago Brazos to aid the land forces in the capture of Fort Brown. The expedition proved a bloodless one, because Fort Brown for some unknown reason was surrendered to Nichols and Ford, without a

single shot being fired. The disgusted Artillery Company returned on the schooner *Shark* and soon disbanded; many of members joined different Confederate regiments.[24]

The foregoing serves to explain why, in March 29, 1862, James reenlisted as a private in the Texas 26th Cavalry, Debray's regiment, which was involved in some meaningful battles to prevent the Union forces from occupying the state. He served until the end of the war, but never saw action outside of the state of Texas, although other Texas regiments were involved in the Virginia campaign and fought at Gettysburg as well as other major battles including Antietam and the Second Battle of Bull Run.

It is interesting to note that three infantry regiments from Texas were involved in the assault on Little Round Top at Gettysburg. Had James enlisted in one of those regiments he would have been on the same battlefield as his brother Calvin, a soldier in the New York 44th Regiment that, along with Chamberlain's 20th of Maine, successfully defended that strategically important position. Thus, a case of "brother against brother" that, as a matter of fortune, was not to be. Ironically, a list of Civil War Veterans buried in Galveston cemeteries includes Calvin and James, both at the Episcopal Cemetery. In "remarks" James is correctly identified as having been a "Private – Twenty-Sixth Texas Cavalry" while inexplicably Calvin is listed as "Private – Fourth Texas Calvary, State Troops Co. F. implying that both fought for the Confederacy.

The Texas 26th Cavalry Regiment was comprised of volunteers from southeast Texas. Its mission was to deny Union forces access to Texas—participating in defending the northern border with Oklahoma along the Red River (thence southward into central Louisiana) and patrolling the coastline, including the protection of Galveston. It was led by Colonel Xavier Debray, a forty-two-year-old immigrant from France who had attended a French military academy. Debray arrived in Texas in 1852 and resided in San Antonio prior to the war. He became commander of the regiment in March 1862, coincidentally the same month that James Preston enlisted as a private. Presumably, as a result of Debray's military background and effective leadership, the regiment was well trained and highly regarded.

Initially assigned to patrol the coast after Union ships established a blockade of Galveston, they subsequently participated in the Red River campaign which included engagements with Union forces in Louisiana, where they received special recognition for performance in battle. Assigned duty in the Atchafalaya swamps of Louisiana near the end of the war, they suffered from scarcity of food and depletion due to malaria. Ordered to return to Texas, they reached Richmond (Texas) when word came of surrender of the Confederacy. They played a role in protecting Houston from the plundering of supplies, until discharged and returning home.

Shortly after the end of the war, James married Emmeline A. McWaters, who was born on May 14, 1849 in Alexandria, Louisiana, within twenty miles of the Atchafalaya. Perhaps the proximity of her hometown to the location where James was stationed is a coincidence, or alternately, they could have met and fallen in love during wartime. They were to live in Galveston and have one child before James' untimely death in May 1870.

Notes

[1] Rev. Charles F. Preston—July 9, 1861. Presbyterian Church in U.S.A. Foreign Mission Correspondence and Reports: 1833–1911, China,

1837–1911, letter book vols. 4,5,8, 9: calendar entry 550, (Philadelphia: Presbyterian Historical Society).

[2] Ruth Painter Randall, *Colonel Elmer Ellsworth*, (Little Brown and Company, 1960).

[3] Captain Eugene Arus Nash, *A History of the Forty-Fourth Regiment, New York Volunteer Infantry, in the Civil War, 1861-1865*, (Chicago: R.R Donnelley & Sons Company, 1911), 7.

[4] William Gilham, *Manual of Instruction for the Volunteers and Militia of the Confederate States*, (Richmond: West and Johnston, 1861), 81–4.

[5] Nash, *A History of the Forty-Fourth Regiment, New York Volunteer Infantry, in the Civil War, 1861-1865*, 89.

[6] Ibid., 224.

[7] Ibid., 90.

[8] Ibid., 101.

[9] Terry Reimer, *One Vast Hospital: The Civil War Hospital Sites in Frederick, Maryland After Antietam*, (The National Museum of War Medicine, 2001), 12.

[10] Ibid., 6.

[11] Alfred Jay Bollet, *American Civil War Medicine, Challenges and Triumphs*, (Tucson: Galen Press, 2002), 258.

[12] The Civil War, NPS.Gov, Park Home, Facts, Casualties. US Department of the Interior. https://www.nps.gov/civilwar/facts.htm

[13] Bollet, *American Civil War Medicine, Challenges and Triumphs*, 231.

[14] Nash, *A History of the Forty-Fourth Regiment, New York Volunteer Infantry, in the Civil War, 1861-1865*, 129.

[15] Robert Underwood Johnson and Clarence Clough Buel, eds., "Battles and Leaders of the Civil War," vol. 3, based on "The Century War Series" of "The Century Magazine," (Castle, A Division of Book Sales, Inc., 1995), 439–440.

[16] Nash, *A History of the Forty-Fourth Regiment, New York Volunteer Infantry, in the Civil War, 1861-1865*, 151.

[17] Reports of Col. James C. Rice, Forty-Fourth New York Infantry, commanding regiment and Third Brigade, O.R.—Series I—vol. 27/1

[S#43] —Gettysburg Campaign, July 31, 1863. https://www.civilwar-home.com/ricegettysburgor.html

[18] Allie Ward, *Bury Them in Peace*, (Gettysburg: The Gettysburg Compiler, Civil War Institute at Gettysburg College, 2012), https://gettysburgcompiler.org/2012/08/16/bury-them-in-peace-by-allie-ward/

[19] Rev. Charles F. Preston—August 9, 1861. Presbyterian Church in U.S.A. Foreign Mission Correspondence and Reports, (Philadephia: Presbyterian Historical Society).

[20] James M. Schmidt, *Galveston and the Civil War: An Island City in the Maelstrom*, (Charleston History Press, 2012), 20.

[21] David Leip, Atlas of US elections, 2109. https://uselectionatlas.org/RESULTS/state.php?f=0&fips=36&year=1860

[22] Schmidt, *Galveston and the Civil War: An Island City in the Maelstrom*, 20.

[23] Ibid., 21.

[24] Dr. J.O. Dyer, *The Old Artillery Company of Galveston*, (1917).

Chapter Six

William and Platt: White Gold

Wait's Mill, ca. 1870.
Photo courtesy of Joe Drazan.

While the Civil War was being fought and the eastern half of the United States was in turmoil, life in the Northwest Territory seems to have been largely unaffected. William and Platt, having given up on Colorado as a place to settle permanently, were on the move again—motivated by declining business prospects in the Denver area and in part by discovery of gold in Idaho and the ensuing gold rush there.

At the very least, they had somewhere to go other than back east and had acquired knowledge and skills that would serve them well until they reached their destiny. Beyond that, whether they had failed as prospectors or not, they had sufficient resources to purchase supplies and transportation for a journey. And the approach they took in business development, combined with involvement in the political process of establishing a territorial government, would serve them well later on. So after liquidating their remaining holdings in and around Golden Gate City, William and Platt acquired wagons, mules, and/or horses; purchased supplies required by miners (including non-perishable food, tools, and clothing); and set off in the spring of 1862. Their route followed the Cherokee Trail, which ran due north through the future site of Fort Collins, and trapper trails to the Oregon Trail at Fort Laramie.

The story of the discovery of gold in Idaho is well documented in the Idaho State Historical Society Reference Series; it parallels that of Colorado in two respects: reports by fur-trade trappers of gold in stream beds were decades old before a serious attempt was made to evaluate them; and the first serious attempt to find gold met with success. In Idaho, during the summer months of 1860,

> Ten prospectors led by Captain E. D. Pierce entered the Nez Perce Reservation in search of gold. After a month of no luck, one of the men, Wilbur Bassett, strikes gold along Canal Gulch. This discovery sets off one of the largest migrations in American history. Within six months, prospectors from all over the west stake another 1,600 claims in Canal Gulch. They come by way of the Columbia and Snake rivers, making Idaho one of only two states settled from west to east.[1]

Canal Gulch is in north-central Idaho, roughly 40 km due east of Lewiston and 30 km north of Elk City.

Immigrants coming from Colorado, "got as far as the upper Salmon River around Fort Lemhi only to discover no easy route to get down the river to Florence,"² a challenge that William and Platt would encounter. In 1861,

As soon as weather permitted prospecting, parties from Pierce set out to examine the surrounding country, and by the middle of May, 1861, fifty-two miners were on their way to the south fork of the Clearwater, where gold had been noticed in 1856 by a white traveler on the Nez Perce Trail. Gold was found before the end of May, and a mining district was organized June 14. The South Fork got off to a slow start, but Elk City was established before the end of July, and some handsome strikes August 1–2 improved the reputation of the district enormously. By then the diggings there were rated as an ounce a day, and the dust was relatively good—about $16 per ounce. Some 800 or 1,000 miners were there by late August, but the rush to Florence swept away almost all the miners by the end of September, so there was little opportunity for big production the first season. Elk City revived in June, 1862, when a surplus of miners overflowed from Florence, but production rates again were rather low. Even though ditches were dug for water during the 1863 operations, the season was a bad one, and recovery was poor.

Fabulous reports of production at Florence startled the entire Pacific Coast in the fall of 1861. Production got underway within six weeks of the original discovery, August 19–20, and during October and November some of the miners there were taking out hundreds of dollars a day. The district was not large, but what there was of it seemed incredibly rich—at least as reported in the newspapers—and except for its isolation and hard winters, Florence was exactly the kind of mining zone that prospectors had dreamed of finding. In spite of an exceptionally difficult first winter, thousands of hopeful miners joined the rush to Florence, and some 10,000 actually reached the mines there the next spring. The trouble was that only about 3,000 could find work there at all, so most had to look for other mines. Production reached about $50,000 per day in 1862, after which most of the best deposits were pretty well worked out. Florence was a good but unspectacular camp in 1863, and then went rapidly downhill.[2]

All of this did not bode well for the Prestons, but they had made their commitment and would have to deal with it. The Preston brothers set their sights on Elk City, and they were accompanied by others from the Denver area. Following the Oregon Trail as far as Fort Hall, they turned northward on the Mormon Missionary trail to Fort Lemhi. Reaching the Snake River when it was near flood stage due to snow melt, they had a difficult decision to make—wait until the water subsided, or cross. They chose the latter,

> using their wagon as a boat. The experiment was a very dangerous one, but they managed to thus safely ferry across camp equipments (sic) and wagons of a large train of immigrants, swimming the stock. On reaching Fort Lemhi, as wagons could not be taken further, they traded their cattle and wagons to some of those in the train who

had become discouraged and turned back, receiving mules for their property. Pack saddles were made and their first experience in the most primitive form of transportation was had. One of the mules rolled down the mountain and landed in the brush hundreds of feet below but further than that no great losses were sustained. After experiencing such hardships as only a packer knows anything about, they at length reached the Elk City mines, where the search to the key to Nature's treasure vaults began.[3]

Upon reaching Elk City via a circuitous route on the Nez Perce Trail, they evidently found that the prospects for striking it rich were minimal.

William went on to Lewiston, about 30 miles to the west, which had become a major supplier center for miners in Idaho and Montana, and became engaged in the business of teaming and draying. Platt went through the mines and in 1864 and 1865 was engaged in merchandising in Warren's Diggings, Idaho.[4]

The following excerpt from *Waitsburg: "One of a Kind"*,[5] based on undated personal recollections of William Preston's son Herbert, provides some insight into the challenges of William's occupation:

There (in Lewiston) he became a freighter, and freighted supplies from Wallula, Washington to Lewiston, Idaho, Wallula being the end of water transportation. The freighting was done by means of covered wagons drawn by eight or ten horses or mules, the driver would ride one of the wheel horses and guide the leader with a jerk line.

The freighters in those days [ca. 1860] travelled together in trains of about forty or fifty wagons as a protection against Indians. They were all of them equipped with crude guns. Although they were frequently attacked by the Indians, there were few casualties, as the troops from Fort Walla Walla would accompany them whenever they expected trouble. Whenever the different Indian tribes would fight among themselves they seemed more savage and danger of an attack on the white people was more imminent.

The trails were so crude and some of the canyons so deep that sometimes they were forced to couple up the horses on a wagon and take one wagon at a time to the summit, which made for very slow travel. They very seldom averaged more than fifteen miles a day.

At night they would usually camp along a stream or by a stage station, where they could obtain water and feed for their horses. For protection against Indians they would place the wagons in a circle, with the horses and men in the center. The Indians were not interested in their supplies or their wagons, but they were interested in stealing the horses.

The modern highway from Pendleton through Walla Walla, Dayton, Pomeroy to Lewiston follows closely the main thoroughfare of the Indians which was known as the Nez Perce trail. The original wagon roads along this route followed almost exactly the old trails. Between Dayton and Pomeroy the old Nez Perce Trail and the first wagon road crossed the Tucannon River farther upstream than the highway.[6]

One of the stage stations they would camp for the night was on Coppei Creek and it was here William G. Preston met Mathilda Cox, whom he later married.[7]

At about the same time that William had given up on seeking his fortune through panning for gold, another individual in the Lewiston area, who by misfortune had been forced to give up his chosen profession of milling, was being encouraged by a resident of the Touchet valley near Walla Walla (Dennis Willard) to move there and build a mill. He was Sylvester Wait, a miller by trade who had previously operated a mill in Oregon but had lost it during a conflict with Native Americans, and was running a dairy farm.

Settling of the region along the Touchet (*Toushay*) River had begun in 1859, immediately after the end of hostilities with indigenous people. A site recorded in the journals of the Lewis and Clark expedition at the confluence of the Touchet River and Coppei Creek was claimed by Robert Kennedy in 1859. Soon, a former soldier in the battles, Albert Lloyd, settled nearby and was instrumental in keeping the peace with the local tribes by permitting them to camp on his land. William Bruce, originally from Indiana, came to the Touchet valley in 1861, seeking a location that would improve the health of his wife. In 1862 he purchased the Kennedy claim and thereby became a neighbor of Willard's.

In the early 1860s, farmers expanded their production of wheat from that required for their own livestock to a much larger quantity for human consumption. When gold was discovered in nearby Idaho, a stagecoach began operating between Walla Walla and Lewiston, passing through the area[8] and stimulating trade with the miners.

Having an abundance of water-power and being in a region where five thousand bushels of wheat per year were grown and then transported to Walla Walla for milling, an attractive alternative was to mill the wheat to flour locally, then have it packed to the mines in Lewiston for sale to miners. The economics were very favorable; the amount paid to farmers for wheat was $1.50 per bushel, the equivalent of about $7 per barrel of flour—whereas a barrel of flour sold in Lewiston for $14. As added inducement, Mr. Willard offered to donate a site for the mill and to encourage farmers to grow more wheat in support of the project.[9]

After giving the matter due consideration, Mr. Wait sold his diary farm and rode to the Touchet River valley, carrying all the money he had, $1,500, in saddlebags.

> Goldsmith Hammer saw him go by and told the story: I remember when S. M. Wait came through this country after he sold his dairy farm near Lewiston. Wait was going to what is now Waitsburg to start a flouring mill, and he had $1,500 in his saddlebags. He lost them in a gulch north of here where Huntsville now is, and rode several miles before he was aware of the loss. He turned back at once but they were not in the road though a few hours later he overtook a man who had put them into a wagon he was driving, without examining the contents of the bags. The farmer's lack of curiosity was as phenomenal then as now but had it not been for his total indifference, there might have been no mill at Waitsburg and no Waitsburg either.[10]

And one might add, no opportunity for the Preston brothers to develop the business into a large and successful enterprise and contribute to the welfare and development of the region.

The initial project was successful. With some ingenuity in locating suitable building materials, a trip to San Francisco to acquire machinery, an agreement with farmers to store their grain until the mill was operational—in May 1865 the first load of wheat was ground into flour. The demand for flour (along with bacon, a major staple of the miner's diet) combined with an increased number of men seeking their fortune in the Idaho mines, quickly led to expansion of the mill along with a store to sell goods at the site. In order to pay for the expansion, Mr. Wait sold a half-interest in the mill to William and Platt Preston, regular customers who were freighting flour and other goods to the mines.

From that beginning, a village grew—starting with a school, store, and post office with mail delivered by a stagecoach and becoming a place where overnight accommodations were necessary—hence, a hotel and so on. In 1968 the citizens of the village, originally called Delta, voted to rename it Waitsburg in honor of the mill's founder and former part owner with the Preston brothers.

To put this into clearer and broader perspective, there have been nearly 160 flour mills in the state of Washington. The first in what is now Washington State, was built in 1816 at Markus Flats, near Kettle Falls. It was powered by animals.

As settlers appeared, the growing of grain and milling to flour was a necessary staple of their diet Early settlers found that eastern Washington was "extraordinarily suited" to growing wheat due to rich soil and no need to irrigate. "Yields per acre were better than back east." There was abundant water-power available.

Walla Walla "became the center of the flour milling industry" due to proximity to rivers for transportation of machinery into the region and shipping flour out of it.

> At one point in time there were seven gristmills operating on a thirty-mile span of the Touchet River.... One of the most interesting aspects is the relationship between millers and the founding and naming of towns.... When a

town was founded, and sometimes before it was founded the first industrial business was a sawmill. The second was usually a gristmill.... Since a gristmill was so important to the success of a town, millers were in great demand. Sylvester Wait was such a miller....[10]

He came west from New York State with experience gained from working in mills in the upstate area.[11]

Sylvester Wait was born in Waitsfield, Vermont in 1822 to Samuel and Hannah Morse Wait. Samuel was the grandson of General Benjamin Wait (of French and Indian War and Revolutionary War fame) for whom Waitsfield was named.[12] Sylvester moved with his family to Gouverneur, New York in 1835, and later to Philadelphia, New York, the latter about five miles from Antwerp, New York. The move gave Sylvester the opportunity to acquire knowledge of flour milling equipment and operations because there were several such mills in that region during the 1840s. This was not the case at his place of birth, where there were neither gristmills, nor related grain production—farming in Vermont being mostly dairy. It is not clear when Sylvester left the Antwerp area for Oregon, but it is known that his marriage to Mary Hargrave of Salem, Oregon took place in October 1853.

Coincidentally, the McAllaster family (sometimes spelled McAllister) relocated from Vermont, to Antwerp during the early 19th century.[13]

Calvin Preston, MD received his medical degree from Fairfield Academy in the Utica, New York area, about ninety miles south-southeast of Antwerp in 1825. He briefly set up a practice in Antwerp, there marrying Margaret McAllaster, before relocating in Galway, New York in 1830, where William and Platt were born. Margaret's sister was Sarah McAllaster, who married the Reverend Adam Platt, William's mentor during the period 1850–1852 (when he explored a career in religion). Margaret and Sarah's brother Alexander married Louisa Wait, great granddaughter of General Wait. Thus, through the McAllaster family connection and the common ancestor General Wait, William and Platt Preston were related, albeit distantly, to Sylvester Wait.

That fact must have become evident to them when they discussed their place of origin. One can imagine at a casual get-acquainted meeting Sylvester saying, "I'm originally from a little village named Philadelphia in upstate New York." "Near Antwerp," William responds. "Yes, I lived next to the McAllaster farm." Followed by a surprised Platt, exclaiming, "Our mother is the former Margaret McAllaster,"and so on, to the revelation of the General Wait connection. A good icebreaker no doubt, and possibly a factor in the development of their future business relationship.

Alternately it is tempting to speculate that William and Sylvester became acquainted when William was visiting his mother's family in Antwerp but there was a narrow window of opportunity for that to happen as Sylvester departed for the west coast as early as 1850.

Incidentally Platt's full name was Platt Adams Preston which seems to be the preferred version although he is referred to occasionally as Platt Adam Preston or Adam Platt Preston - but in any case a name selected by Dr. and Mrs. Preston out of respect and fondness for the Reverend Adam Platt.[14]

Platt Adams Preston, ca. 1880. Photo courtesy of the family of Laura Preston Chase.

Wait was an honest and popular man and became county commissioner in 1867. The Townsmen soon voted to name the town Waitsburg. Wait then helped Jessie Day start a mill downstream and that town became Dayton. Pomeroy is named after a miller, as are Dartford, Elberton, Post Falls, and Meyers Falls.[15]

So Sylvester Wait started the mill, rapidly paid back the money borrowed from investors, used the funds from the sale of a half-interest in the mill to the Preston brothers for expansion, then sold his remaining interest to them and moved on to a similar venture nearby. The motivation that the Preston brothers had in becoming Mill owners is understandable in these terms:

Capacity of the original mill was about fifty barrels a day,[16] so a production run of five thousand bushels of wheat ground to a little over one thousand barrels of flour could be milled in twenty days. During the Civil War, interruption of the supply of cotton forced mills to use paper sacks, which were less expensive then cloth. There was no charge for power for the milling operation because

Waitsburg Mill with wheat fields in the background, ca. 1974. Photo courtesy of the family of Laura Preston Chase.

the source was flow of river water and the mill maintenance cost was minimal. Taxes were low, sixteen mills on the dollar so the only significant fixed cost was debt service, probably at 4 percent. Thus, on the $15,000 revenue from the sale of wheat—after

accounting for labor, packaging, cost of wheat, and debt service—about $6,000 remained to be distributed as profit, freight
charges, and reduction of the loan balance. Because Mr. Wait
was able to "rapidly pay back the money borrowed from investors," perhaps $2,000 was assigned to that purpose. In the end,
Wait had approximately $4,000 from the initial production
run to share with the freighter and himself. Both he and the
freight service had leverage in the negotiation, Wait certainly
more, because there was competition between freight operators. Perhaps they split the amount 75/25 percent with Wait
netting $3,000—or approximately $36,000 per year for full-time
operation. Keeping in mind that the initial income resulted
from less than one month of activity, and that a yearly income
of $1,200 was an average living, the mill was a remarkably suc-
cessful venture. The added importance of this to the Preston
brothers was that they operated a freight service and thus could
profit from both the milling, as well as the distribution and
sales activities.

In 1870 they became sole proprietors and subsequently gained
control of the local industry. By 1882 the capacity of the mill had
expanded to 130 barrels of flour per day, and the Prestons were
cultivating eighteen hundred acres of wheat in the Waitsburg
area, which provided about seventy thousand bushels, or fifteen thousand barrels of flour. While prices for wheat and flour
fluctuated—constantly driven by factors like the weather—reve-
nue on the basis of fourteen dollars per barrel would have been
$200,000, exclusive of milling done for other wheat farmers
in the area. For a number of years, the mill was solely owned
by the Preston brothers, later becoming the Preston-Schaffer
Milling Company, which operated until 1957 with mills at
multiple locations.

William, through vision, hard work, and perseverance, assisted by his brother, achieved success in business and found a beautiful area in which to live. But the story is not complete without including the actions he took to support and protect his other siblings when fortune turned against them. For example: Calvin survived the Galveston Hurricane of 1900 (which remains the US natural disaster resulting in the greatest loss of life), barely managing to rescue his family of five and suffering a daunting financial loss; Charles, upon returning home from Canton, China after twenty-three years there as a missionary, died in Hong Kong, leaving his widow and six young children in a difficult situation; and Maria, suffering from dementia, was left at the mercy of her husband's relatives after her husband's death in Florida. William and Platt (prior to the latter's untimely death) came to their rescue.

William G. Preston, ca. 1890. Reprinted from *An Illustrated History of Southeastern Washington* (1906).

Notes

[1] Idaho Mining Association, www.MineIdaho.com/education/history, 1860.

[2] "Mining in Idaho," Information supplied by Ernest Oberbillig, Idaho State Historical Society Reference Series 9, 1960, revised 1985, Pages 8–9. https://history.idaho.gov/wp-content/uploads/2018/08/0009.pdf.

3 Frederic A Shaver, *An Illustrated History of Southeastern Washington: Including Walla Walla, Columbia, Garfield and Asotin Counties*, (Western Historical Publishing Co., 1906), 245.

4 Vance Orchard, compiled by, *Waitsburg: "One of a Kind"*, (Waitsburg Historical Society, 1976), 41.

5 Ibid., 43.

6 Gerald J. Tucker, *History of the Northern Blue Mountains* (Umatilla16), 1940, Page 20. https://www.fs.usda.gov/lnternet/FSE_DOCUMENTS/ fsbdev7_015563.pdf

7 Orchard, *Waitsburg: "One of a Kind"*, 43.

8 Ellis and Elvira Ellen Laidlaw, *Wait's Mill. The Story of the Community of Waitsburg, Washington*, (Chicago: Adams Press, 1970), 66.

9 Ibid., 71–2.

10 Norman Reed, "Flour Milling in Washington — A Brief History." historylink.org/file/9474, 2010.

11 Matt Bushnell Jones, *History of the Town of Waitsfield, 1782-1908, with Family Genealogies*, (Lowell: Courier-Citizen Press, 1909), 501. https://archive.org/details/cu31924028838600/page/n11

12 Ibid., 3–4.

13 Descendants of Richard McAllister (R04), William Worth, Clan McAlister of America, 2011, 109, 110, https://www.clanmcalister.org/ wworth2.html

14 Orchard, *Waitsburg: "One of a Kind"*, 19.

15 Reed, "Flour Milling in Washington — A Brief History."

16 Orchard, *Waitsburg: "One of a Kind"*, 21.

Chapter Seven

Charles Preston:
The Treasury Street Chapel
and His Final Rest

Treasury Street, Canton, China 1860. Felice Beato.
Photo Courtesy of the Library of Binghamton, Collection Ref. 4232.

*T*HE MORTALITY RATE of missionary children in China may not have been exceptional for the nineteenth century, but letters to the board containing the sad news are not hard to find. On November 13, 1862, Charles wrote the following to the board on the Kerr's sad experience:

When the last mail was dispatched I was at Macao with my family—Mrs. Preston and the children were there about a month—myself 16 days. You will have (heard of) the bitter bereavement of Dr. & Mrs. Kerr in the loss of both of their children—They are truly afflicted—God grant unto them the consolations of his grace. We fear the cholera may be making its way to the South—There have already been several victims here.....[1]

And soon it made its way too close to home. Cholera, generally caused by sewage-contaminated drinking water is now highly treatable through the use of intravenous hydration to combat dehydration resulting from diarrhea—and antibiotics to kill the bacteria.

Not long after, Charles expressed his sadness at the death of his daughter, Maggie:

23rd January 1863

My Dear Mr. Lowrie,

Little did I think when I mentioned in my last note to you that little Maggie was sick that it was her last illness—But such was the will of Our Heavenly Father—After a sickness of two weeks she fell asleep on New Year's Day—and we firmly believe was carried by angel to Abraham's bosom— we had for our confirmation of our faith in the covenant many evidences that she was a child of God—Nobody so sweet as Jesus is there Mamma? was her remark very often—She has learned to read the Bible with a good deal of fluency and in addition to a general ideas of her fitness we have an impression of her willingness to die—that she might get to be one of Jesus' little "lambs."

It is a great affliction to us—no one can tell how great—for no one can know what a sweet child she was—nor how great the vacancy caused by her loss.

She was singing all day her beautiful hymns—as if already preparing as she was for the event—now all is silent—and the light of our dwelling has been put out—or rather I should say taken away to shine with a more brilliant light above. We feel that she is not lost but only taken a little before—and we are comforted in remembering the many pleasant speeches which showed her simple faith in the Gospel.....[2]

Sadly, this reminds one of the secular perspective: "we tell ourselves stories in order to live." —Joan Didion

On the positive side (while concerned about the Civil War, his brother James' role in it, and the division of the Church into North and South factions) Charles Preston had an opportunity he had been waiting for since arriving in China eight years previous: to preach the gospel in the Chinese language in a chapel of his own. Apparently with board acceptance, he began to solicit funds independently for a long-term lease of a property on Treasury Street for the building. His letter of September 22, 1863 describes the outcome:

My Dear Mr. Lowrie,

In your letter received by the last mail you requested me to send you a plan of the new Chapel on Treasury Street. Herewith I send a single sheet with measurements and at the same time a record of Expenses and Subscriptions. The negotiations for the site and building were protracted and involved but I hope the accompanying statement may make all plain ....

The building is quite substantial and very light and well ventilated, I preach there in the hottest weather with great comfort. I hold a lease for 15 years at an annual rent of $82.60. After 15 years the rent will be $168 per annum—I hope before that time however it may be purchased or a more desirable site secured—But even then the rent would be cheap for the situation—as it is in a very expensive part of the City. There is never any difficulty in securing a fine audience as to members and quality—while a very crowded street it is not a noisy one ....

[It] is acknowledged to be altogether the best site for a chapel in Canton—One of my English friends calls it our Cathedral. The entrance is attractive and over the door is a large sign in gilt letters "Gospel Hall"—and on each side also in gilt characters the scripture "Glory to God in the highest, peace on earth and good will to men." Over the entrance in the Depository is a large sign with gilt green & black characters—"There is but one God only" I wish to have many more passages of Scripture suspended around the walls With not very many exceptions I have had a daily service there since it was opened—It would be a great addition if I had a native assistant. The audiences are very respectful and attentive—Newcomers are much struck with the high ceiling and the appearance of the hall....[3]

Presumably, they were also struck by the quality and enthusiasm of Rev. Preston's preaching. The following was written after Rev. Preston's untimely death:

Charles F. Preston ... was justly regarded as the most fluent of all foreigners in the use of the difficult Chinese language. With the exception of the time occupied in one visit to this country [US], he has held a daily service for many years, in which he generally addressed from four hundred to eight hundred people. Though an unimpassioned speaker in his native tongue, he was always enkindled to an unusual degree when addressing his Chinese audiences, and suc-ceeded beyond most preachers in winning attention. His chapel in Treasury Street was like an eddy in a great peren-nial stream. It drew from the thousands of passers-by many each day who had never before heard of Calvary. Coming, it may be, from distant interior provinces, they saw this ear-nest foreigner, and before him an attentive body of listeners, and turned aside to see and hear. It was not the usual theat-rical performance of the temples, as they soon learned, nor any speculation of a zealous vender of earthly wares; but, strangely enough to them, it was the message of a disinter-ested man, who had crossed the ocean to tell them of God's great love to men, of a Redeemer dying upon the cross for their salvation. Many, filled with wonder, came again and again. Some found the way of life speedily, but many more went away pondering the word in their hearts...."[4]

The chapel where he enthusiastically preached the gospel was a glowing success in Rev. Preston's life. Years later, in 1918 a Galway resident who knew the Prestons would comment in an oral history segment for the Galway Historical Society "never heard he had much success in converting the heathen Chinese," a statement that reflects a striking lack of knowledge and appre-ciation of a life well spent.

Furloughs granted by the mission board provided an opportunity for missionaries to travel to the United States, communicate directly with the church members about their experiences, and receive gratitude for accomplishments in the field—the gist of which was contained in a June 1865 letter to the board from Rev. Preston. He had been in China for eleven years at that point and presumably was fending off feelings of homesickness. His father, while in good health, was sixty-six years old, still living in the family home on East Street in Galway, New York with his second wife and youngest daughter, Maria, while married daughter Sophia lived close by. So a trip to Galway would have been timely and appropriate. It took several years before the board granted his request, and then without enthusiasm.

In early 1866 Rev. Preston raised the issue of furloughs again, proposing a policy of regular furloughs at intervals of ten to sixteen years, and stated that he did not want to be looked upon as guilty of running away from duty but wanted to come home. An April letter contains "possible plans for return to the U.S." Then his attention turned to "Mission Difficulties" which apparently included Dr. Happer's outside activities and earnings. Dr. Kerr then joined the discussion with a "statement of various matters which have agitated us," followed by a letter of complaint from Mr. Preston that "there seems to be no idea (on the part of the General Assembly) of what is called for—no conception of the work to be done," and another letter describing "differences in the mission" and deferring a visit to the U.S. Dr. Happer then wrote that, "regarding the differences, 'misunderstandings cleared up.'"

The problem, that of conflict on goals, approaches, and methodology, was not one confined to the Canton Mission. Elsewhere in China there were quarrels between missionaries explained in terms of strong-willed, intelligent, and driven individuals of differing perspectives within the same religion in conflict over such matters as the proper Chinese phrase for God being "Shen" (Deity), or "Shang Ti" (Supreme Deity).

A scholarly historical study[5] of the American Presbytery in China summarizes the Canton situation as one reflecting "a sharp rivalry between John G. Kerr and Andrew Happer ... two extremely able missionaries, each of whom made lasting contributions to the Chinese movement but who simply could not get along." Incidentally, Rev. Preston was a close associate of Dr. Kerr.

In 1867, the advent of steam-powered ships on the ocean changed time of travel and communications between the missions and the board. Rev. Preston would make note that the faster pace of mail by the Trans-Pacific Mail seems to bring us much nearer to the mission home.

In 1869, Preston finally got approval for a furlough, which included travel with his entire family to the US. His ship, the steamer SS *America*, left Hong Kong on March 19, 1870. After arrival in San Francisco his entourage, which included a Chinese servant for the purpose of helping his invalid wife with luggage and the children, arrived in Galway, New York via a cross country trip on the newly operating First Transcontinental Railroad, which had recently started operations.[6]

Galway 6th May 1870

My Dear Mr. Lowrie,

I am happy to say that by the good hand of God upon me I have brought my family safe to my father's house—I should have written to you upon arrival from San Francisco but I was very busy and Mr. Loomis said write to the Mission House in regard to my arrival. I spent the Sabbath at Omaha where I met Dr. Clark of Boston—on his way to the Saudi Islands. While in California I only spoke to the Chinese but in Omaha I spoke to the Sabbath School—Dr. Clark gave a stirring speech in the evening. I expect to spend a few days here and then on to New York on my way to Windham to visit my wife's family—thence to Philadelphia to the General Assembly—after which I have no plans except to see old friends and make news— for myself and the Chinese Mission especially at Canton. I telegraphed to Condit and he met me at Girard and rode with us for two hours—the people in California are very much interested in the Chinese and I think now is the time to set all sail—for I am afraid the enthusiasm will not con- tinue for long—By a little direction it may be made of good account. I am overwhelmed by the pleasure in seeing my friends and aged father. I shall see you in a few days and speak of many things which I have no time to write.

Believe Me
Yours very truly

C.F. Preston

Rev. Preston's time in the United States was spent preach- ing at Presbyterian churches in the Galway, New York area—at Cohoes and Albany, for example. He and his father, the lat- ter named a commissioner, attended the General Assembly in Philadelphia together. During their visit to Windham, where his wife's family lived and coincidentally was his father's place of birth, arrangements were made for son Walter's living accom- modations because he would attend school there and not return to China with the family. Walter was ten years of age at the time; sadly Rev. Preston would not see him again.

At this point in time it appears that Rev. Preston's plan was to return to Canton for several years and then secure a position with the mission on the West Coast, where immigration had resulted in a large Chinese population. On August 24, 1871 he wrote:

> My Dear Mr. Lowrie:
>
> It is perhaps the time to begin to arrange for out return to Canton. We will be glad to stop a little time in San Francisco and to leave on the steamer of Oct. 1st. So we are set to leave here suppose sometime between the 10th to the 15th of Sept.........[7]

The Prestons arrived in Canton in early November 1871, the trip from New York to Canton taking forty-five to fifty days, by use of the transcontinental railway to San Francisco and steamer to Canton, compared with the 160 days of his 1854 voyage there by sailing ship via the Cape of Good Hope. While certainly a more comfortable and rapid means of travel, it made more frequent trips to and from China a practical matter, provoking a negative response from the Mission Board. Reacting to a growing concern of the Board regarding the frequent return of missionaries to the U.S., Dr. Happer would eventually state his position on the matter as summarized in the mission log of correspondence:

> Canton—The return of missionaries to the United States. I do not wonder that the Board is alarmed. The facilities of steamers present great inducements. Comparison of present days with former days of sail boats. The length of time

on a sail boat was enough to deter anyone undertaking it, except for sufficient reasons. Five or six months was the time to China. Six weeks on a steamer with every comfort and luxury and by cars is a pleasure excursion. Suggested rules for return. Board to call upon missionaries to endure hardness. The number may be diminished. The quality will be improved.[8]

And so, it is not surprising that when Rev. Preston initially requested a transfer to the US to work among the Chinese immigrants on the West Coast, he did not get much sympathy, even as his chronic illness worsened.

From the time of his return until his final departure from Canton, Rev. Preston would continue to preach the gospel at the Treasury Street chapel while engaging in translating the New Testament into Chinese and preparing a hymn book. The second Presbyterian Church of Canton was organized in 1872 and he became its stated supply. He also preached regularly at the chapel of the Medical Missionary Society adjoining the hospital as well as his residence.

Charles Finney Preston, ca. 1877. Photo courtesy of the family of Laura Preston Chase.

In 1876, he began the process of seeking approval for a position for the mission among the Chinese immigrants on the West Coast of the US. The board turned him down perhaps because of scarcity of funds in the treasury to support it, and possibly also to keep a missionary of his capability in service in China. His letter of May 1877 is a plea to the board to reconsider his application for a change of assignment, containing a reference to his health along with a doctor's ominous advice regarding a change of climate. Reading between the lines and summarizing briefly, Rev. Preston was critically ill with dysentery or chronic diarrhea and struggling to find an accommodation from the Board to relocate him from the mission in China to the US. No doubt the future of his family weighed heavily on his mind, yet his tone is polite and deferential.[9]

Canton May 9, 1877

My Dear Mr. Ellenwood

Enclosed I have sent you an account of my trip down the west coast. When I returned I found your letter of the 6th inst. I cannot say I am altogether surprised—and while I am sorry the Board still responds with so much disfavor at my application, I am not inclined to complain or find fault. I try to regard the matter in the light of a providential indication that my way is still up before me and I trust that light will arise from an unexpected quarter—so that in the end it will be manifest that this decision at this time was for the best.

I am pleased at your assurances of fraternal regard & friendship—& [accept] gladly the explanation that your former letter was an attempt to alleviate the crisis. I appreciate all you say about advice to a brother—but I am compelled to confess that after all the assessment of the Board I am of the same opinion still—I am confident that were you in my place you would feel as I do and be anxious to keep the application I have made before the Board—I do not know that I can add very much to what I have already said in favor of my scheme—well perhaps to say that the

consideration of my health may render the changes necessary—The surgeon of the US hospital gave his opinion most
decidedly that a change of climate is called for and that my
complaint will yield to nothing else. I hope he is mistaken
and that I may recover—I have lost 30 pounds in weight in
the past month & I find my spirits are very depressed. I feel
that this aspect of the case is one that requires proposing
advice for the vote of the mission—when I gave myself to
the Board it was with the intention of self sacrifice to the
service of the church—and in my application I had no idea
of anything inconsistent with that idea—I believe I am ready
to keep my children in China—send them as you say you
do to Boarding school or to take them to California seems
the best plan. What is right under the circumstances? I will
feel my way and do as God directs. I have two brothers living in Washington Territory—the number of Chinese is
increasing in that region and in Oregon. Is it possible the
Board would look with favor upon my removing there for a
season? I might do as Mr. Condit is doing preach in English
with a house in Portland—would perhaps be free from the
objections to San Francisco or Oakland.

I am very sorry the Board have not seen the way clear to
assisting Dr. Kerr's mission work in California. I am quite
sure that Dr. Loomis, Mr. Condit and Dr. Speer would
agree with my opinion that there is work enough there. Dr.
Loomis indeed frequently complains in his letters ... China
is the proper place for missionary labor far more important
California—but there is a call to do much in California—
The mission there is very necessary and much more may
be done than has been done—No persons are better fit-
ted for doing this work than such as from various reasons

called away from Canton—the two fields are intimately connected together and the church has a special interest in the work in California per their circumstances.

I wish very much that the Board could see its way clear to give me a place somewhere on the Pacific Coast for a few years—I think I can do good work there—my health I believe requires the change and I could keep my family together while the children are at school. Should my health permit I am content to remain in Canton—but if the physicians advise a change in climate my desire is still to labor for the Chinese under the direction of the Board. I trust this matter may be reviewed by the Committee and left to be decided when a fresh application is made. The convictions expressed in my letter remain & I trust the principle argued as important may be accepted without reference to my individual case.

I trust you do not suppose I wanted a bad meaning out of your letter—I did not intend to do violence to the plain sense of it. I suppose the matter must rest at present—the Board evidently wished to have it dropped but I imagine Dr. Loomis will not keep silent if he is understood to be in so want of help— He will probably try to correct that impression. I cannot withdraw my application and perhaps it would be unwise to urge it any more just at present. I still think the cause supported by my letter the best for all concerned—But in this difference of opinion I trust you will give me credit for true fraternal feelings—I have made no charges and only endeavored to reply to your letter in the fairest manner possible.

Believe me, Yours respectfully

C.F. Preston

According to John Hays of Galway, husband of Rev. Preston's sister Sophia, the board resisted providing Rev. Preston relief even limited to a vacation. In the words of Mr. Hays:

> He worked so hard and the climate was so hot, that he must have a change, go back to his native air. He wrote to the Board in New York and they replied that funds were so low in the treasury that they couldn't give him a vacation. The doctor, as soon as he heard of the Board's decision, told Mrs. Preston that he must go somewhere at once, so they bundled him up for Hong Kong. He stopped the first night with a missionary and he just gave out. His wife was sent for and he only lived 5 days.[10]

Charles Finney Preston passed away on July 17, 1877, just days before his forty-eighth birthday. It is difficult to overlook the fact that in his last letter to the board he was pleading for a change in location that meant the difference between life and death. He was buried at the Hong Kong cemetery, ironically in a locale named Happy Valley. A monument erected by his three surviving brothers bears the inscription:

In memory of Rev. Charles F. Preston—a member of the American Presbyterian Mission. Arrived in Canton May 15, 1854, and fell asleep in Jesus July 17, 1877. I am only resting.

Charles F. Preston monument. Courtesy of Chris Nelson.

At some point later, the board consented to bring Mrs. Preston and their five children, ages five to fourteen, to the West Coast, where they were temporarily provided accommodations in a home for Chinese women. Dr. Preston wrote the board shortly after her arrival in San Francisco:[11]

Galway, N.Y. 18th Mar. 1878

Rev. F.F. Ellenwood D.D.

My Dear Sir

I have just received a letter from my Dear Boy's widow announcing her safe arrival in San Francisco with her Family where she is now occupied in the Home for Chinese Females. I have written to advise her to retain her connection with the mission if desired.

She has been talking of going to Waitsburg, Walla Walla County, W.T. where I have two sons in business.

She requested me to ascertain if the Board will furnish the means to send her eldest son to that place who is now in school in Norwich, Conn. Would it not be well to retain Her influence and family on that coast as they are familiar with the Canton dialect and there are so many Emigrants on that coast from that province.

Now my Dear Brother allow one to suggest to you the idea of making a short notice this life and labors in the interest of the Master and of his grace which might be noticed in some paper—

With High Esteem

I am my dear sir

Yours truly

C.Preston

The date of Dr. Preston's letter suggests that Mrs. Preston left Canton at the end of January 1878, approximately six months following Charles' death. According to Presbyterian Historical Society records, she had resigned her position with the mission before year-end 1877.

Many articles were written honoring Rev. Preston. An excerpt from one in the Union College archives reads as follows:[13]

Mary B. Preston and Frederick— Hong Kong, ca. 1877. Courtesy of the family of Laura Preston Chase.

I knew very well Charles Preston of the class of '50, the son of the village Doctor at Galway, Saratoga County where Samuel Nott preached. When I knew him he was a portly man. He carried all before him. That, however, did not interfere with his activities. He learned the Chinese language as few foreigners learn it. He became the most effective preacher among our missionaries and filled Canton with his Gospel. In this revolutionary period Canton has been governed by a group of men the majority of whom are Christians.

Left to right: Frederick and Laura Preston with Annie Bennett, (San Francisco, 1878). Courtesy of the family of Laura Preston Chase.

Rev. Preston's family would have had a challenging existence had it not been for the resources and compassion of his brothers William and Platt in Waitsburg. His wife and five children who travelled with her from China relocated there and were reunited with Walter, who had completed his education in Windham, Connecticut and taken a position in the brothers' mill. After finishing her education, Rev. and Mrs. Preston's eldest daughter, Sophie, inspired by her father's work, became a missionary and traveled back to Canton alone by steamer and arrived safely at the house where she was born. Her childhood amah (nursemaid) welcomed her back, and her knowledge of the Chinese language returned. She met a young missionary from Oberlin, Ohio, and they married and stayed at that same location and house for twenty-two years until his illness forced them to return to the States, where he became a professor of language at Oberlin College[14] (incidentally— where Charles Grandison Finney was once a professor and subsequently president). So history repeated itself, but with a happier ending.

Notes

[1] C.F. Preston, Presbyterian Church in U.S.A. Foreign Mission Correspondence and Reports, 1833–1911, China, 1837–1911, letter book vols. 4,5,8, 9. (Philadelphia: Presbyterian Historical Society, 1862), calendar entry 595, November 13, 1862.

[2] Ibid., 599, C.F. Preston, January 13, 1863.

[3] Ibid., 622(a), C.F. Preston, September 22, 1863.

[4] Memorials of the Foreign Missionaries of the Presbyterian Church U.S.A., William Rankin, (Philadelphia: Presbyterian Board of Publications and Sabbath School Work, 1895), Necrological Record 278.

[5] G. Thompson Brown, *Earthen Vessels and Transcendent Power: American Presbyterians in China, 1837-1952* (American Society of Missiology Series, 1997), 71.

[6] C.F. Preston, Presbyterian Church in U.S.A., calendar entry 276, May 6, 1870.

[7] Ibid., 137, C.F. Preston, August 24, 1871.

[8] Ibid., Mission Board Log, A.P. Happer, September 29, 1876.

[9] Ibid., calendar entry 117, C.F. Preston, May 9, 1877.

[10] Elizabeth Robb Quinby and Ethel Robb, *Historical and Genealogical Notes of Galway, New York,* 2 vols., Galway Preservation Society Archives Section P – December 19, 1918 letter, John Henry Hays to Mrs. Quinby.

[11] C.F. Preston, Presbyterian Church in U.S.A., calendar entry 25, March 11, 1878.

[12] Quinby and Robb, *Historical and Genealogical Notes of Galway, New York,* February 3, 1919 Letter, John Henry Hays to Mrs. Quinby.

[13] "Charles Preston, Class of 1850," Union College Archives, 1912.

[14] Quinby and Robb, *Historical and Genealogical Notes of Galway, New York,* February 3, 1919 Letter, John Henry Hays to Mrs. Quinby.

Chapter Eight

Calvin and James: Galveston, Texas

Calvin W. Preston, ca. 1890.
Reprinted from *An Illustrated History of Southeastern Washington* (1906).

Y THE END of the Civil War the citizens of Galveston were simply tired of the conflict; a period of occupation by the Confederate army was at least partially responsible for that attitude. Related evolving ambivalence to the emotional issues that were the driving forces of the conflict, slavery and state's rights, may have helped Galveston's economy recover faster than that of other areas of the state and the South in general. And while James' relationship with his family in New York may have suffered from his support of the Confederate cause, (unlike his brothers, there is a dearth of information available about him in the upstate area of New York) his bond with Calvin was apparently unaffected.

Calvin returned from the war apparently not content with resuming his occupation as a farmer in quiet, upstate New York. He relocated to Galveston in 1866 and found employment in a drug store, Barstow and Morris. Subsequently, he and a partner, A. Robira, opened a drug store of their own. Records of Calvin's training for the profession are not available. Any formal training he received would have occurred in the period 1864 to 1866, while living in New York. A logical place for such would have been at the Albany Medical College, but a check of their records indicates that he did not attend. However, it was common during that period for druggists to receive training by internship, and his father would have been a natural choice. Calvin's residence address in Galveston, listed in the 1875 City Directory is at the corner of Avenue H and 10th Street, the same location of James' in 1868. Whether they shared the same quarters for a period of time cannot be determined, but it seems obvious that James encouraged Calvin to move to Galveston.

Calvin's support of the abolitionist cause might have caused him to have reservations about moving to Texas, where slavery was, to say the least, a widely accepted practice prior to the end of the Civil War. But shortly after the end of hostilities an event occurred in Galveston that probably allayed his concern.

General Robert E. Lee's surrender on April 9, 1865 reached Texas later in the month, coinciding with the appointment of

Colonel Ashbel Smith as Commander of the remnants of the Second Texas Infantry for the defense of Galveston.[1] The news, initially "denounced as Yankee Lies and Propaganda," was followed by that of President Abraham Lincoln's assassination. While the military leadership continued to encourage the troops to maintain readiness, it was clear by the end of April that the war was over, and the Confederate garrison in Galveston disbanded. The Army of the Trans-Mississippi, which included Texas, was the only Confederate force still active, surrendering on June 2. On June 18, Union Army General Gordon Granger arrived at Galveston Island with 2,000 federal troops to occupy Texas on behalf of the federal government. The following day (legend has it), standing on the balcony of Galveston's Ashton Villa, Granger read aloud the contents of "General Order No. 3," announcing the total emancipation of those held as slaves:

> "The people of Texas are informed that, in accordance with a proclamation from the Executive of the United States, all slaves are free. This involves an absolute equality of personal rights and rights of property between former masters and slaves, and the connection heretofore existing between them becomes that between employer and hired labor. The freedmen are advised to remain quietly at their present homes and work for wages. They are informed that they will not be allowed to collect at military posts and that they will not be supported in idleness either there or elsewhere."[2]

Galveston's ex-slaves rejoiced on hearing the news....... The day has been remembered ever since as "Juneteenth," a portmanteau of the words "June" and "nineteenth," also "Emancipation

Day" or "Freedom Day"). Beginning in 1866, African Americans in Galveston and throughout the state began annual celebrations of Juneteenth with church services, parades, readings of the Emancipation Proclamation and more. Still, it would take time for that freedom and equality to be fully realized.[3]

Indeed, total equality is an objective not yet achieved today....

A fifth-generation member of a Galveston African American family explains[4] that, in addition to being the founding location of the Juneteenth movement, there were other underlying factors of the city's unique race relations that contributed to Calvin's comfort level in settling there:

> Galveston's inter-ethnic history is a bit complicated. The main context that I can provide is that Galveston's status as an international seaport ensured that a steady stream of outsiders kept the city's culture from being as isolated as other locations across the U.S. South. Sailors and the like came from ports around the world. The port trade was lucrative enough to provide employment for a wide cross-section of society.
>
> The presence of various European ethnics ... was significant as well, as it added nuance and dimension to the framework of what constituted "race," in much the same way that one might find in northern urban centers. Notable among those segments were those who emigrated from Italy, Greece, Germany, etc. *Island of Color*[5] points out that in Galveston's pre-*Jim Crow* era, legally-enforced racial separation was not a preoccupation there.
>
> Galveston at that time was by no means a racial-harmony utopia. Separation existed, as an expression of tradition. Resources were still allocated along racial lines

(schools and houses of worship were segregated), generally reflecting preference toward white citizens. But informally, people lived in close proximity with one another, and found common ground. The city's Reconstruction era civic leaders prominently included individuals like Norris Wright-Cuney (1846-1898), a biracial man who was the chief customs official for Galveston's port, and can be given credit for much of the development in Texas of the Republican party (then the party of abolitionists). Considerable detail about his life can be found in [*Island of Color*].

Another individual profiled in [*Island of Color*] is Jack Johnson (1878-1946), the 1st black heavyweight boxing champion. His story has been chronicled in movies, books and other media around the world. But he also signifies a discomfort that occurred upon the enactment of Jim Crow laws. His childhood came before Jim Crow laws significantly took effect in Galveston, and one could interpret his brashness with white women as being a celebrity protest much like one finds in the 21st century among activist celebrities. Johnson was from the same neighborhood where I grew up more than a half century later (I was born 10 years after his death), and I've been told that he was a friend of both of my grandfathers. During his childhood, Jim Crow taboos had not manifested themselves in Galveston until the 1890s or so.

Much of the legacy of the 19th century continued though the lifetime of my own father, whose teenage years coincided with WWII. My father explained to me that during his young adult years, he learned that law enforcement officers in other parts of Texas were somewhat leery of blacks from Galveston, based on an assumption that

Galveston's black people were unaccustomed to the burdens of Jim Crow. Yes, they attended segregated schools and churches. But excluding those who were extremely wealthy or poor, Galveston's citizens of all racial/ethnic groups resided in close proximity, albeit while maintaining a distance under most social situations.

That situation was likely not much unlike what occurred during the late-mid 1800s with Calvin Preston as a neighbor to my great-great grandfather.

Unfortunately, James' and Calvin's life together in Galveston were ended with the death of James about four years after Calvin's arrival. His passing was described in the May 8, 1870 issue of the *Galveston Daily News* and termed "mysterious," (a notch down from suspicious), which was evidently sanctioned by the authorities. An obituary was published in the May 15, 1870 *Flake's Daily Bulletin*. Together the articles contained these images: An elder German immigrant engaged in collecting shells at the eastern end of the island found James' body "lying with face slightly embedded in the sand," clothed only in undergarments. He informed two passersby who notified the police. Upper clothing was found nearby along with a watch and forty-five dollars. According to the *Galveston Daily News* article, the watch was running, the body limp and not yet cold. Two men watched over the body until arrival of the coroner. The impression of Judge Johnson was that he drowned, although Chief of Police Smith thought the cause of death was apoplexy (i.e., cerebral hemorrhage or a stroke). Noteworthy is the information that James had been complaining of ill health for several days prior.

✻ ✻ ✻

FROM A LAYMAN'S perspective there are three types of strokes: ischemic, in which a blood clot obstructs flow of blood to a portion of the brain; hemorrhagic, caused by a blood vessel on the brain surface rupturing and filling the space between the brain and skull with blood; and a so-called TIA (transient ischemic attack), a brief interruption of the blood supply to part of the brain that causes a temporary impairment of vision, speech, or movement. By contrast, a cerebral hemorrhage is characterized by the bursting of an artery in the brain, which fills the surrounding brain tissue with blood

Ischemic strokes account for about 90 percent of all instances. Stroke is currently the number five killer of adults in the US— behind heart disease, cancer, lower respiratory diseases, and accidents. The symptoms of ischemic stroke include but may not be limited to:

- Sudden numbness or weakness of the face, arm or leg— especially involving one side of the body
- Loss of vision in one or both eyes
- Trouble walking, dizziness, loss of balance or coordination
- Sudden, severe headache with no known cause

Ischemic strokes are further classified as associated with small blood vessels (lanunar) or large blood vessels (thrombosis). Thrombotic strokes are the most common, accounting for 80 percent of ischemics.

Prompt medical attention is the key to minimizing damage to the brain resulting from an ischemic stroke. A recognized medical team objective is administering clot-dissolving medication within a maximum of one hour from the onset, but sooner is obviously better. Some insight into the reason for this is found in "Time is Brain—Quantified" by Jeffrey L. Saver, MD. [6]

As noted by Dr. Saver, the title, (a takeoff of the phrase, "time is muscle") which is associated with the need for quick action in acute coronary care, has its roots in the Benjamin Franklin aphorism, "Time is Money." Using Dr. Saver's figures, the number of neurons (nerve cells) in the human forebrain is 22 billion, and during a typical large vessel stroke, 120 million nerve cells are lost each hour. Compared with the rate of nerve cell loss due to aging, the patient's brain ages the equivalent of 3.6 years each hour without treatment, or by simple extrapolation ~90 years per day. But perhaps more important, functions like vision, balance, and muscular control are lost.

* * *

GOING BACK TO James' situation, if a stroke had been his affliction and the reason for his death, probabilities point to an ischemic large vessel stroke, the case explored by Dr. Saver. But the several days of illness prior to death related to suffering a stroke would certainly have precluded a walk on the beach prior to collapse, because the remaining brain function would have been minimal. Therefore, a cerebral hemorrhage appears to be a more likely cause.

Seventy-five years later, at 3:35 p.m. on April 12, 1945, President Franklin Roosevelt succumbed to a cerebral hemorrhage in Warm Springs, Georgia. He had awakened that morning at 8:30, complaining of a headache and stiff neck. Suffering from sustained high blood pressure and weak physically, he was in a state of precarious health. Those close to him described him as slipping away. Prior to his collapse, he had endured periods of listlessness consistent with the episodic nature of the disease.[7]

James Preston could have been experiencing episodes of cerebral hemorrhage symptoms in the days before his death. On May 8, 1870, he apparently had the energy and sense of balance to walk from his house to the eastern tip of Galveston Island on his own, a distance of two to three miles. He may have been preparing to bathe in the Gulf waters when the activity associated with his walk triggered a final episode. He fell near the water's edge and the tide partially covered him, which would explain his face embedded in the sand when he was found, and giving the appearance that he had drowned. It is conceivable that the death resulted from a combination of either incapacitation and loss of consciousness due to a cerebral hemorrhage, or hemorrhagic stroke followed by asphyxiation due to drowning.

There was an inquest, and the Jury "determined" the cause of death "unknown"—a non sequitur, for certain. An autopsy could have been performed but would have to have been requested by the coroner, an elected official in 1870 Galveston. However, during that time period autopsies were not guided by well-recognized pathologists' procedures and were most often conducted in the interests of justice. In the opinions of the Chief of Police and Judge after the viewing the body, apoplexy and accident by drowning probably tipped the scales in the direction of foregoing an autopsy.

At the time of his death James was married with two small children. Research failed to locate any details of their lives. He was apparently employed for some time by E. S. Jemison, a major cotton brokerage firm, but also listed as a bookkeeper for A.J. Ward at the Headley Building on the Strand. The body was released to Calvin for burial.

Calvin continued to prosper and grow professionally after James' death. His drugstore business evidently developed beyond a two-man operation, adding a porter and clerk to the staff, according to the Galveston business directory of 1876. At that time the store was located at 180 Market Street, a few blocks from his home.

A pamphlet describing drugs available at the Preston and Robira drugstore under the title "Elegant Preparations" is presented as a "Physicians' Dose List" with "quality and strength" guaranteed. Included are about two hundred items, most of them in the form of elixirs, or tonics. Noteworthy in the list are elixirs containing strychnine, arsenic, opium, and morphine—along with tonics with ingredients of beef, blackberry root, iron, calisaya bark, eucalyptus, and hops.

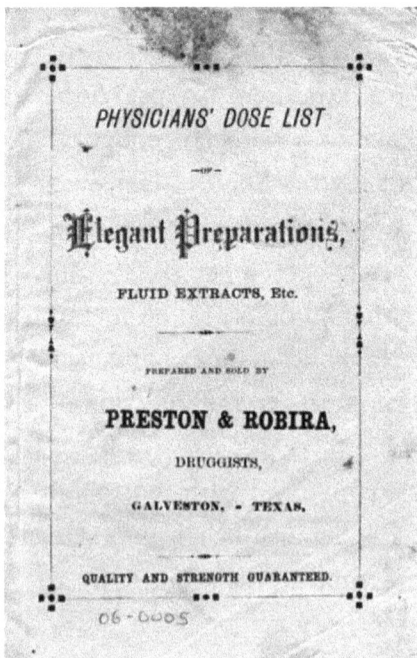

PHYSICIANS' DOSE LIST

—or—

Elegant Preparations,

FLUID EXTRACTS, Etc.

PREPARED AND SOLD BY

PRESTON & ROBIRA,

DRUGGISTS,

GALVESTON, - TEXAS.

QUALITY AND STRENGTH GUARANTEED.

06-0005

Courtesy of "1900 Storm" collection, Rosenberg Library, Galveston, Texas.

Strychnine is a deadly poison with a history of use in homicides. In sufficient doses it kills by constricting the muscles of the chest so that the victim is unable to breathe, and dies in an alert state—slowly and painfully from asphyxiation. In reduced doses it has a history of use for improving athletic performance during competition. It was reportedly used widely by cyclists in the early days of the Tour de France, and is defined as a stimulant in the World Anti-Doping Agency's current list of banned substances. During the

2016 Olympics, bronze medalist weightlifter Izzat Artykov was stripped of his medal after he was found to have strychnine, a.k.a. "rat poison," in his system. Preston and Robira list the strychnia elixir, which also contains arsenic, another poison of choice by murderers, as "5 minims Fowler's Solution, 1–64 [1/64] grain Strychnia in a teaspoon full," and describes it as an "alterative and tonic." "Alterative" is an obsolete medical term applied to a substance that tends to restore health. Presumably, the bottle containing the elixir had a very clear warning about the dangers of overdosing.

Opium had wide use in nineteenth-century medicine until its addictive property became well-known. Due to its tendency to cause constipation, it was used to treat diarrhea, malaria, and dysentery. As a sedative, it was used to tranquilize the mentally ill. It was prescribed to women for relief of menstrual pain, to people suffering from tuberculosis and pneumonia for relief of coughing, and as a pain killer. Preston and Robira's Elegant Preparations describe it as a narcotic and stimulant. Narcotics are generally used for relief of pain, stimulants for treatment of respiratory problems such as asthma. The Preston and Robira dose was described as 1 grain (65mg) in a teaspoonful. If, as one source suggests, 200 milligrams of Opium can be a lethal dose, then the dose

Courtesy of "1900 Storm" collection, Rosenberg Library, Galveston, Texas.

Courtesy of "1900 Storm" collection, Rosenberg Library, Galveston, Texas.

recommended by Preston and Robira is dangerously close to the limit

While some of their products put their clients at risk and others were essentially placebos, their approach appears to be more or less routine for a late nineteenth-century drug store—and the business prospered. A business announcement in the *Galveston Daily News* of February 8, 1880 entitled "Notice of Copartnership" provided a new name for his firm: "C. W. Preston & Co. Dealers in Drugs, proclaims Medicines and Chemicals, Providing personal attention to Physicians Prescriptions, Pharmacie Française French, German and American Proprietary Medicines. And introduces a new member of the firm, Mr. E. L. E. Castleton PH.G."

One troublesome question related to James' death, completely speculative but reasonable to entertain is: with Calvin's access to poisons such as strychnine and arsenic, his residence in close proximity to James', and the fact that, shortly after James died, Calvin married his widow—could James' death have been caused by poisoning carried out by Calvin with or without Emmeline's knowledge and consent? Certainly, Calvin had opportunity and means—the remaining issue being motive, perhaps a love triangle? There is no way to know for sure, but keeping in mind that the Prestons were a deeply religious family, an intriguing alternate explanation for the marriage comes from the scriptures, Deuteronomy 25:5—

"When brothers live together and one of them dies and has no son, the wife of the deceased shall not be married outside the family to a strange man. Her husband's brother shall go in to her and take her to himself as wife and perform the duty of a husband's brother to her."

In 1876 Calvin built a home at Eleventh and Ball Streets (Avenue H). By July of 1888 his firm had relocated to a more prosperous section of the downtown, at Market and Twenty-Second Street (a.k.a. "Preston's Corner"). In 1889 he filed for a Trademark on a headache remedy, "Preston's Hed-Ake."

An astute businessman, Calvin put some effort toward assimilation into Galveston society. Based on his service to the Union during the Civil War, some resentment would naturally be expected, particularly from those who had fought for the Confederate cause. But by the end of the war the population was weary of it, and the "occupation" of the city by Confederate soldiers had caused friction. So it is not surprising at the end of the nineteenth century that the Chief of Police was a former Yankee soldier and that circumstance certainly overshadowed Calvin's similar background and eased his development of business relationships. Beyond that, he took steps to join the right social societies, including the Free Masons, and the Texas Society—Sons of the American Revolution. He was also a member of the Texas Volunteer Guard, where he held the position of Major and Inspector General, which accounts for the use of the title "Major" in his obituaries published in newspapers in New York and Washington.

All was well as the end of the century approached; then two events would occur that brought sadness and abrupt changes to Calvin's comfortable life.

Notes

[1] James M. Schmidt, *Galveston and the Civil War: An Island City in the Maelstrom*, (Charleston History Press, 2012), 120.

[2] Ibid., 123.

[3] Ibid., 126.

[4] Roy Collins III, in conversation with the author, October 23, 2018.

[5] Izola Ethel Fedford Collins, *Island of Color, Where Juneteeth Started*, (Bloomington: Authorhouse, 2004).

[6] Jeffrey L. Saver, MD, "Time is Brain—Quantified," *Stroke—Journal of the American Heart Association*, (January 2006).

[7] Joseph Persico, *Franklin and Lucy: President Roosevelt, Lucy Rutherford and the Other Remarkable Women in His Life*, (New York: Random House, 2008).

— Chapter Nine —

Maria and the First
Transcontinental Railroad

Currier & Ives—Across the Continent (1868)
Library of Congress Prints and Photographs Division Washington, D.C.

1869 WAS AN important year in the life of Maria, the
youngest daughter of Dr. and Mrs. Preston. Maria Chapin
Preston, her middle name selected as a tribute to Margaret

Anna Platt and Maria Preston—Antwerp, New York, ca. 1870. Courtesy of the family of Laura Preston Chase.

Preston's dear friend with whom she prayed for their sons to become missionaries to China, was born in 1842. She displayed musical talent very early in life and as a child became the organist at the Presbyterian church following the untimely death of her predecessor. A church member for her entire life, at Galway she participated in the Young Ladies Prayer Meeting Society. In 1861 she graduated from the Ladies Collegiate Institute in Ballston Spa, New York. She became a music teacher and played keyboard instruments at social events and church services. Her photo, taken in Antwerp, New York with a cousin, shows a refined and attractive woman in her mid- to late-twenties.

The reasons for her move from a comfortable home with her parents in Galway to Waitsburg, Washington to live near her brothers William and Platt are not recorded. However, she had much in common with them, including an interest in music, the Presbyterian religion, and a fondness for the finer things in life (for example, beautiful, expensively and artistically furnished homes). And while the manifest destiny phrase "Go West, young man, and grow up with the country" is gender-specific, it is difficult to imagine that it did not strike a responsive chord in young women.

She must have been aware through correspondence of the financial success her brothers had achieved in the milling of flour to supply miners with a food staple—and they would have described attractive features of the region and the rapidly growing village centered by the mill. In "Wait's Mill," an excerpt from the book *All Over Oregon and Washington—Observations on the Country* by Mrs. Francis F. Victor (copyright 1872) describes the countryside and the town of Waitsburg, in particular, in glowing terms:

> A ride through the Walla Walla valley along the line of the stage road, shows us the most cultivated portions. The face of the country is undulating—covered with grass and flowers. Fat, sleek-sided cattle feed in herds on a hundred hills. The only game which we notice is ... prairie hens and curlews. The latter amuse us much with their noisy, silly ways and awkward style of running or flying.
>
> A ride of 18 miles brings us to the Touchet, a beautiful stream with a gravel bottom, wooded banks, picturesque bluffs and an open, handsome valley. And here at the crossing is the promising new town of Waitsburg ... which today has an appearance of the most enterprising and thrifty of any town except Walla Walla in the whole valley. Judging by the farm wagons, the sleek horses the well-dressed farmers' families and the brisk trade at the stores, we should say that the Touchet was the farmer's land of Canaan.
>
> Good morals and good order seem fashionable in Waitsburg—a great recommendation to a new place in a new country. There is considerable outfitting for the mines done at this place which is on the direct road to Idaho.
>
> Here, as everywhere that the bunchgrass grows, we observe the fine looks of the stock subsisting entirely on it. Beyond Waitsburg the road follows the Touchet valley for twenty miles, past a constant succession of farms,

with neat commodious dwellings and a neat commodious white-painted schoolhouse every few miles of the way.

At that time the town boasted 109 souls and thirty-five dwellings, and a church with a circuit riding pastor was being talked.[1]

The date of Maria's relocation to the adopted town of her brothers is not known precisely. According to federal census records, she lived in Galway with her parents in 1870; the 1875 census lists only Dr. and Mrs. Sarah Preston and an 1880 Waitsburg, Washington census lists her as part of the household of Platt and Laura Preston, describing her as "sister, single" with an occupation of music teacher. It is reasonable to assume that, sometime in the five-year period between 1870 and 1875, she travelled west to join them and that it happened shortly after transcontinental rail service began in 1869—which made coast-to-coast travel significantly easier, reducing the travel time from six months to two weeks, according to one source.

Prior to transcontinental train service, travel in the US from the East to the West Coast was either by: train to Nebraska followed by stagecoach across the plains and mountains; steamship to the isthmus of Panama, then travel by rail to the Pacific Ocean followed by steamship to a US West Coast port; or steamship around Cape Horn, South America.

The first option, train and stagecoach, would appear to be the quickest. Train travel to the Midwest was well established and stagecoach lines to California existed, starting about ten years before the First Transcontinental Railroad was completed. On the basis of a 2,000-mile stagecoach route and an average speed of 10 mph for eight hours per day—that part of the journey took approximately four weeks. Add to it a week from New York to the stagecoach route by train, another week by steamship from San Francisco to Wallula, Washington, and a one-day stage-coach ride to Waitsburg—the total comes to slightly more than six weeks, exclusive of time lost to make connections, so per-haps seven weeks total under the best of conditions.

Long-distance travel by stagecoach had its challenges, including rough roads, outlaws, hostile Native Americans, limited weather protection, and rustic (to say the least) nightly accommodations.

The second-most attractive option on the basis of time alone was steamship from New York to the Isthmus of Panama rail-head, rail travel to the Pacific Coast, followed by steamship to San Francisco. Total travel by sea took about six weeks, includ-ing the small amount of time to cross the Isthmus. Add a week for the voyage to Wallula and overland travel to Waitsburg, plus an allowance for connections, and the total was about the same as by railway and stagecoach. Unfortunately, travel through Panama could result in contracting an infectious disease. In fact, a central figure in development of the transcontinental rail-way, Theodore Judah, contracted yellow fever during a trip via Panama and died in New York City a week after arrival.

The last option, passage by steamship around Cape Horn, approximately seventeen thousand miles to San Francisco would have resulted in a journey of about a five-month duration, including transportation from San Francisco to Waitsburg.

All of the options for travel from Galway to Waitsburg prior to 1869 had limitations, and none would appear to be suitable for an unescorted woman. The First Transcontinental Railroad changed that overnight, offering coast-to-coast travel in approx-imately one week or less with excellent sleeping accommoda-tions in Pullman cars, a dining car, limited need to change trains, and a fare of approximately $150 that was probably within Maria's reach. Maria would have taken the stagecoach from Galway to Albany; boarded a New York Central train to Buffalo; changed to the Lake Shore and Southern Michigan train for Chicago; thence on the Chicago, Rock Island, and Pacific to Council Bluffs; and by ferry or bridge (depending on the date of her travel—the bridge not completed until 1872), to Omaha, where she would board the Union Pacific Train to Promontory Point, Utah. There she changed to the Central Pacific train for Sacramento, and via the Western Pacific and San Francisco & Alameda railways, traveled directly to San Francisco. In San Francisco she boarded a steamship to the Columbia River mouth at Astoria, and traveled up the river to Wallula, Washington. She completed her journey by stagecoach to Waitsburg. A lingering question is: Did she make this journey unescorted? Perhaps one of her brothers traveled to Galway to help her with her personal effects, ensure her safety, and assist her in making the necessary travel connections.

Coincidentally, in 1870, the Preston brothers acquired sole interest in the Waitsburg Mill and, responding to demand, installed four additional millstones. Clearly, they were doing well and could have easily afforded to provide Maria funds for first-class accommodations on the transcontinental railway.

Maria would travel back to the Galway area at least once in her lifetime to visit her sister Sophia, as reported in a Saratoga newspaper society column of 1907, and undoubtedly it was easier and more direct, because the Northern Pacific railway passed close to Waitsburg, connecting with Chicago, and the Oregon Short Line branched off from that to the south, connecting with the Union Pacific railway in Wyoming.

The first mention found of Maria in Waitsburg is related to the Methodist church, erected in 1871. In the 1925 recollections of Waitsburg resident E. Chester Davies is found the following:

Those were the days when there was only one church in the "burg": Methodist ... when there was only one church instrument, the Estey Harmonium, owned by Miss Maria Preston. And many's the time we have toted that instrument from her residence and back after lifting up our voices [in] praise. Harmony or discord made no difference we done the best 'we uns' could.[2]

Surprisingly, given the time that must have been required to develop and run a successful business, her brothers were accomplished musicians; the same source mentions a quintet composed of "Miss Preston, pianist; Platt Preston, violinist; Bill Preston, cellist....[3]

The Waitsburg Presbyterian Church, organized in 1878, included Maria Preston as an original member. In 1885 she married Alexander Stewart, a wealthy Waitsburg businessman. They had a good life together until Maria's illness led to an unfortunate turn of events.

Notes

[1] Elvira Ellen Laidlaw, *Wait's Mill, The Story of the Community of Waitsburg, Washington*, (Chicago: Ellis and Adams Press, 1970), 84.

[2] Vance Orchard, compiled by, *Waitsburg: "One of a Kind"*, (Waitsburg Historical Society, 1976), 56.

[3] Ibid., 57.

— Chapter Ten —

Calvin and the 1900 Galveston Hurricane

Painting: "Tremont Street, Galveston During the Hurricane of September 8, 1990,"
Courtesy of "1900 Storm" collection, Rosenberg Library, Galveston, Texas.

he year 1900 was one of major changes in Calvin Preston's
life and circumstances. It started with the death of his
brother, Platt, while visiting with his daughter in March,
and culminated with the Galveston Hurricane in September, the
effects of which caused him to move with his family from the
city that had been his home for thirty-five years.

Information on Platt's medical problem is not readily available; it is known that he took
a trip with his daughter, Laura
Maria, to "Mexico" (more probably New Mexico), quite possibly seeking relief from tuberculosis, and then stopped at
Calvin's home in Galveston on
the return to Waitsburg. There,
after a month-long stay, he
died.[1] His body was shipped to
Waitsburg, where a funeral was
held under the auspices of the
Grand Lodge of the Masons of
the state of Washington.[2]

Laura Maria Preston at the time of her
engagement, 1906. Courtesy of the family of
Laura Preston Chase.

Born in Galway on November
1, 1837, Platt was destined, judging from the historical record, to
live in the shadow of his older brother William. While there is no
doubt that they shared the same passions and drive, references
to Platt in historical documents are less frequent and detailed.
And the fact that he succumbed to an unknown chronic illness
in 1900 at the age of sixty-three may have diminished the impact
that he had on his adopted hometown of Waitsburg, Washington.

In brief summary, he joined his brother William in the
operation of a ferry and shipping steamboat enterprise on the
Missouri river in 1855; followed him to the Denver, Colorado
area during the Gold Rush; then travelled with him to the Elk
River, Idaho and worked in mining and merchandising. In 1866
the brothers relocated to Waitsburg, Washington, where they

became partners in the flour mill developed by Sylvester Wait, becoming sole owners and operators of that enterprise in 1870. He and his brother made significant investments in farmland to provide wheat for the mill.

But Platt also had meaningful achievements on his own. For example, he served in the Washington State Senate from 1889 to 1893 (1889–91) for District Eight, 1891–93 for District Ten, and as mayor of Waitsburg for several years. As a commissioner of the State Penitentiary in Walla Walla he contributed to the construction and initial operation of a jute mill, the principal stated purpose of which was to provide prisoners with an opportunity for exercise and a meaningful occupation. Described in *An Illustrated History of Southeastern Washington*[3] as one of the most completely equipped factories for grain bags and jute fabrics in the country, when operating at full capacity it employed over 245 men. The output of the mill averaged 140,000 grain bags per month while at the same time producing hop cloth, mattings, special bags, and twine. For the period of two years ending in September 1900 the profit exceeded $10,000. While the Preston's mill obviously benefited from the operation, southeastern Washington had numerous other grain mills which presumably took advantage of local supply of bags.

Platt married Laura Jane Billups of Waitsburg on November 12, 1869 and had seven children, only three of whom survived beyond the death of their parents. Laura passed away on June 13, 1896. Their daughter, Laura Maria, was only thirteen years of age when she accompanied Platt to Mexico seeking a cure for his illness. Platt's obituary in the March 13, 1900 issue of the *Galveston Daily News* states that Calvin accompanied Laura Maria in transporting Platt's remains to Waitsburg for burial. One supposes that during this visit Calvin reconnected with William, and that the renewed relationship would be of comfort to him following the events that would unfold later in the year.

Platt's obituary in the *Columbia Chronicle* closes with the following prayerful tribute:

Laura Jane Billups Preston, ca. 1880. Courtesy of the family of Laura Preston Chase.

> Platt A. Preston, the pioneer, one of the builders of an empire ... surrounded by the budding trees he loved so well ... we leave you to your last long sleep. Soft and safe to you be this earthly bed. Bright and glorious be thy rising from it. Fragrant be this sprig that here shall flourish. May the earliest buds of spring unfold their beauties over this your resting place. And may the sweetness of summer's last rose linger longest.

Turning to the daunting challenge that Calvin would face later in the year, his obituary in the *Amsterdam* [New York] *Evening Recorder* dated July 1, 1905, likely written by sister Sophia (his only remaining close relative in the area), reads in part:

> Soon after the close of the war, Major Preston went to Galveston, Texas, and was a resident of that city for thirty-five years, being most of the time in the drug business. ... He was elected city assessor, and held that office at the time of the flood in Galveston.
>
> Major Preston's experience at that time was most thrilling. In the afternoon of the day of the great storm, he learned at his office that the water was sweeping the city

from the gulf. Immediately starting for home, he found on his arrival that his house was surrounded by water, the depth of several feet. Securing the help of two men who had a boat, he floated on this to the house, rescued his wife and daughters, who were then obliged to stand on the dining room table, and walking in water to his shoulders, he pushed the boat containing his family ahead of him until he reached a place of safety.

The "Great Storm" was the Galveston hurricane of 1900 which flooded the entire city, destroying much of it and resulting in eight thousand deaths—six thousand in the city itself. After all this time it remains the greatest natural disaster to occur in the US, while ominously appearing to be a microcosm of the present climate change debate and potential impact. The hurricane has been the subject of popular books based on survivor accounts, newspaper articles, National Weather Service records, and photographs of the devastation. The 1900 Storm exhibit of the Rosenberg Library is an excellent source of information on all aspects of the hurricane. Familiar topics include prior failure to build a seawall that might have greatly reduced the carnage and loss of life; US Weather Service station chief Isaac Cline's characterization of hurricane damage fears as "absurd delusions" (he was to suffer great personal loss from the storm); disagreement between Cuban meteorologists and the US Weather Service on the hurricane track (unfortunately, the Cubans were right); US Weather Service internal politics that downplayed storm severity until it was too late; the harbinger of doom represented by the internal collapse of Ritter's Saloon during lunch hour; the death of ninety of the ninety-three occupants of St. Mary's orphanage; the violence of the storm as reflected by accounts of survivors, many of whom elected to shelter in place rather than seeking a large public building for refuge, combined with miraculous stories of survival after having spent terrifying hours clinging to floating wreckage at the height of the storm; wind-driven missiles, including roofing slate and shards of glass that severed limbs and caused decapitations; the immediate aftermath, which included the daunting and heartbreaking task of disposing of corpses; and, finally, the construction of a seventeen-foot-high seawall (which would have greatly mitigated the destruction caused by the hurricane) and the elevation of the remaining buildings to match the seawall height.

Missing in these popular accounts is a detailed description of the hurricane's characteristics in terms of size, speed, wind velocity, storm surge, barometric pressure, and rainfall. Without this information it is difficult to understand the scale and ferocity of the monster that tore Galveston apart or to envision the challenges that Calvin Preston overcame in the rescue of his family.

Approximately 200 miles in diameter, moving at 11 miles per hour, the hurricane reached Galveston during the late morning of September 8, 1900—the eastern boundary of the eyewall passing just east of the city in the evening. Preceded by a storm tide, it was initially perceived as another flooding event citizens tolerated as status quo on the island. The first sign of a problem was an unusually high tide in opposition to the predominate direction of the wind.

Shown below are profiles of wind speed, barometric pressure, wind direction, and storm surge water depth—with the timing the Ritter's Saloon collapse, Calvin's rescue mission, and the lull in the storm superimposed.

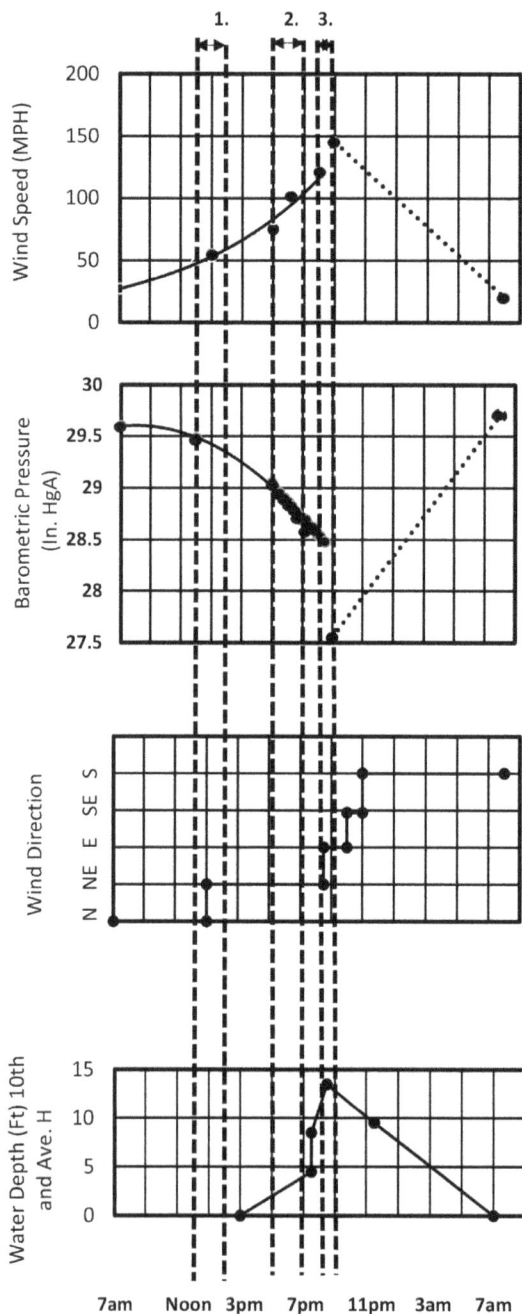

Estimated Time
Intervals – Hurricane
Events:

1. Ritter's Café
   Collapse 12-2pm
2. Calvin's Rescue
   Mission 5-7pm
3. Storm Lull 8-9pm

Data to reconstruct the characteristics of the hurricane come from a report written by Dr. Isaac M. Cline, Director of the US Weather Bureau at Galveston during the event.[4] While not as complete as one would like, there is sufficient information to provide estimated profiles of wind speed, barometric pressure, wind direction and storm surge depth as function of time.

Wind Speed

Four points are given, some cryptically, for the time period from 1:00 p.m. on September 8, 1900 to 8:00 a.m. September 9:

1. "A storm velocity was not attained until 1:00 p.m." Here "storm velocity" is taken to mean a velocity consistent with Level 10 on the Beaufort Scale equal to 55 mph.

2. "The wind speed increased steadily and reached a hurricane velocity about 5:00 p.m." A Category 1 hurricane has a minimum sustained wind speed of 74 mph by the Saffir-Simpson Scale—or alternately, greater than 73 mph corresponding to Level 12 on the Beaufort Scale.

3. "The greatest velocity for five minutes was 84 mph at 6:15 p.m. With two minutes at the rate of 100 mph.

4. "It is estimated that prior to 8:00 p.m. the wind attained a velocity of at least 120 mph.

5. "At 8:00 a.m. on the morning of the 9th was blowing at the rate of 20 mph from the South.

Also useful is the information that: a) "For a short time, about 8:00 p.m., just before the wind shifted to the east, there was a distinct lull, but when it came out from the east and southeast it appeared to come with greater fury than before; and b) other sources give the maximum wind speed achieved as between 130–145 mph, which is consistent with statistical correlations of minimum barometric pressure with wind speed given in[5] assuming a minimum pressure range of 890–940 millibars, or 26.7–27.8

inches of mercury. Lowest pressures quoted for the Galveston hurricane are 27.5–27.6 inches of mercury or 931 – 935 millibars, in that range.

Combining the above data and information in graphic form with reasonable trend lines results in the plot of wind speed versus time provided above.

Barometric Pressure

Barometric pressure and wind speed are linked by the conservation of energy principle formally expressed in Bernoulli's equation, named after Daniel Bernoulli, a member of a family of brilliant eighteenth-century Italian mathematicians. Bernoulli's equation states that, for a fluid in motion, pressure and speed have an inverse relationship—in other words, as speed increases, pressure decreases.

Barometric pressure is relatively easy to measure with a simple instrument, and the measurements can be made in the shelter of an enclosure, in contrast to wind speed, where a portion of the instrumentation system is directly exposed to the elements. Pressure measurements were made by Galveston station personnel during the hurricane, before and after the anemometer used to measure wind speed was ripped from the rooftop of the weather station—and while limited in time span, when combined with other data gathered by NOAA, a graph of pressure versus time can be constructed with reasonable confidence.

The emotional impact of falling pressure on the layman may be limited, as it certainly does not have the visual or sound effects of wind speed, but it does reflect the worsening conditions as the hurricane moved through the Galveston area and serves as a means of judging the accuracy of wind speed estimates.

From 1971 to 2008, hurricanes were characterized in terms of wind speed, barometric pressure, storm surge, and resulting flooding using the Saffir-Simpson Scale. An adjustment was made in 2009 to eliminate all but wind based on an anomaly related to storm surge. Since then the rating of a hurricane has been on the basis of wind speed alone, in brief summary shown below (source: National Hurricane Center):

Category	Sustained Wind Speed Range (mph)	Potential Property Damage (due to wind, not storm surge)
1	74–95	No real damage to building structures
2	96–110	Some roofing material, door and window damage
3	111–129	Structural damage to small residences
4	130–156	Complete roof structure failures on small residences
5	>157 or greater	Complete roof structure failures on industrial buildings

Interestingly, it is reported[6] that around 6:30 p.m. with the wind speed exceeding 100 mph "the roofs the roofs of houses and timbers were flying through the city as though they were paper and it appeared suicidal to attempt a journey through flying timbers" (to reach the safety of a substantial building in the center of the city), which seems to be in agreement with "Potential Property Damage" of "some roofing material" and " Structural damage to small residences" on the Saffir-Simpson Scale. And perhaps some of the debris resulted from storm surge damage that subsequently became airborne.

Beyond the challenge faced by Calvin Preston in his attempt to rescue his family there is an interesting aspect of wind speed versus time related to a harbinger of the disaster to unfold.

The collapse of the second floor of Ritter's Saloon and Café onto diners below during the initial period of the hurricane is legendary. Located in the business district, it was a popular place for businessmen to have lunch. On the day of the hurricane, as the city streets began to flood and the wind increased in strength, a group of business leaders met there during the lunch hour in apparent denial of the threat. While the exact time of the tragic event is not readily available, at some point during the period from, say, noon to 2:00 p.m., the second floor of the building (used as a print shop and containing heavy machinery) collapsed onto the first floor dining area, killing at least two individuals instantly and causing mortal injuries to several others—thereby drawing attention in a dramatic way to the rapidly worsening conditions. This signal that the storm was no ordinary event undoubtedly saved lives as people started to seek refuge in substantial buildings, rather than sheltering in place or simply ignoring the storm altogether.

In retrospect, an interesting thing about the Ritter's internal collapse is that during the "lunch hour" the sustained wind velocity was in the range 45–60 mph, not likely (with reference to the Saffir-Simpson Scale related damage estimates) to cause such destruction. To be more specific, according to various sources, a Category 1 hurricane, with sustained winds in the 74–95 mph range, causes minimal *structural* damage, damage being limited to removal of roof shingles and appendages such as gutters and shutters. Since the force exerted by wind is proportional to the speed squared, sustained wind in the 45–60 mph range has 40 to 66 percent of the force corresponding to the Category 1 wind speed lower threshold—which, again, is incapable of substantial damage.

By one popular account[7]

> "a powerful gust of wind tore off the building's roof. The 'blast effect' caused by the wind's sudden entry into the closed space of the second floor apparently bowed the walls to the point where the beams supporting the ceiling of Ritter's slipped from their moorings" and the ceiling collapsed into the dining room.... [with the] brutally heavy printing presses.

A second popular account[8] attributes the collapse to wind entering through open second floor windows, causing the walls to flex and joists to lose their purchase.

The first theory, attributing the failure to a powerful wind gust is initially attractive, because wind gusts are common during such events, and depending on the time-averaging basis for sustained wind and gust measurements, the probable maximum gust speed can be (with reference to the Durst correlation) a maximum of 1.6 times the sustained wind speed. However, conventional wisdom based on Saffir-Simpson Scale correlation with structure damage would be in conflict with this failure explanation, because while the subject scale is based on sustained wind speed, the correlated structural damage implicitly includes the effects of gusts, which are a feature of winds associated with storms.

Regarding the second theory, with all due respect to its author, the notion that the windows on the second floor were open is difficult to comprehend as it was windy and raining at the time, thereby exposing the working area of a print shop to the elements (think in terms of flying papers and running ink!), as well as water penetrating the ceiling and falling on the diners below. The possibility that wind-borne debris broke some windows is conceivable at the time of the collapse, but then the question is: how many—one, several, all? In addition, the effect of wind entering the second-floor space at a speed well below Category 1 and flexing the walls sufficiently to dislocate the joists, does not seem to be a particularly convincing argument.

For sure, at some point in time during the passage of the Category 4 hurricane, the café (which was exposed to perhaps an hour of sustained wind at 145 mph with gusts up to or exceeding 180 mph) with windows and roof missing looked like a bomb had exploded inside. But this is probably not the condition of the structure when the diners lost their lives.

"Ritter's Restaurant—Where Several Prominent Men Were Killed." Courtesy of "1900 Storm" collection, Rosenberg Library, Galveston, Texas.

So, what caused the collapse? A reasonable question to ask is: were the printing presses operating that day, and if so was failure simply a result of vibration of the machinery? But without an engineering failure analysis, and more information to support it including evaluation of the failed structure components, it is not possible to say. It may have been that the dead weight of the heavy printing equipment, possibly far in excess of a safe floor-load, was the predominant factor, requiring only a small amount of wind-related vibration from a storm of much lesser intensity than a Category 1 hurricane to bring it down. In other words, no powerful wind gusts required here— it was ready to go with just a little help. Or, with reference to the Goodman Diagram (a recognized basis for structural failure analysis) the joist stress imposed by the dead weight of the printing machinery may have been so great that it was only a matter of time before vibration of the printing equipment, possibly operating that day, weakened the floor sufficiently to cause failure. An accident waiting to happen, hurricane or not, so to speak. And while it tragically caused the deaths of some of the diners below, the overall impact of convincing citizens that a storm of major intensity was on the way may have saved many more lives.

Returning to the challenges faced by Calvin Preston according to the account in his obituary, in the afternoon when he arrived at his house the water depth was "several feet". He borrowed a boat, and "walking in water to his shoulders, he pushed the boat containing his family ahead of him until he reached a place of safety." Data available on the water depth as a function of time is shown in the graph at the beginning of this section.

The data tends to contradict the statement that in the afternoon, upon hearing of flooding, he immediately started for home. To put this in perspective, Calvin was about five feet six inches tall, so walking in water up to his shoulders, say four feet or more in depth, would mean that the rescue was well underway at 6:00 p.m., and certainly over by 7:30 as the sudden increase in storm surge at that point increased the water depth to nine feet. In all probability he stayed at his shop until closing, working feverishly to move his goods on the first floor above the expected high-water mark. According to[9] that was three feet above the floor—a failed effort for certain as water eventually reached the second floor. This was the first of two instances that day in which a proactive effort on Calvin's part led to an unexpected outcome.

Leaving the shop at Market and Twenty-Second Streets around 5:00 p.m., his probable route was south four blocks on Twenty-Second Street to Ball Street, thence east on Ball Street eleven blocks to his home at the corner of Ball Street and Eleventh Streets, a distance of 1.3 miles wading in water two-to-three-feet deep with wind-driven steady rain (not to mention debris) at sustained speeds of 80–100 mph. Under those conditions his rate of travel was slow, perhaps 1–2 mph—with progress toward his destination made by clinging to fences and lampposts and resting momentarily on the lee side of buildings to catch his breath. True, on the longest and most difficult leg of the journey he was headed directly east, while the wind direction was predominantly from the northeast, affording him some protection, but he was fifty-five years old, so the effort must have been close to his capability and fraught with danger. In the process he managed to borrow a rowboat from two men whose role in the actual rescue is not clear. The report suggests he transported his wife and four daughters to the place of sanctuary pushing the boat by himself.

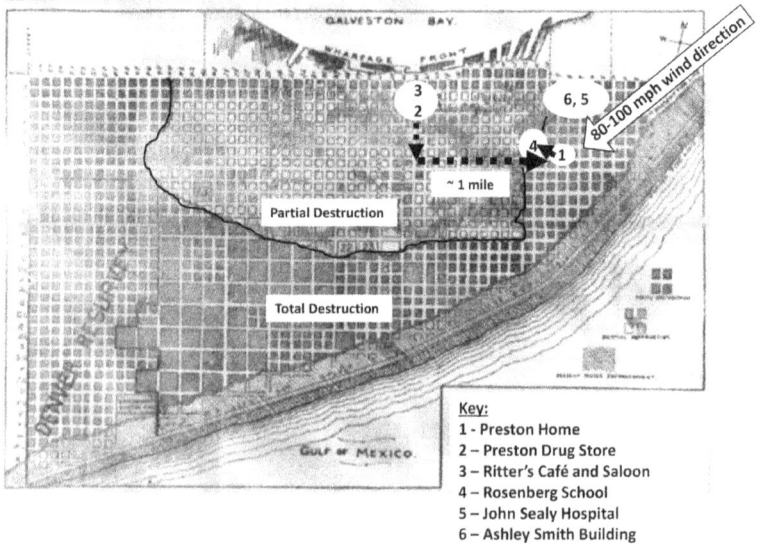

Key:
1 - Preston Home
2 – Preston Drug Store
3 – Ritter's Café and Saloon
4 – Rosenberg School
5 – John Sealy Hospital
6 – Ashley Smith Building

"Calvin's Rescue Mission" Map 456B—"Galveston Storm—Saturday, September 8, 1900." Courtesy of the "1900 Storm" collection, Rosenberg Library, Galveston, Texas.

With his family of five in the boat, having a probable capacity of six hundred pounds and therefore overloaded, he had to
push it to a sturdy public building nearby. His choices were medical buildings, the John Sealy Hospital, and the Ashbel Smith
Building (a.k.a. Big Red)—six
blocks north of his house, or
the Rosenberg School—one
block to the northwest.

The medical buildings were
undoubtedly used for shelter
during the hurricane. Both are
substantial, four-story structures constructed of stone, but
they both suffered significant
damage. A survivor story from
John Sealy Hospital provides a
vivid portrayal of the terror felt
as the storm came ashore:

John Sealy Hospital. Courtesy of the "1900
Storm" collection, Rosenberg Library,
Galveston, Texas.

"a.m. It does not require a great stretch of the imagination
to imagine this structure a shaky old boat out at sea, the
whole thing rocking like a reef, surrounded by water said
water growing closer ever closer.

Have my hands full quieting nervous hysterical women.
12-Noon. Things beginning to look serious water is to the
first floor in the house all over the basement of the hospital, cornices, roof window lights shutters blinds flying in
all directions.

Noon. The scenes about here are distressing, everything
washed away, poor people trying vainly to save their bedding & clothing, methinks the poor nurses will be trying

to save their beds in short order. Now flames in the distance. It is a grand, fine sight our beautiful bay a raging torrent. 3pm. Am beginning to feel a weakening (sic) desire for something to cling to should feel more comfortable in the embrace of your arms. You hold yourself in readiness to come to us should occasion demand. Darkness is overwhelming us, to add to the horror. Dearest—I reach out my hand to you, my heart—my soul." (Saturday, Sept 8, 1900 at Sealy Hospital.)[10]

The Rosenberg School was built by Henry Rosenberg, Galveston business leader and philanthropist, to provide the best

Rosenberg School cornerstone, 2019.
Photo by John Huoni.

possible opportunity for education of the white children of the city, on land described as the east side of lot 311 on Eleventh Street, between Winnie and Ball streets. Lot 250, containing Calvin Preston's home, is on the opposite side of Ball Street, one block east. The school, demolished in 1966, was an imposing three-story brick stucco structure 206 by 90 feet, built at a cost of $75,000. The cornerstone was laid with a Masonic ceremony in June 1888, and construction was completed in February 1889.

Ruins of the Rosenberg School.
Photo courtesy of "1900 Storm"
Collection, Rosenberg Library,
Galveston Texas.

The Rosenberg School was Calvin's most likely destination, because it was in the general direction of the wind, which required less effort to move the boat, made visibility better, and, most importantly, the distance was much less. In addition, Calvin was a prominent member of the Masonic Temple, his name engraved on the cornerstone, so he would have felt comfortable seeking shelter there.

While the School was a robust-looking structure, survivor accounts indicate that, like the John Sealy hospital, it was nowhere near a comfortable place to stay that night. Reportedly, the refugees spent most of the night seeking to keep doors shut from the force of the wind and water, some choosing to stay in east-west-oriented corridors because they were more sheltered from the wind. At one point a chimney collapsed into the interior, instantly killing a group of people huddled on the floor below. In an interview with Annie McCullough, one of the many individuals who found shelter at the School, tape recorded in 1972 when she was ninety-five years old, the raw emotion associated with her recollection of the strength of the storm and the pandemonium inside the school is notable:

Mrs. McCullough, age twenty-three, and her husband lived at Eighth and K streets, several blocks from the Rosenberg School, which was at 11th and Ball. As the severity of the storm increased, her Uncle Ed, who owned a dray pulled by a mule, loaded a mother and her children (neighbors) in it for transportation to the school. Annie decided to walk on her own. When she got to the corner of Ninth and Broadway the wind was strong and waves were coming, so out of fear for her safety she momentarily stopped and was carried across by a passerby.

> When we got to the school, water was comin' in so fast , the wagon was floatin' and the mules were swimmin'. Dray was in the water. We got on the dray, the wagon. The men lay flat on their stomach on each one holding the little children.

When we got to 10th and I [saw] water wasn't quite as deep as on Broadway [Avenue]] When we [hit] Rosenberg School, water hadn't come on there but the wind! Oooh. Those men that was in the school, all they could do was stand up against those doors, try to hold them closed, keep them from blowin' open.

My husband's people were over there, came in from 8th and H. They were so glad to see him come in. Upstairs, people was hollerin' and cryin', hunting their folk, couldn't find them. Oh, it was an awful thing! You want me to tell you. But no tongue can tell it!We didn't go upstairs. We sit in the hall going east and west, sit in the

"Part of the wreck of the Rosenberg School—8 Killed in One Spot." Courtesy of the "1900 Storm" collection, Rosenberg Library, Galveston, Texas.

"Looking southwest toward the beach from Twelfth and I, September 1900."
"The Great Storm" collection.
Courtesy of the Texas State Library and Archives Commission.

hall. It was crowded. No—first [we sat] in the hall going north and south. They was screamin' and hollerin'. It was so crowded. Men trying to hold the doors. My husband says come sit in the hall going east and west. We got up there. When we left that place where we had just come from, we had just got from under it [and] the lightning streak come, knocked the flue in. It killed 15 people from where we moved![II]

The next morning the storm was gone, the sky was blue, and there was a breeze of 20 mph blowing from the south. From a vantage point on the second floor of the school, Calvin could look toward the Gulf and see very few houses standing, but one of them was his. Ironically, his house somehow withstood the wind and storm surge, was eventually restored, and is now listed as a 1900 Hurricane Survivor.

Over three thousand homes were totally destroyed, having an estimated value at the time of $5.5 million, along with damage to buildings, personal and other property in Galveston County of $30 million, for a total of $35.5 million, or the current equivalent of $1 billion—a negligible amount relative to recent losses related to hurricane damage along the southern coast of the US. But, of course the loss of life exceeds by a huge factor that attributed to recent hurricanes, the difference

Calvin Preston Residence—1900 Storm Survivor, 2009.
Photo by Elizabeth Rogers Alvarado.

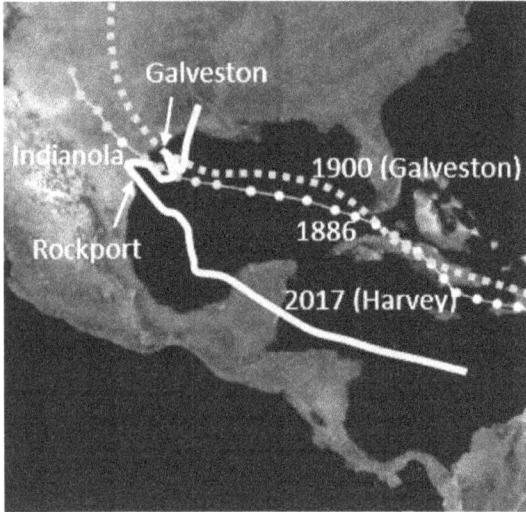

Tracks of Harvey, Indianola and 1900 Galveston Hurricanes. Image courtesy of Wikimedia Commons. https://commons.wikipedia.org/wiki/User:Nilafanion

reflecting advance notice of storm track and mandatory evacuations.

In this regard, it is interesting to compare and contrast the characteristics and effects of the 1900 Galveston hurricane with those of hurricane Harvey, which came ashore along the Texas coast on August 25, 2017. Both were Category 4 hurricanes at landfall, approximately two hundred miles in diameter and travelled along similar, parallel paths from the Caribbean, as shown in the adjacent figure. The minimum barometric pressure recorded for Harvey was 937 mb, while Galveston's is given as 931 mb with the expectation that the sustained maximum wind velocity for the latter would have been slightly higher; a maximum sustained velocity of Harvey's 132 mph makes the frequently quoted figure for Galveston's of 145 mph seem a bit high.

Major differences for the two events include storm surge, total rainfall, duration of time at the landfall location, destruction of property, and loss of life.

Storm surge and storm tide are distinct; storm surge is the total amount of water elevation due to the storm. Storm tide is the combined height of the tide and the surge at the time of the storm. For hurricane Harvey the maximum values are 6.7 and 12.5, respectively. Insufficient information exists to provide storm surge height for the Galveston hurricane. The storm tide maximum value was approximately fifteen feet.

Total rainfall for the Galveston hurricane is quoted by one source as nine inches, whereas the maximum total for hurricane Harvey is sixty inches in one location, with many reporting as much as forty. While the property damage and loss of life at Galveston was mainly related to storm surge, in Harvey's case the cause was catastrophic inland fresh water flooding. The huge amount of rainfall is attributed to stalling of the tropical storm that Harvey evolved, spending five days along the Texas coast before heading northward.

Loss of life during hurricane Harvey, while tragic, was very small compared with Galveston. A total of less than seventy individuals died as a result of the event, due again to rainfall-related flooding. In Galveston's case the lives lost numbered six thousand in the immediate area and as much as eight thousand, total—most due to storm surge and the failure to evacuate in anticipation of it.

Estimated Hurricane Deaths

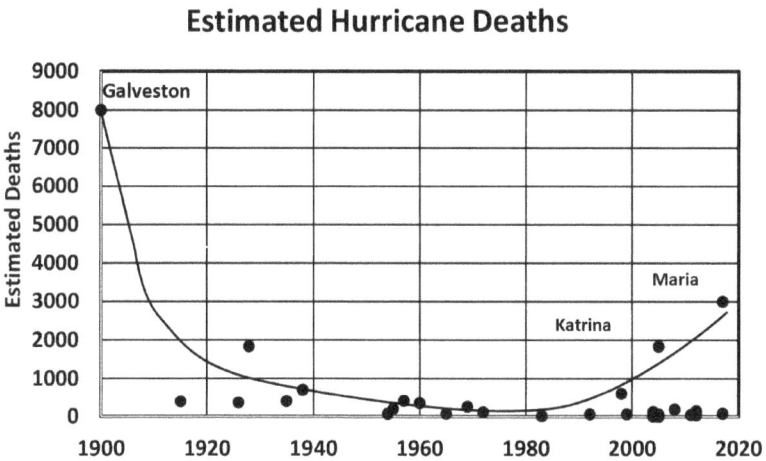

The property damage story is the reverse of the loss of lives comparison; the number of homes and businesses damaged or totally destroyed in the region due to hurricane Harvey totals two-hundred thousand, whereas the only readily available figure for Galveston is 3,636 homes totally destroyed. Be that as it may, the property damage estimate for Harvey stands at $125 billion, compared to an estimated $1 billion on a current value of the dollar basis for Galveston.

In general, the trend for property damage due to hurricanes making landfall in the United States has been sharply upward since about year 2000. This is primarily due to the growth in population of coastal communities. The worst may be yet to come as sea level and water temperature rise, the latter related to increased hurricane intensity due to the effects of climate change.

Estimated Hurricane Property Damages

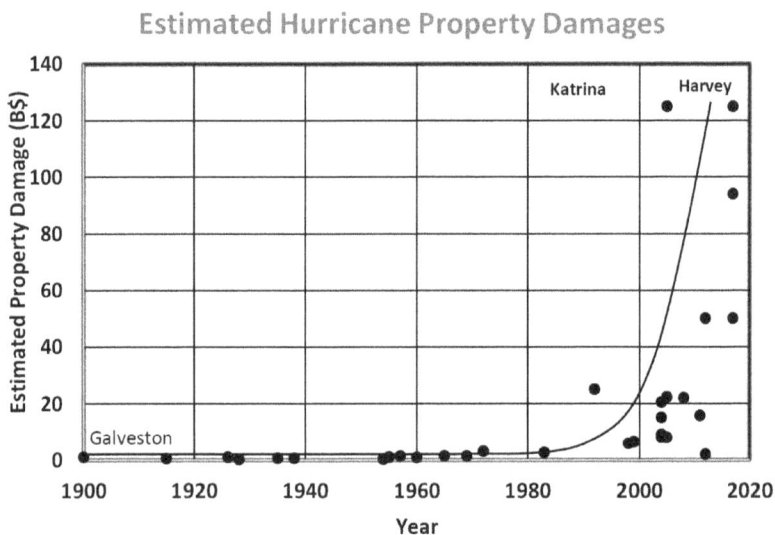

The general trend for deaths due to hurricanes in the US is downward until approximately year 2000, followed by higher death tolls, particularly related to hurricanes Katrina and Maria. In these instances, there was a higher death-rate among the most vulnerable of the population: the sick, elderly, and those of lower income—involving failure to evacuate and interrupted continuation of medical treatment. Hopefully, steps are being taken by private entities and all branches of government to reverse this trend.

Calvin stayed in Galveston through the initial phase of cleanup and played a role in gaining relief funds as a member of the Masonic Temple. But the hurricane left him in a precarious position financially, and the effort required to recover was undoubtedly daunting. And he was forced to relive the carnage of his Gettysburg experience.

His brother William, knowing of his plight, invited him to move to Washington State, offering him a job as a bookkeeper for the Preston grocery company in Walla Walla. In 1901 he resigned from his position as Galveston City tax assessor and with his family moved first to Walla Walla and then to Waitsburg, where he was elected mayor. The concern and care that William demonstrated toward Calvin would be evident later in actions he took to protect Maria.

Notes

[1] "Hon. P. A. Preston Dead. A Pioneer of Washington Died at the Home of His Brother," *Galveston Daily News*, March 13, 1900.

[2] "Honor Brother's Memory. Large Number of Masons Attend Funeral of Platt Preston," *Columbia Chronicle*, March 20, 1900.

[3] *An Illustrated History of Southeastern Washington, Including Walla Walla, Columbia, Garfield and Acotin Counties*, (Western Historical Publishing Co., 1906), 136.

[4] Isaac Cline, "Special Report on the Galveston Hurricane of September 8, 1900," U.S. Department of Agriculture, Weather Bureau Office of Chief Clerk, Washington, D.C., October 5, 1900 Circular., Local Forecast Official and Section Director, Paragraphs 6, 7, 11.

[5] R.D. Wooten, "Statistical Analysis of the Relationship between Wind Speed, Pressure and Temperature," *Journal of Applied Sciences* 11 no. 15 (2011): Figure 2a–b

[6] Cline, "Special Report on the Galveston Hurricane," Paragraph 10.

[7] Erik Larson, *Isaac's Storm*, (Crown Publishers, 1999), 159.

[8] Al Roker, *Storm of the Century*, (New York: HarperCollins 2015).

[9] Cline, "Special Report on the Galveston Hurricane," Paragraph 9.

[10] Anonymous Letter Written at John Sealy Hospital, Courtesy of the 1900 Storm Collection, Rosenberg Library, Galveston, Texas.

[11] Izola Ethel Fedford Collins, *Island of Color, Where Juneteenth Started*, (Bloomington: Authorhouse, 2004,) 280–1.

Chapter Eleven

Maria, Sophia:
Old Age, Dementia,
and the Power of Love

Mr. and Mrs. Alexander Stewart, with House Maid. Stewart House, Waitsburg, Washington. Ca. 1910. Courtesy of the family of Laura Preston Chase.

N CONTRAST TO Calvin's life, or for that matter all of her brothers' lives, Sophia's was ordinary, and there is a sense that she devoted herself to the wellbeing of her father. Born in Galway in 1835, she lived a quiet life relative to her siblings. Maria traveled home at least once to visit her sister, Sophia

Preston Hays, as reported in a column in the *Amsterdam Evening Recorder* on July 22, 1907.

Sophia married John H. Hays of Galway in 1862. They lived for a time in Galway village on East Street, several houses away from Dr. Preston, at a home once occupied by Joseph Henry, a prominent scientist and the first Secretary of the Smithsonian Institute. Five years before his death in 1885, Dr. Preston transferred title of his home and a fifty-acre parcel east of the village to Sophia. Two years after Sarah Anderson Preston died in 1893, Sophia sold the properties to Eugene Brundige. At that time Sophia and family lived in Saratoga Springs. A number of society-page articles mention Sophia as an organizer or participant in events in Saratoga. She and her husband had three children. In perhaps the final instance of a Preston family member leaving the Galway area to live in Waitsburg, Washington, Sophia's daughter Margaret visited her relatives there and subsequently married a wealthy lumber distributor, Arthur McCoy, in 1909.

A society page of a Saratoga newspaper mentions a visit from Sophia's sister, Mrs. Alexander Stewart, in 1907. This brief article does not provide details, and most probably the reason for Maria's visit was a private matter not likely to be shared outside the family.

In 1885 Maria had married Alexander Stewart, a wealthy Waitsburg businessman. They lived very comfortably, as described in a newspaper article dated August 20, 1909:

Alexander Stewart's new mansion has been under construction for the past two years. Cost is approximately $15,000. Without furnishings. Building is of cement structure 21/2 stories high with a large veranda and full basement.

Floors are of parquetry mahogany, white maple and oak. The walls are of hard plaster and the remainder of the interior woodwork is of Douglas fir, stained a deep mahogany. There are 14 rooms including eight bedrooms (chambers). One staircase, a grand affair, winds from the reception hall upwards and is designed for servant's use. The spindles are common fir. A beaded moulding is used above the baseboards. The windows are all of French beveled glass and enormously heavy.

The doors are beveled plate mirrors and besides the doors there are 30 other mirrors so that whichever way a visitor turns he will observe himself.

Over the inlaid floors are spread Persian rugs, covering all the elaborate work. The electrical fixtures are very elaborate and steam heating plant are all the latest patterns.

Celebration of the 25th wedding anniversary of Mr. and Mrs. Alexander Stewart observed with their new house opening held on January 8, 1910.[1]

They evidently also spared no expense related to transportation, the same source reported:

April 28, 1910... First limousine or closed body car ever seen in Walla Walla county was the auto of Alexander Stewart of Waitsburg. Cost: $5,200.[2]

But while their wealth supported a very comfortable life, coincident with their growing affluence and display, Maria's mental health descended to insanity. The combination of these circumstances would place Maria in harm's way not long after.

As early as 1904, Alexander Stewart was concerned about his wife's deteriorating mental condition. The diagnosis of her mental illness is not readily available but was not of an intermittent nature. It is reasonable to speculate that she suffered from age-related dementia of the most common type, *Alzheimer's*. Alexander, seeking to slow or arrest the rate of decrease in her mental capabilities,

> "took her east and consulted eminent specialists on mental diseases in her behalf and ... when he returned ... he stated nothing could be done for her."[3]

Interestingly, her 1907 visit with her sister in Saratoga Springs is consistent with the timeframe of consultations with specialists. Coincidentally, the following year marked a report by German clinical psychiatrist and neuroanatomist, Alois Alzheimer, on "a peculiar severe disease process of the cerebral cortex" later named after him. The fact that Maria's disease slowly progressed until her death in 1916 is consistent with Alzheimer's, as is the condition she was found in when apparently abandoned five years later.

The situation related to his wife's illness, their advancing years, and the probability that he had chronic health issues of his own evidently motivated Alexander Stewart to pursue an arrange-ment with other members of his family to provide for his and his wife's care when they were both incapacitated. His plan was to enter into a contract with them to provide that care in exchange for transference of property owned by him and his wife. A prob-lem with the plan was that some of the property he intended to transfer was owned separately by Maria. She had acquired these properties as a gift, most probably from her brother William, so because she was not mentally competent, she could not legally enter into a contract to transfer them. Nevertheless, Alexander had a deed transferring the properties to him drawn up, and on April 20, 1906 it was executed under their signatures.

In 1911, Mr. and Mrs. Stewart travelled to Idaho to stay with family members; during October of that year, Alexander executed a contract with five of his relatives stipulating that—in return for real and personal property transferred to them in Florida, Washington, and other states—the relatives would support and maintain him and his wife for as long as they should live. In September 1912 they went to Miami, Florida, where Alexander died in November 1912. At that time all his property and investments, including the land fraudulently transferred from Maria, had already passed into the control of his relatives, some of whom lived in that state.

Barr P. Stewart, Alex's nephew, was appointed administrator of his estate and was initially responsible for Maria's care, but that changed quickly. Based on subsequent information describing her condition, caregiving was not high on his list of priorities. On January 25, 1913 D. J. Heffernan was appointed guardian of Maria Stewart conditional on taking an oath and entering into a bond of five hundred dollars prior to the Dade County court order taking effect. However, Mr. Heffernan failed to act on the bond until July 30. Perhaps he expected Maria to pass away quickly from the neglect she had already endured.

At about that point in time, William Preston must have become aware that Maria's wellbeing was in jeopardy, possibly through a business associate or acquaintance in the Miami area. The information he received was undoubtedly alarming and detailed, because his reaction was swift, decisive, and resourceful. Elderly and not in condition for a long trip or strenuous activity and dealing with complex legal issues—in February 1913 he employed an attorney, Mr. M. O. Pickett, and the attorney's wife (the latter to provide health care and personal supervision) to travel to Florida and return with Maria. There they found her "in a neglected, pitiable and filthy condition; that she was in feeble health and unable to care for herself ... almost without clothing and in the most abject want ... kept in this abject condition by the relatives of her husband."[4]

One could reasonably conclude that she had been left on her own, to die.

Before the Mr. Pickett could obtain permission to return Maria to Washington State he was required to sign a written contract with the relatives on behalf of William which described the purpose of Maria's journey as one of "paying a visit to her brother" (because a change of climate would be beneficial to her health) and stipulated that no charges for her care and transportation be incurred by the estate. More importantly, it stipulated that the contract between Alex Stewart and the Stewart Family would not be altered as a result of the visit. It also placed a requirement on William to report the physical condition of Maria to Barr Stewart and D. J. Heffernan every three months (or more frequently if they so desired). Further, it decreed that she should have kind, considerate care—and if mistreated, the visit must end immediately. That William agreed to the onerous, disingenuous contract terms simply reflects his intent to get Maria out of the control of the Stewart relatives and deal with the issues later.

After the contract was executed, Mr. and Mrs. Pickett purchased suitable clothing for Mrs. Stewart, and by easy stages and with the assistance of nurses and hospital attendants secured at various points along the road of travel brought Mrs. Stewart to Walla Walla County [state of Washington] where her health and physical condition ... rapidly improved although her mind [seemed] to be utterly gone.[5]

The next step was to block any attempt by the Florida guardian, Mr. Heffernan, to return her to Florida and recover her land in Washington. William was in an awkward position to take the lead in these actions, having authorized signature of the contract prohibiting such on his behalf, but her friends in Waitsburg—most likely responding to a request by William and understandably sensitive to Maria's predicament—came to her rescue applying to the superior court of Walla Walla County to appoint a guardian. On March 29, 1913 Mr. R. E. Butler was appointed. Mr. Butler then commenced legal action to recover Maria's property in Walla Walla County against Charles Stewart, Alexander's half-brother, to whom the lots had been fraudulently conveyed. After this action had begun, Mr. Heffernan filed his bond with the Dade County court and began proceedings in Walla Walla County court to have Mr. Butler's appointment vacated.

In the trial to recover Maria's property, R. E. Butler, acting on behalf of Maria, requested that the deed conveying the lots to "Alex" Stewart be set aside and annulled and that a later deed from Alex Stewart to Charles Stewart also be annulled—both on the basis that Maria was mentally incompetent at the time she transferred her property and that she could not have understood the deed she executed.

The defendants denied that Maria had been insane at the time of execution of the deed to Alex and maintained that Mr. Butler's appointment was invalid because Maria was a resident of the state of Florida, and therefore he had no legal capacity to sue.

The trial judge, upon reviewing the evidence found that both Alex and Charles Stewart were aware of Maria's insanity when her property was transferred to Alex, issued a decree setting aside the deeds in question and quieting the title on November

11, 1913. The Stewarts appealed the action to the Supreme Court of Washington, Ref: Stewart v. Stewart, #11872.

The legal action brought at about the same time by D. J. Heffernan against R. E. Butler challenged Butler's appointment as Maria's guardian, arguing that he should be discharged and the order appointing him vacated. Charles Stewart, claiming to be a party in interest, joined as a petitioner. The judge issued an order dismissing the application and Heffernan appealed to the Supreme Court of Washington State. Ref: Heffernan et al. v. Butler, #11873

The Supreme Court decisions on both cases are dated April 20, 1915.

In Stewart v. Stewart the appellants, Charles P. Stewart and company contended:

1. that the original complaint related to transfer of Maria's property to Alex does "not allege that Alex knew she was insane;"
2. "that the trial judge erred in holding R. E. Butler was qualified as guardian;" and
3. "that the trial judge erred in its [sic] finding that Maria C. Stewart was insane when she executed the deed to her husband, that her husband knew she was insane and that the appellant Charles B. Stewart knew she was insane when she conveyed the lots."[6]

In response, the justices pointed out that:

1. the complaint "alleges that Alex Stewart was the husband of Maria Stewart, and that she was insane when the deed was executed. The reasonable inference from these facts would be that he knew of her insanity."
2. "On a trial ... the application to vacate the appointment [of R. E. Butler] was dismissed and we have this day affirmed

that the judgement." (Case #11873, Heffernan et al. v. Butler.)

3. Finally, after carefully examining the evidence related to the issue of Maria's mental condition at the time of transferring the property, the justices concluded that, "it clearly preponderates [is greater in number, influence and importance] in the respondents favor and sustains the findings made [by the trial judge]." Further that Charles B. Stewart had "ample opportunity for observing her incompetent and insane condition, which is clearly shown by the evidence and must have been apparent to him. Although he denied knowledge of her condition his credibility was for the court [to determine]. He was an interested party. It is manifest that the trial judge refused to credit his statements and we are satisfied that he was justified in so doing. ...The judgement of the trial court is affirmed."

In Heffernan et al. v. Butler, the appellants required "R. E. Butler to show cause why he should not be discharged as [Maria's] guardian and why the order appointing him should not be vacated," appealing the trial court's order dismissing the application. The appellants contended that: 1) Maria C. Stewart is not a resident of Walla Walla County, Washington; 2) that she has no property or estate within Walla Walla County; 3) that Maria C. Stewart is a resident of Florida; and 4) that D. J. Heffernan on January 26, 1913 was appointed guardian by the court of Dade County in that state.[7]

In response the justices pointed out that:

Alexander Stewart...and Maria C. Stewart were married in the year 1885; that at all times thereafter, and until the year 1911, their unquestioned residence was in Walla Walla County, Wash.; ... that in 1911 he took his wife to Idaho where they remained with relatives for about one year; that in September 1912 they went to Florida where Alex Stewart died in November 1912; that as nearly as can be ascertained all of his property and investments in the state of Florida passed into the hands or control of his relatives, a number of which lived in that state........Maria Preston remained in Florida with the relatives of her deceased husband until removed to Washington.[8]

The record shows that for many years prior to the 1906, Maria C. Preston owned and held title to certain lots in Waitsburg, Walla Walla County, Wash. As her separate estate; that on April 21, 1906 she conveyed these lots to her husband, Alex Stewart so as to make them his separate estate; that thereafter on September 18, 1912, shortly before his death he conveyed them to Charles B. Stewart, his half-brother; that respondent R. E. Butler as guardian for Mrs. Stewart, claiming that she was insane, that the deed was fraudulently obtained, that Alex Stewart conveyed the lots to Charles B. Stewart without consideration and that Charles B. Stewart then knew she was insane and incompetent when she had conveyed the lots to her husband, commenced an action in the superior court of Walla Walla County against Charles B. Stewart, his wife and others to set aside the deeds and quiet the title.

The record does not convince us that Alex Stewart or his demented wife ever obtained a legal residence in the state of Florida, or that he intended to remain there.

It was after the commencement [to set aside the deeds and quiet her title] that appellant D. J. Heffernan filed his

bond in county court of Dade County Fla. As guardian of
Maria C. Stewart and instituted this proceeding to vacate
the appointment of R. E. Butler.[9]

Saving the most critical assessment of the appellant's conten-
tions for last, the justice opined:

> *Appellants seem to predicate some rights upon the contract
> which Mr. Pickett executed when in Florida, insist that he and
> Mr. Preston have violated the agreements therein contained,
> and claim that by virtue of the contract and its violation they
> are entitled to have Mrs. Stewart returned to Florida in order
> that D. J. Heffernan may discharge his pretended duties as
> guardian in that state. This contention is scarcely worthy of
> passing notice. The entire record is convincing to the effect
> that what the Florida parties sought to accomplish by their
> written contract was to rid themselves of the expense of car-
> ing for Mrs. Stewart, although they had seized all the Florida
> property of her late husband and had contracted to care for
> and maintain her in comfortable circumstances. It was not
> until they feared they were about to lose property interests
> they hoped to control in this state they concluded that their
> contract had been violated by Mr. Preston and Mr. Pickett
> and that they in some manner caused the Florida guardian
> to institute this proceeding. It was then that they concluded
> that the courts of this state had no jurisdiction to appoint a
> guardian for Mrs. Stewart, or protect her interests and insisted
> that she be returned to the state of Florida. Such contentions,
> under the facts here known, do not commend themselves to a
> court of justice. The judgement is affirmed.[10]*

And that ended the matter. As a result of the Supreme Court rulings the Stewarts lost control of Maria's properties, but apparently there was no impact on the other real estate and personal property obtained by contract from Alex; the Stewarts profited greatly from the transaction and provided nothing in return.

The general problem of elder financial abuse has not diminished with time. The state of Maine is currently the oldest state in the nation based on a median age 44.9 years, with an estimated number of people over sixty-five totaling about 20 percent of the population.[11] So one would expect that elder abuse might be a prominent issue in the state—as it is. As described in a December 26, 2017 editorial in the *Portland Press Herald* under the headline "Elder Financial Abuse Often a Family Affair," a report by Legal Services for the Elderly and the Maine Office of Aging and Disability Services (prepared by the University of Southern Maine's Muskie School of Public Services) indicates that the mostly likely perpetrators are family members—the vast majority the victim's child—and the most likely to be victimized are the unmarried or widowed, particularly if living alone.

The study analyzed records from Maine Adult Protective Services and Legal Services for the Elderly cases from 2010 to 2016, and estimated that older Mainers lost as much as $451.5 million because of financial exploitation over the six study years.

Continuing, the report found that the most prevalent form of exploitation involved loss of a house in which the family member arranged to have title transferred to their name and then evicted the elderly relative. It called for new means of detection to prevent exploitation before it occurs, encouraging all parties with connections to the potential victim to be on the lookout for abusers and increasing the ability to recover lost personal resources.

In response to this crisis a Bill, L.D. 316, "An Act to Protect Adults 66 Years of Age and Older from Financial and Other Types of Exploitation through Theft by Deception," sponsored by State Representative Anne Carney is under consideration for passage in 2019. "If enacted, L.D. 316 will raise four crimes – theft by deception, theft by misapplication of property, theft by unauthorized taking and misuse of entrusted property – to felony levels when the owner of the property is dependent on others for physical or emotional support."[12]

In Maria's case the perpetrators were her deceased husband's relatives, but the action they took was very similar in the transfer of real property, followed by abandonment of his widow. Had it not been for her brother's sense that something had gone terribly wrong, her fate would have been to die alone in unspeakable conditions. Maria Preston remained in Waitsburg in the care of William and his family until her death.

Notes

[1] Vance Orchard, compiled by, "Truly Mansion of Magnificence," in *Waitsburg: "One of a Kind"*, (Waitsburg Historical Society, 1976), 110–1.

[2] "Keiser Had the First Car Here," Ibid., 61.

[3] Stewart v. Stewart, Opinion per Crow, J. *Washington Reports: Cases Determined by the Supreme Court of Washington*, vol. 85, (Bancroft-Whitney Company, 1915), 205.

[4] Heffernan et al. v. Butler, no. 11873, Supreme Court of Washington, April 20, 1915, *Pacific Reporter*, vol 147, (St. Paul: West Publishing Co., 1915), 1154.

[5] Ibid., 1155.

[6] Ibid., 1158.

[7] Ibid., 1153.

[8] Ibid., 1154.

[9] Ibid., 1155.

[10] Ibid., 1155–6.

[11] Peter McGuire, "Maine retains its distinction as nation's oldest state," *Portland Press Herald*, September 14, 2018.

[12] Anne Carney, "Rep. Carney: Bill Aims to fight financial exploitation of older Mainers," *Portland Press Herald*, May 22, 2019.

— Chapter Twelve —

Epilogue and Closure

Approaching Waitsburg from the south.
Photo by Bill Rodgers: www.billrodgersphotography.com.

A T THE BEGINNING of the twentieth century, the surviving children of Dr. and Mrs. Preston had dwindled to four: William, Calvin, Sophia, and Maria.

CALVIN died suddenly from an attack of pleurisy on June 20, 1905. He was survived by four daughters, a son, and his wife. He was interred in the Waitsburg cemetery. An homage to him contains the following thoughts:

Major Preston was a man of the most genial and generous impulses and he had a host of friends. He had literary taste and his writings showed marked abilities. As an after-dinner speaker he had few equals and he was always ready to assist in public functions by his ready wit and eloquence. His speeches were impromptu and flowed directly from a true heart, warm with real sympathy and love.

The tribute concludes with the words of William Shakespeare: His life was gentle and the elements so mixed in him that Nature might stand up and say to all the world, "this was a man."[1]

Left to right: Mrs. Dale Preston, Mrs. Anderson, the dog Duke, Cora Laidlaw, William G. Preston, Ivan Bruce, Standford Anderson, Ellis Laidlaw, Markham Anderson and Hubert and Vernita ? in front of the Preston home on Orchard Street, Waitsburg (1908). Reprinted from *Wait's Mill.* Courtesy of Lisa Zigweid.

WILLIAM used the last years of his life productively, engaging in philanthropic projects, strengthening his legacy as a much-admired community leader. Having served in the state legislature and as the first mayor of Waitsburg, he was well-connected politically and had numerous business interests, including bank-ing and merchandising.[2] And he somehow found time to play instruments in local bands. A touching tribute to him and his wife Matilda is found in *Wait's Mill*:

> To the north of us, at the street intersection, lived William and Matilda Preston, known to most as Uncle Will and Aunt Tillie, half of the inhabitants being related to them and the rest, like us, merely copying the more intimate term. As befitting for one of the oldest owners of the flour mill that had given the town its start, the Preston dwelling was distinguished by a corner turret enclosed with win-dows to the second story, two parlors and a music room embellished with tile fireplaces and ceiling rosettes of plas-ter cupids and roses, and a small backyard abode for Billy Clark, the horse trainer, and for a short time, a Chinese cook which was a mark of opulence in that day.
>
> Uncle Will Preston had hired the cook but his wife could not endure such extravagance for long. Although she now lived in gracious comfort, Aunt Tillie, born on the Oregon Trail to pioneers, Julia and Anderson Cox, could not forget or put aside economies that necessity had forced upon the family during hard years on the western frontier. In the midmorning she might appear at our kitchen door, hold-ing a covered kettle by its bail.
>
> "I noticed you had a fire on your range," she would say to mother, "and just thought there was no need of me build-ing up one too, if I could set this pot of beans on the back of your stove and let it simmer for a while—if it won't be any trouble to you."[3]

And, of course, it wasn't.

In 1912 William made a decision to donate a new public school to the City of Waitsburg, his intent clearly inscribed on a panel above the doorway:

ERECTED FOR THE PEOPLE BY
WILLIAM G. PRESTON
TO PROMOTE HEALTH, INDUSTRY, AND RECREATION
TO ENCOURAGE A PRATICAL EDUCATION

Preston Hall, ca. 2010. Photo by Joe Drazan.

Preston Hall, completed in 1913 and dedicated on November 27 of that year, is a rectangular three-story, hip-roof, brick-and-concrete building in neoclassical-revival style, measuring eighty-four feet wide and seventy feet deep. Cost of construction was $30,000 with an additional $5,000 allocated to furnishings. The interior included a first floor eighteen by forty-foot swimming pool, and a bowling alley, as well as storage and maintenance areas. On the second floor were a gymnasium and manual training and shop facilities. Rooms on the third floor were science classrooms.[4] While modifications to the interior have been made, including elimination of the swimming pool and bowling alley, its "historical integrity is almost totally intact."[5] Preston Hall is currently used as a middle school with approximately seventy students, grades six through eight.[6] It is listed on the National Register of Historic Places.

Where did William get the idea to embark on such a project? Quite possibly, it was from his brother Calvin. The Rosenberg

School in Galveston—where a cornerstone inscribed with his name was placed during dedication ceremonies and where Calvin and family spent a terrifying night on September 8, 1900— was a very similar project.

The home William shared with Matilda still stands at the corner of Eighth and Orchard Streets. Actions taken to honor William's contributions to Waitsburg include naming a main street and an adjoining park after him. According to a local source,[7] he was recognized as Waitsburg's foremost progressive citizen. His obituary, published in a local newspaper,[8]

Home formerly occupied by William and Matilda Preston (2019). Photo by Skip Winchester.

states that William died on February 20, 1916 at the home of his son Charles in Portland, Oregon, cause of death attributed to old age. Referred to as "one of the best-known pioneers of the Inland Empire" he had been living with his son for some time. At the time of his death, he and his wife owned a home in Walla Walla, but apparently no longer one in Waitsburg. His will, dated December 10, 1912, listing real community property held by him and his wife as well as separate personal and community personal property, totaled an estimated $280,000 at the time of his death (roughly the equivalent of $6.5 million in current value). Not as wealthy as General Carpentier by a huge margin, but much admired, which the General apparently was not. The bulk of the estate went to his wife and two surviving sons, with smaller but significant bequests made to relatives, the largest to his sister Sophia in Saratoga Springs, New York. She would not benefit from this, because she passed away on September 3, 1914.

His obituary summarized his life experiences and noted that he and his wife frequently visited Los Angeles, California, the location of some Preston family descendants. His grave is in Waitsburg Cemetery.

SOPHIA: After moving to Saratoga Springs, New York in about 1895, Sophia Preston Hays became involved in benevolent organizations and the Second Presbyterian Church. She was a noteworthy member of society there, and her activities were occasionally recorded in the local newspaper, including the marriages of her children, her visits to relatives, and her attendance at events. She passed away at the Saratoga Cure and Infirmary near the home she shared with her husband at 10 Madison Street.

MARIA, the last of the surviving siblings, passed away on October 18, 1916 and was buried in Waitsburg Cemetery. Her husband, Alexander Stewart, is buried in Florida.

The seven children of Dr. and Mrs. Preston had widely differing lifespans. In order of birth year, and using round numbers: Charles, forty-eight years; James, thirty-nine; William, eighty-four; Sophia, seventy-nine; Platt, sixty-three; Maria, seventy-four; and Calvin, sixty. The average lifespan is sixty-four, more or less in line with that of the overall population of the US in that time period. Interestingly, Dr. Preston, born in 1799 and passing away in 1885 at the age of eighty-six, exceeded the lifespan of each of his children.

The Mill

The Preston-Parton Mill, ca. 2007. Photos by James Miller: www.millpictures.com.

AS TIME WENT on, the Preston brothers' involvement in the Waitsburg Mill diminished, while the company expanded. At the time of his death, William was president of the company, though he did not take an active role in its management. By 1950, the facility had grown in size to a five-story building, used electric power to drive the mill equipment, had a capacity of 750 barrels a day, and operated twenty-four hours a day with a twenty-man crew.[9] The company was incorporated twice—first, in 1891 under the name Preston–Parton, and in 1911 as the Preston–Shaffer firm.

In 1904 the company added a new mill in Umatilla County's grain belt to meet increasing demand. This was followed in 1917 with a third mill in Freewater (Oregon), and in 1925 with the purchase of a mill in Pendleton. The offices of the company were moved to Walla Walla in 1939. The total payroll at that point in time was two hundred. During World War II the armed services sustained an increasing demand for products. The non-exempt

Preston-Shaffer Milling Co. flour sack, ca. 1940. Courtesy of the family of Laura Preston Chase.

military status of mill workers resulted in a crew of elderly men or men rated 4-F by the draft.[10]

The Waitsburg Mill would continue to operate until 1957 when the stockholders made a decision to close it down, part of a general trend of Washington State mill closures as the export of wheat became more financially viable than milling to flour. According to one source, there have been 160 mills in the state of Washington with the industry reaching its zenith around 1890.[11] In 2005 there were two mills operating there. For a period of time, the Touchet Valley Grain Growers used the Waitsburg Mill for office space and grain storage, eventually deeding the deteriorating property to the Waitsburg Historical Society. The buildings continued to deteriorate, and in 2005 were placed on the state's list of most endangered historical properties. With the help of the City, the Historical Society took steps to stabilize the buildings, adding temporary roofing and raising funds for major repairs. In the early morning hours of September 6, 2009, the buildings caught fire and became a total loss.

"Destruction of the Waitsburg Mill by fire, September 6, 2009."
Photos by Erica Peters-Grende (*left*) and Skip Winchester (*right*).

A year later, there are few if any clues about the cause of the fire, which was nonetheless ruled "suspicious" by

investigators late last year. Despite citizens' rewards totaling $10,000 for information leading to the arrest of a possi-
ble arsonist, lead investigator Walla Walla County Deputy
Sheriff Brian Bush said officials aren't any closer to knowing why or how the mill met its fiery end.[12]

Interestingly, the abandoned, badly deteriorated, and partially fire-damaged Parkis Mill of Galway met a similar fate
thirty years earlier as a result of condemnation proceedings or
just common sense, and as noted previously was intentionally
destroyed in a controlled burn.

A proposal to commemorate the mill based on a plan developed by an architectural firm providing ten thousand square feet
of enclosed space for a museum, offices and exhibition areas, and
a gift shop at an estimated cost of $7.5 million did not move for-
ward.[13] Today, the mill site is an open area occupied by a parking
lot and two exhibits related to mill history, merging with a field
on gently rolling terrain, bordered by railroad tracks on one side
and the Touchet River on the other.

Waitsburg

Main Street, Waitsburg, looking south.
Photo by Bill Rodgers: www.billrodgersphotography.com

Source: Google

WAITSBURG AND THE mill grew together, from initial operation of the latter until the middle of the twentieth century. A comparison of the population growth with the increase in capacity of the mill shows how they were linked from the period 1865, when the mill opened, until 1950. A decrease in population occurred during the Great Depression, followed by a slow improvement as the nation as a whole recovered, and continued during World War II and the immediate post-war recovery. But foreign competition for milling led to a

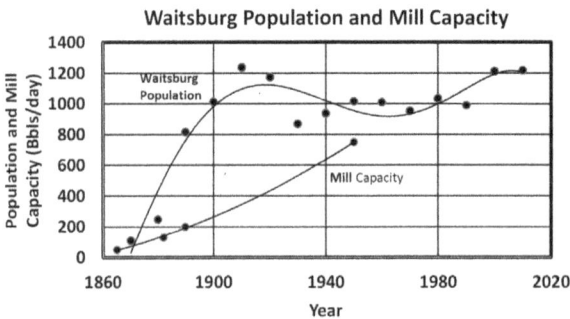

Waitsburg Population and Mill Capacity

demise of the mill in Waitsburg and elsewhere in Washington State. Wheat farming remains a leading occupation for the area. A local version of "amber waves of grain" reflects this, as captured in the photograph below.

Wheat harvesting, Waitsburg (2019).
Photo by Bill Rodgers: www.billrodgersphotography.com.

The city is roughly one square mile in area, with a population of approximately twelve hundred people. The demographics are 93 percent white, and 5 percent Hispanic, with the median age of the population approaching 49 years.

In 2007, in preparation for the 2015 sesquicentennial (after years of thoughtful consideration and pursuit of funding grants) the Waitsburg community embarked on a revitalization of the downtown with a reconstruction of Main Street described as "curb to curb," including beautifying improvements such as historically correct street lamps, trees, and flower planters. In addition, three works of public art in bronze were commissioned: one to honor the founder of the public library; another modeled after the Washington Monument in Washington, D.C. and a third depicting the founding fathers—William Bruce, Sylvester Wait, and William Preston—in the act of carrying on a discussion

Bronze Statue depicting the Waitsburg Founding Fathers: William Preston, Sylvester Wait, and William Bruce (left to right). Photo by Skip Winchester.

Wait's Mill water turbine, shaft, and pulley recovered from remains of the fire. Photo by Skip Winchester (2019).

Wait's Mill kiosk. Photo by Skip Winchester (2019).

while transporting sacks of flour on a hand truck.[14]

A fourth display of historical significance was completed and placed at a park on the site of mill in time for the celebration: a water turbine, shaft and pulley recovered from the ashes of the Waitsburg Mill fire, including a written description of the hardware and its place in local history.

At the edge of the parking area is a kiosk consisting of a shed roof over the original mill vault with framed information panels briefly describing the history of the mill, the town, and the immediate area. The latter includes a description of the land contained in the diaries of the Lewis and Clark expedition, which passed through the future site of the town in 1806. The tribute is undoubtedly appropriate, but upon reflection there is an emptiness to it, hopefully suggesting a work in progress.

Other features of the city memorializing the town fathers include a museum located in the William Bruce house, which is also the headquarters of the Waitsburg Historical Society. A very meaningful memorial to their lives is found in the numerous streets bearing their names, including Preston St., Bruce St., and Willard St., and their beautiful homes.

Bruce Memorial Museum, 2019. Photo by Bill Rodgers: www.billrodgersphotography.com.

Galway, New York

AT THE BEGINNING of the twentieth century, Galway village was a resort destination in the midst of a thriving agricultural region. There were 229 farms supported by a large segment of town's population of 1,350. Vacationers came from the surrounding cities of Amsterdam and Schenectady, and as far away as New York City, to enjoy recreation at nearby Galway Lake. There were two hotels and boardinghouses at the center of the village to accommodate visitors. This came to an end suddenly in September of 1908.

An early morning fire started in a hay barn and swept through the center of the village, destroying eight buildings, including the two hotels, and with that event the character of the village changed forever. Manufacturing facilities vanished shortly afterward, lured to nearby communities with railroad access—the Parkis Mill moving to Ballston Lake in 1926. Growth of manufacturing in nearby Schenectady at the General Electric and

American Locomotive Company plants drew workers from the farms—a trend accelerated in the 1940s by World War II due to the huge effort to build radar and radio systems, ship propulsion turbines, and weapons. The farms suffered as there was no labor available to keep fields clear of brush. By 1950 the number of farms was reduced to about forty.[15]

Satellite Image: Galway Village, 2019.
Source: Google.

Today, the Galway village occupies a square area (a half-mile long at each side) and has a population of approximately two hundred with a median age of thirty-seven. There are several small businesses in or in close proximity to the village, including a bank branch, restaurant, and medical facility. There are three churches and an elementary school and a high school. The elementary school, named in honor of Galway's leading historical figure, Joseph Henry, opened in 1958.

✳ ✳ ✳

JOSEPH HENRY (1797–1878), a physicist who became the first Secretary of the Smithsonian Institute in Washington DC, spent seven years of his childhood from age eight to fifteen living on a farm about a quarter-mile east of Galway Village with his grandmother. This is the same farm later owned by John Henry Hays, husband of Sophia Preston Hays. Legend has it that, when pursuing a pet rabbit that had disappeared into a hole in the foundation of a village church, Joseph found his way through the crawlspace to the church vestibule where the village library was kept.

Taking a book from the shelves he began reading and forgot about the rabbit. The experience stimulated his intellect and reading became a habit, which eventually led to his discovery of the world of science when he chanced upon Dr. Gregory's Lectures on Experimental Philosophy, Astronomy and Chemistry.[16] He graduated from Albany Academy, took a teaching position there, and during that period of his life started experimenting with electromagnetism, developing more powerful magnets and a very early (albeit crude) direct current motor. He discovered the principle of self-inductance, the property of an alternating current (ac) electric circuit that results in an induced voltage opposing the flow of the current. In recognition of his pioneering work, the unit of inductance is called a "Henry." Later at the College of New Jersey (which would become Princeton University) he continued his experiments, gaining recognition for his ability as a researcher that led to his appointment as the first Secretary of the Smithsonian.

Joseph Henry. Photo by author (2019).

The Galway home he lived in was destroyed by fire many years ago. A state historical marker at the site calls attention to his brief stay in Galway.

* * *

THE HOME OF the Preston family still stands—with minor modifications to the exterior although modernized inside.

Home formerly owned by Dr. and Mrs. Preston, 2019. Photo by author.

Central heating (first, coal in 1930 and later, oil) was added when electricity became available, accompanied by indoor plumbing and a septic system. The coal and wood-fired stoves located in upstairs bedrooms were removed along with brick chimneys supported on sturdy closets, an approach that undoubtedly violates present day building codes.

The usual arrangement consisted of a rectangular cross-section closet constructed with framing lumber with a height that left about 3 feet of vertical space relative to the ceiling. A gable end of the room was the preferred location, the chimney center aligned with the roof peak. Midway between the chimney base and the ceiling a circular opening was provided in the chimney for a stove pipe. A sturdy wooden platform covered with 2-3 inches of concrete formed the chimney base. The chimney, made of brick approximately 2x3 feet in cross-section extended upward from the base, through the ceiling then outward through the roof, terminating 2-4 feet above the peak. The total height of the chimney was typically 10-15 feet, the dead weight on the order of 5000 to 7500 lbs. As

Home formerly owned by Horace Carpentier. Photo by author (2019).

expected, this amount of weight would, in time, cause severe deflection of the floor-supporting structure, twisting the sub-header and forcing it outward—sufficient reason for dismantling it to avoid collapse with the chimney suddenly falling to the first-floor level.

Finally, a fireplace with a "heatilator" was added in the first-floor hallway.

On adjoining properties (one on either side) are two churches, Baptist and Catholic. Locust trees along the front and sides of the house seemed old in the 1950s but remain standing today, as do the forsythia hedges planted by my parents sixty years ago. Along the streets of the village, the homes mostly date back to the same period with an occasional ranch or cape cod style home and a 1940s-era bungalow here and there. Essentially a bedroom community, it is a pleasant place to live. A Methodist church stands on the corner that is the site of the Presbyterian church the Prestons attended, which was destroyed by fire in 1947. Diagonally across to the north is the home that General Carpentier occupied, now a three-family in deteriorating condition recently acquired by a bank through foreclosure. The watering trough he donated to the village still exists. Restored to a presentable state after a truck backed over it, it is a mute reminder of days past.

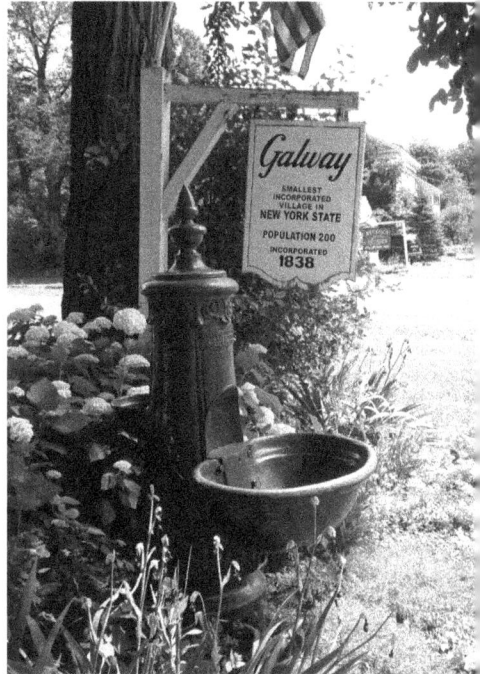

Galway Village water trough (2019). Photo by author.

Closure

WILLIAM PRESTON LEFT his childhood home in 1850, seeking adventure and a rewarding career, and with no intention
of returning. In the end, accompanied by his younger brother
Platt—after several false starts (religious leader, seaman, riverboat captain, hotel owner, pack train operator) and travel
of 3,000 miles over a ten-year period—he achieved something
remarkable. He found a place very similar to his home of origin
but with the opportunity to make a comfortable living at something familiar. And there he gathered his family around him.

Galway of the 1850s was mostly a farming community, as
was Waitsburg. Galway's climate and gently rolling terrain
at the foot hills of the Adirondack Mountains bear a similar-
ity to that of Waitsburg—the latter with the same terrain, the
Blue Mountains in the distance, and even a possibly more
moderate yearly fluctuation in temperature. Major economic
advantages of Waitsburg were the presence of a river to supply adequate water power, a climate and soil that provided the
best possible growing conditions for wheat, the availability of
transportation to move the product to market, and a substantial local market for flour. One has to look no further than a
comparison between the gristmills in Galway and Waitsburg to
understand this.

In terms of milled product, in 1870 the Parkis Mill of Galway
produced 29,500 pounds including meal, feed, and flour with a
total value of $1,670. In 1865, the first year of operation of the
Waitsburg Mill (during which the supply of wheat was limited),
it produced 20,000 pounds of flour with a value of $14,000,
based on demand at the nearby Idaho gold mining region. So
the Waitsburg Mill was substantially more profitable.

Very quickly, William and Platt became wealthy and influential members of the Waitsburg community. What was missing from their lives was the companionship of their brothers and sisters. They must have been a very close-knit family while growing up, because there is no other explanation for the mass relocation that followed.

The reunion happened slowly. Unfortunately, James passed away not long after William and Platt arrived in Waitsburg, and Calvin was committed to his business in Galveston. But Maria came soon after the First Transcontinental Railroad began operations (1869) and while Charles, seeking to get approval from the Presbyterian Mission Board for a transfer to Washington State from China, died in the process, his wife Mary and six children found their way to Waitsburg in 1878. Calvin's arrival with his family was delayed until 1901, following the great Galveston hurricane of 1900. The only holdout of the group was Sophia, although she, her husband, and daughter Margaret visited Waitsburg in 1907. As a result, Margaret married Arthur McCoy of Waitsburg in 1909 and lived there for the remainder of her life.

Surrounded by brothers, a sister, and their families for whom he cared a great deal, William must have been very comfortable in his role as the patriarch. There was sadness for sure—deaths of children, brothers, and spouses at an early age (even for that time period). But there were also good times during the period from the 1870s to 1900 when he, Platt, and Maria played music together—William on cello, Platt on violin, and Maria at the keyboard—and talked of the old days in that large home in a small, rural upstate New York village.

With Platt's death in 1900 came the pain of losing the brother with whom he had the closest relationship and shared the struggles of the search for opportunity. But the pain of that final separation was diminished when circumstances quickly resulted in Calvin's arrival. For the next five years, William had the company of Maria and Calvin. Calvin's sudden death and Maria's rapidly declining mental health probably found William depending more on the support of his wife Matilda and children and led him to consider his legacy for his adopted community. Thus, the donation of Preston Hall.

William's last act, the rescue of Maria, must have given him a great deal of relief and satisfaction. He died shortly after she was returned home, and she passed away not long after he did, leaving his sons and wife to share in his fortune and live comfortably.

The Prestons had interesting, productive lives, the record of which is archived here and there across the United States and in letters from China. Hopefully, this account puts the pieces together in a coherent and interesting manner. Immediate descendants of Dr. and Mrs. Preston's children, with a few exceptions, lived on the West Coast of the US, from San Jose to Seattle. Their descendants can undoubtedly be located with a sufficiently detailed genealogical study. A family source indicates there is still a small core of descendants in Southern California but the rest are scattered around the world.

Notes

[1] F.A. Shaver et al., compiled by, *An Illustrated History of Southeastern Washington, Including Walla Walla, Columbia, Garfield and Asotin Counties*, (Western Historical Publishing Co., 1906), 229.

[2] Ibid., 245.

[3] Ellis and Elvira Ellen Laidlaw, *Wait's Mill, The Story of the Community of Waitsburg, Washington*, (Chicago: Adams Press, 1970), 120.

[4] National Register of Historical Places Registration Form, United States Department of the Interior National Park Service, January 1993, 1–5.

[5] Ibid., 3.

[6] Preston Hall Middle School, https://www.greatschools.org/washington/waitsburg/2091-Preston-Hall-Middle-School

[7] Vance Orchard, compiled by, "Streets Named for Pioneers," in *Waitsburg: "One of a Kind"*, (Waitsburg Historical Society, 1976,) 45.

[8] "Death of Wm. G. Preston, Pioneer and Philanthropist of Waitsburg Claimed by the Grim Reaper," Columbia Chronicle, February 23, 1916

[9] Vance Orchard, compiled by, "Mill had a 92 Year History," in *Waitsburg: "One of a Kind"*, (Waitsburg Historical Society, 1976,) 22.

[10] "Four-fifths of Century is Observed. Preston-Shaffer Milling Co., Operating Four Plants, Had Inception in 1865 at Waitsburg, Walla Walla," Union Bulletin, February 25, 1945.

[11] Norman Reed, "Flour Milling in Washington—A Brief History," HistoryLink.org, Essay 9474, July 11, 2010, https://historylink.org/File/9474

[12] Imbert Mattee, "A Vision for Wait's Mill," *Waitsburg Times*, Sept. 9, 2010.

[13] Jillian Beaudry, "Commemoration Ideas Emerge," *Waitsburg Times*, June 28, 2012.

[14] Ted Katauskas, "Culture Club, Washington Cities Inspire Civic Engagement by Resuscitating, Reinforcing and in Some Cases Redefining Community Identity," *City Vision Magazine*, May/June 2017, 18–20.

[15] Dennis Yusko, "Community effort creates book on Galway's history," *Times Union*, January 4, 2015.

[16] *A Memorial of Joseph Henry*, Published by Order of Congress, (Government Printing Office, 1880), 504.

— Appendix —

*T*HE LOCATION OF all the Preston descendants cannot be known in the absence of a complete genealogy study. Cemetery listings in Waitsburg, Washington; Galveston, Texas; Glens Falls, New York; and Galway, New York provide information on the final locations of some of the Preston family members. A limited genealogy study was undertaken in 1935 by Ralph A. Chase, husband of Laura Maria Preston (daughter of Platt Preston), and is the source for much of the following information. The Chases, at the time, lived in South Pasadena, California.

Preston monument, Galway Cemetery (2015). Photo by author.

A list of individuals interred in Galway Village Cemetery includes four Prestons: Calvin Preston, MD; Margaret (his first wife); Sarah (his second wife); and John (his brother). While John's name appears on the monument, no dates are included. A monument engraved with *his* name along with dates of birth and death is located on plot seventy-eight of the Schuylerville, New York Prospect Hill Cemetery. There are no known Preston descendants in the immediate Galway, New York area. John Preston and his wife had no children. The same is true of the sons of John and Sophia Preston Hays, who lived in Glens Falls until the time of their deaths.

CHARLES FINNEY PRESTON died in Hong Kong in 1877 and was buried there in the Happy Valley Cemetery. His wife, Mary, and six surviving children relocated to Waitsburg after his death. Mary subsequently moved to Portland, Oregon and lived with her daughter Laura.

Their children who survived to become adults were Walter Byrne (b. 1860), Mary Byrne (b. 1863), Sophie Gray (b. 1864), Annie Carrie (b. 1866), Laura Condit (b. 1867) and Frederick Brewster (b. 1869). Walter Bryne married Mary Moore in Walla Walla, Washington in 1894, and they had one child: Louisa Byrne. Mary Bryne married Alvin Kinnear in Waitsburg, and they had two children: Mary Elizabeth and Charles Campbell. Sophie Gray returned to the place of her birth, Canton, China and married Frank Wisner there. They had three children: Margaret Byrne, Carl Chauncey, and Francis. Subsequently, they moved to the Oberlin, Ohio area. Annie Carrie married Lincoln Bennett in Portland, Oregon, and they had one child: Mildred May. Laura Condit married Robert Campbell in Santa Monica, California, and there were two children: Preston Dunnett and Morrison. Finally, Frederick Brewster married his cousin, Margaret (daughter of Platt and Laura) in San Jose, California. They had two children: Frederick Platt and Calvin Glen. After Margaret's death in 1914, Frederick married Thetis Ann South in Los Angeles.

JAMES EDWIN PRESTON married Emeline A. McWaters in Galveston, Texas on August 30, 1866. They had two children before James passed away on May 7, 1870. James was buried in the Episcopal Cemetery, Galveston, in a grave next to one reserved for his brother, Calvin, which is presumably empty. James' two children are: Martha Flint (b. 1869, d. 1884) and Sophie Alexander (b. 1870). No further information on the children is provided in Ralph Chase's 1935 study. After his death, James' wife married Calvin Walbridge Preston, and they had four children.

WILLIAM GOODELL PRESTON and his wife Matilda had four children: Herbert Platt (b. 1872), William Chester (b. 1874), Charles Bliss (b. 1876), and Dale Hays (b. 1879). William Chester died as an infant. Herbert and Charles relocated to Seattle and Portland, respectively. Herbert died in 1955, and Charles in 1948. The fourth son, Dale, died in 1910, possibly in Waitsburg. The 1935 research suggests that Charles and his second wife had an adopted daughter but contains no details on the families of Dale or Herbert.

William, Matilda, and William Chester are buried in Waitsburg.

SOPHIA JANE PRESTON married John Henry Hays in Galway on January 8, 1862. They had three children: Stephen Alexander (b. 1863), Edwin Preston (b. 1871), and Margaret Sophia (b. 1874). Stephen and Edwin moved to Glens Falls, New York and had no children. Margaret went to Waitsburg, Washington where she visited briefly and subsequently married a wealthy lumber distributor, Arthur M. McCoy in 1909. They had two children: Arthur Hays (b. 1911) and Robert Holmes (b. 1912). Arthur M. McCoy died in 1926, Margaret in 1950. They and Arthur's first wife Elizabeth are buried in the Waitsburg Cemetery.

Sophia Hays died in 1914, followed by her husband in 1923; both are buried in Pineview Cemetery in Queensbury, New York.

PLATT ADAMS PRESTON and Laura Preston had seven children, but only three survived to adulthood: Laura Maria, Platt Waite, and Margaret. Platt's wife Laura died on June 13, 1896, and Platt died on March 12, 1900. Children Anna, Edwina, and William pre-deceased both parents; and son Glen Calvin died on July 4, 1900 (shortly after Platt, leaving Laura Maria to be raised by her sister, Margaret). Son Platt Waite was age twenty at that time.

Laura Maria, who accompanied her father on his final trip seeking a cure, married Roger Arthur Chase in December 1908 in Los Angeles. The couple had four children: Evelyn Louise (b. 1911), Margaret Adele (b. 1913), Leland Preston (b. 1916), and Janet Kathryn (b. 1918). During

Chase family gathering, ca. 1923. Courtesy of the family of Laura Preston Chase.

a 1923 visit to Waitsburg they posed for a photo taken by Laura Maria at the McCoy Farm. Ralph Chase is the gentleman in the back row, far right. The Chase children are in the front row. From left to right: Janet is second from left, then Leland, Margaret, and Evelyn. The Chases lived in South Pasadena from 1923 to 1974 in a house that was later used for filming "Beethoven," a 1992 comedy about a family and their St. Bernard.

Platt Waite Preston married Emma Gaskill in June of 1906. They had two children, born in Calexico and Los Angeles, California.

Chase home, South Pasadena, California (1923–1974). Courtesy of Laura Preston Chase.

Left to right: Margaret, Laura, Platt, and Glen Preston, ca. 1900. Platt and Glen died in 1900, predeceased by Platt's wife Laura. Courtesy of the family of Laura Preston Chase.

Margaret married her cousin, Frederick Brewster Preston, son of Rev. Charles and Mary Preston, in San Jose, California on June 6 1900. She died in October 1914 in Los Angeles, Ca.

Platt Adams Preston and wife Laura are buried in Waitsburg Cemetery along with daughters Annie and Edwina, and son Glen, all of whom died in childhood.

MARIA CHAPIN PRESTON passed away on October 18, 1916 and was buried in Waitsburg Cemetery, as noted previously. Her husband, Alexander Stewart, is buried in Florida. There were no children.

— Acknowledgments —

ESEARCH FOR THIS book would not have been successful without the help of many. Here is my best
attempt at a complete list. The information on the
Prestons' lives came either in large, self-contained documentation (such as the archived letters of Rev. Charles Preston and the
legal records of Dr. Preston v. the Caverts) or in fragments (for
example, Calvin's life story). Hence, the latter section is longer
than might otherwise be the case.

The basis for the book started with the document, "Historical
and Genealogical Notes of Galway, New York by Elizabeth Robb
Quinby, on Galway history provided by Galway Preservation
Society archivist Arlene Rhodes. This led to contact with Jozef
Malinowski, historian–Town of Deerfield, New York, who
responded with a number of old newspaper articles and an
assortment of documents, a key item of which was an obituary detailing Calvin Preston's Galveston connection. A subsequent inquiry made to Sean McConnell, senior archivist at the
Rosenberg Library in Galveston, resulted in information on James
Preston's presence there. In parallel, Gail Gwinn of the Waitsburg
Historical Society recommended two books on Waitsburg history, *Wait's Mill* and *Waitsburg: One of a Kind*, containing interesting information and photos related to the Prestons' life in
that community. Sandra Torres' genealogy study of Waitsburg
1858–1900 was useful in filling in some of the blanks, and she was

helpful in reviewing a very early summary of the Preston story. Phyllis Keeler, Town of Galway historian, provided contact information for Platt Preston descendants in California who freely shared photos of the Preston family and useful genealogical information. While the Reverend Joseph Shook suggested some potential local sources of information on Presbyterian missionaries, his recommendation to contact the Presbyterian Historical Society in Philadelphia was by far the most rewarding. From that point on, the research preceded along many paths in pursuit of information on all seven of the Preston children.

Photos are important toward providing context. While some of the events described in this book occurred when photography was in its infancy—surprisingly, there were enough photos available from various sources for the period 1855–1900 to support the storyline with visual input. One in particular that stands out is the 1860 photo of Treasury Street in Canton, China (an especially foreign world to a native of rural upstate New York), which Rev. Preston inhabited with surprising ease for twenty-three years. Taken by Felice Beato it was provided by Paul Taylor, Archives and Collections Coordinator, the Library of Birmingham, U.K. Other photos—such as the fire that consumed the Waitsburg Mill, and the still-existing historical structures and current scenes of interest in places like Galveston and Waitsburg—were taken recently by a number of individuals who were most generous in providing their support.

Contributions to the material upon which this book is based is listed below according to Preston family member.

Dr. Preston:
Information on his family of origin and medical training was found in several documents forwarded by Jozef Malinowski.

Arlene Rhodes contributed a charming anecdote contained in a mid-nineteenth-century Galway newspaper on Dr. Preston and friend's journey down the Ohio River on Captain William Preston's side-wheeler riverboat, as well as other information on the Doctor's life.

A comment made by a Galway farmer in the Quinby notes on a legal complaint against Dr. Preston suggested that there might be legal documents archived somewhere related to the matter. Patricia Sanders of the Saratoga County Historical Society's Brookside Museum provided the location (the Saratoga County Clerk's Office in Ballston Spa, New York) and the number of the file that contained many documents on the case. In addition, she found interesting information on the lawyers for the plaintiff and the defendant. Kathleen Coleman of Brookside provided the portrait photo of Jesse L'Amoreaux, Dr. Preston's attorney.

At the Saratoga County Clerk's Office, Brigette Hebst facilitated locating and reading microfiche images of the legal documents. She and Lauren Roberts, Saratoga County historian, also located some interesting documents and newspaper articles related to the Cavert v. Preston matter and Mr. Cavert's subsequent legal problems.

CALVIN:

A book by Eugene Nash on the history of the New York State 44th Volunteer Infantry Regiment (a.k.a. Ellsworth Avengers) contained useful background information on Calvin W. Preston's service in the Civil War. This led me to a visit to the New York State Military Museum and Veterans Research Center where Christopher Morton, assistant curator, arranged for a viewing of Ellsworth's tunic, bullet hole clearly visible, and provided an image. The Mechanicville (New York) Public Library provided a portrait photo of Elmer Ellsworth.

Related to the beginning of Calvin's Civil War experience, Allynne Lange, curator of the Hudson River Maritime Museum, located a vintage photo of a towboat with barges similar to the one that transported eleven hundred members of the 44th Regiment from Albany, New York to New York City in the fall of 1862 on the way to war. Kian Flynn of the University of Washington Suzzallo Library located an obituary of Calvin published by the *Columbia* (Washington) *Chronicle*.

Roy Collins III, fifth-generation member of a Galveston family, contributed a scholarly and interesting assessment of race relations in Galveston during the period that Calvin lived there.

Elizabeth Rogers Alvarado is the source of the photo of Calvin's home, a Galveston 1900 hurricane survivor, and directed my attention to locating a source for a photo of the Rosenberg School cornerstone engraved with Calvin's name, which was obtained with the assistance of John Huoni.

Photos of places pertinent to the story following the 1900 Galveston hurricane, along with images of Preston and Robira's drug list, were located with the help of Sean McConnell of the Rosenberg Library.

JAMES:
Information on James' stay in Galveston, including his mysterious death, was supplied by Sean McConnell, Rosenberg Library archivist.

CHARLES:
Information on his education and biographical sketches were obtained with the help of Marlaine DesChamps, archives

specialist–Union College (Schenectady, New York). Lisa Jacobson, senior reference archivist of the Presbyterian Historical Society, provided an index to letters written by Charles during the period that he was a missionary to China, and reference archivists Charlene Peacock and David Koch provided assistance in understanding the relationship between the index and microfiche tapes containing the letters' images. The tapes were provided by Cengage Company with the assistance of Alan Boucher. David Koch also provided personal files on Rev. Preston and his wife related to their service as missionaries in China, as well as biographical information on Rev. Adam W. Platt.

Information on the good ship *Horatio*, upon which Charles sailed to China, was provided by Kelly Page, registrar of the Maine Maritime Museum. She recommended that I contact the New Bedford Whaling Museum for a digital copy of an 1855 watercolor of the *Horatio* by Benjamin Russell. Mark Procknik assisted me in obtaining this item from the museum.

Photos of Charles and family, one circa 1855, were provided by the family of Laura Preston Chase.

Photos of the grave in Macao of the Reverend Charles Preston's infant son and Charles' grave in Hong Kong were found on Findagrave.com. The contributor Chris Nelson gave permission for use in this book.

WILLIAM AND PLATT PRESTON:
The photo of Galway's Parkis Mill, where William may have gained experience and knowledge of milling operations, was contributed by Arlene Rhodes. The portrait photo of William included in the book *Waitsburg: One of a Kind* is courtesy of Rick Hamm, and those of Platt and family are courtesy of the family of Laura Preston Chase.

Arlene Rhodes contributed information on the Galway argonauts. The photo of Golden Gate City was supplied by Richard Gardner, Golden City historian. His work is also the source of information on the Prestons' activities at Golden Gate City, and he contributed a personal assessment of the factors leading to its demise and the departure of the Prestons, as well. Sarah Gilmor, reference librarian–History Colorado, provided deeds related to William's land holdings in Denver and notes on his involvement in the 1859 constitutional convention, representing Douglas City.

Joe Drazan contributed the photo of the original Wait's Mill obtained by him from noted Waitsburg historian Jeffrey Broom, as well as a current photo of Preston Hall.

Twentieth and twenty-first century photos of Wait's Mill (a.k.a. the Preston-Shafer Mill) were supplied by the family of Laura Preston Chase and James Miller. Photos of the Waitsburg Mill in flames are by Skip Winchester and Erica Peters-Grende. Cathy Wickwire of the Washington Trust for Historic Preservation was helpful in identifying a photo source. Skip Winchester also generously supplied his own photos of the historical displays at the mill site, the statue of the founding fathers located on Main Street, and the former William Preston home. Bill Rodgers supplied three photos in which he captured the natural beauty of the Waitsburg region and city, as well as one of the Bruce Memorial Museum.

Present-day Galway photos were taken by the author, with the exception of one of the former Preston home in 1950, which was taken and contributed by the author's mother, Elsie Maddaus.

Lisa Zigweid gave permission to use a charming anecdote about William and Matilda Preston contained in her parents' book, *Wait's Mill*, along with a photo of the Preston family and friends. Susan Donegan gave permission on behalf of the

Waitsburg Historical Society to use passages and photos from *Waitsburg: One of a Kind.*

Maria:

Photos of Maria were provided by the family of Laura Preston Chase. Jozef Malinowski contributed a short item from the July 22, 1907 issue of the *Daily Saratogian* about Maria's visit with her sister during a trip to the East Coast for medical advice on her increasing dementia. Bruce Connolly, reference librarian–Union College library, provided advice on possible copyright restrictions associated with documents related to the "Matter of the Guardianship of the Person and Estate of MARIA C. STEWART, a Person of Unsound Mind." Permission to use a description of "The Touchet Valley," an excerpt from the book *Wait's Mill*, was given by Lisa Zigweid, and permission for excerpts from *Waitsburg: One of a Kind* was given by Susan Donegan.

Sophia:

Patricia Sanders' research is the source of newspaper clippings, federal census data, and other documents.

* * *

Susan VanOmmeren generously contributed the time required to read the initial manuscript and suggested several additions, all of which were adopted.

I am greatly indebted to my editor, Dory Mayo, who suffered through the numerous errors in syntax, word use, punctuation, sentence construction, and other manuscript flaws—hopefully typical of a first-time author. It's been a fine education. Thank you, Dory.

Thanks are also due to Colin Rolfe who designed the book—including jacket and interior—achieving unexpected clarity for a number of 19th century, pixel challenged images and transforming rough concepts on interior arrangements of photos and, in particular, jacket design, into a pleasing finished product.

Finally, I must acknowledge the help and understanding of my wife, Barbara, an English Major who reviewed chapters of the book, provided frank assessments, and accepted long hours of my absence as I pursued the myriad of details incorporated in this work. Here, Barbara, is what I have to show for the time together we managed to do without.

— Index —

www.ingramcontent.com/pod-product-compliance
Lightning Source LLC
Chambersburg PA
CBHW030422100426
42812CB00028B/3070/J